Philosophy and Computing

"*Philosophy and Computing* is a stimulating and ambitious book that seeks to help lay a foundation for the new and vitally important field of Philosophy of Information. The author undertakes the challenging task of explaining central aspects of information techology – like databases, hypertext and networks – in ways that reveal important, and sometimes surprising, philosophical implications. Thought-provoking comments abound on a variety of philosophical topics, including logic, reasoning, meaning, belief, knowledge, intelligence, society, ontology, aesthetics and time – to name only a few examples. This is a worthy addition to the brand new and rapidly developing field of Philosophy of Information, a field that will revolutionise philosophy in the Information Age."

Terrell Ward Bynum, *Director,*
Research Center on Computing and Society, Southern Connecticut State University

"Floridi's helpful, informative and often fascinating book is a welcome arrival. Floridi writes calmly and with good sense on topics that others have hyped mercilessly."

B. Jack Copeland, *The Turing Project, University of Canterbury*

"In his seminal book, Luciano Floridi provides a rich combination of technical information and philosophical insights necessary for the emerging field of philosophy and computing."

James Moor, *Dartmouth College*

"Luciano Floridi's book discusses the most important and the latest branches of research in information technology. He approaches the subject from a novel philosophical viewpoint, while demonstrating a strong command of the relevant technicalities of the subject."

Hava T. Siegelman, *Technion, Israel Institute of Technology*

Luciano Floridi is research fellow at Wolfson College and lecturer in philosophy at Jesus College, Oxford University. He is the author of *Scepticism and the foundation of Epistemology* and the consultant editor ... Philosophy on CD-ROM.

Philosophy and Computing

An introduction

Luciano Floridi

London and New York

First published 1999
by Routledge
11 New Fetter Lane, London EC4P 4EE

Simultaneously published in the USA and Canada
by Routledge
29 West 35th Street, New York, NY 10001

Routledge is an imprint of the Taylor & Francis Group

© 1999 Luciano Floridi

Typeset in Times by RefineCatch Limited, Bungay, Suffolk
Printed and bound in Great Britain by
Clays Ltd, St. Ives PLC

British Library Cataloguing in Publication Data
A catalogue record for this book is available from the British Library

Library of Congress Cataloguing in Publication Data
Floridi, Luciano, 1964–
    Philosophy and computing: an introduction / Luciano Floridi.
        p.   cm.
    Includes bibliographical references and index.
    1. Computer science – Philosophy.   I. Title.
    QA76.167.F56   1999
    004'.01 – dc21   98–47915
                                                                            CIP

ISBN 0–415–18024–4 (hbk)
ISBN 0–415–18025–2 (pbk)

. . . ὑπὸ δ' ἀμφίπολοι ῥώοντο ἄνακτι
χρύσειαι ζωῆσι νεήνισιν εἰοικυῖαι.
τῆς ἐν μὲν νόος ἐστὶ μετὰ φρεσίν, ἐν δὲ καὶ αὐδὴ
καὶ σθένος, ἀθανάτων δὲ θεῶν ἄπο ἔργα ἴσασιν.
αἳ μὲν ὕπαιθα ἄνακτος ἐποίπνυον· . . .

Iliad xviii, 417–421

. . . Handmaids ran to attend their master [Hephaestus],
all cast in gold but a match for living, breathing girls.
Intelligence fills their hearts, voice and strength their frames,
from the deathless gods they've learned their works of hand.
They rushed to support their lord . . .

The Iliad, tr. by R. Fagles, p. 481

Contents

Preface

A philosophy textbook is always a risky project. We expect the author to introduce all the basic elements in the field clearly and succinctly, while providing an interesting perspective from which to interpret them fruitfully. This doubles the chances of getting things wrong and generates a paradoxical tension between originality and lack of novelty. In an attempt to get round the latter problem, I have written this introduction to information and communication technology (ICT) with two kinds of philosophy students in mind: those who need to acquire some ICT literacy in order to use computers efficiently, and those who may be interested in acquiring the background knowledge indispensable for developing a critical understanding of our digital age and hence beginning to work on that would-be branch of philosophy I define the "philosophy of information", which I hope may one day become part of our *Philosophia Prima*.

To members of the former group I wish to say that a lot of the basic material provided in the following chapters can also be found scattered elsewhere. It would require some effort to select, collect and order it appropriately and clearly from many different sources that philosophers are unlikely to consult, but I freely acknowledge that I have often simply tried to explain or rephrase more clearly, and with an eye to its philosophical relevance, what is really standard knowledge in computer science, information theory and ICT. (For more technical introductions to computer science see Brookshear 1997, a very valuable and clear overview; Cohen 1997, Dewdney 1989 and 1996; and Tunnicliffe 1991; on information theory see Shannon and Weaver 1975; Shannon 1993 and the more philosophical Devlin 1991; two good textbooks are Reza 1994 and Van der Lubbe 1997; on the philosophy of technology see Mitcham 1994). I must warn members of the latter group of students that whatever originality there may be in the text, in terms of interpretation, arguments or analyses, it may well be controversial. I aimed to provide an unbiased introduction to ICT from a philosophical perspective, but the closer the topic came to the conceptual debate, the more I found myself failing in that aim. It is easier to be intellectually neutral when talking about different types of data storage than when dealing with the concept of text or the possibility of artificial intelligence. By the time the reader has reached Chapter 5, I can only hope that my "logocentric" or "neo-Cartesian" views (both labels with negative connotations for many philosophers who write about the topics covered by this book) will be sufficiently clear to allow an open discussion of their value. It is up to the reader to judge whether I have been able to keep a reasonable balance.

Let me now briefly introduce the contents of the book.

In Chapter 1, I outline the nature of the digital revolution, sketching the profound transformations that it has brought about in four areas: computation, automatic control, modelling and information management. In the second part of the chapter, I consider the impact that the digital revolution has had on the world of organised information, which I more broadly call the *infosphere*. I discuss how ICT has provided a new physics of knowledge and describe the three stages in which the infosphere has been digitised. In the last part of the chapter, I focus on the relations between philosophy and the digital, thus introducing the following chapter.

In Chapter 2, I explain what a computer is, first by analysing the conceptual steps that led to the construction of the first machines, then by concentrating on the nature of a Universal Turing machine and its Boolean logic. In the second half of the chapter, I move on to the description first of a Von Neumann machine and then of a commercial PC.

In Chapter 3, I introduce the Internet as a basic technological innovation. I first summarise its history and explain in more detail what the Internet is and what it can be used for. I then devote some space to the analysis of electronic mail, interpreted as a new form of communication, which I call the *silent dialogue*. In the second half of the chapter, I explain the nature of the World Wide Web and then go on to analyse the new kinds of problems that the growth of a network of information and communication has given rise to in the field of organised knowledge.

In Chapter 4, I begin by describing the context within which we can best understand the development of databases, textbases and hypertexts; I provide a more technical introduction to the nature and types of database available today, and then briefly discuss some philosophical issues arising from this technology. The last part of the chapter is dedicated to the nature of hypertext, the analysis of some mistaken views about it, and the development of an interpretation of hypertext as the logical structure of the infosphere. I conclude with some remarks about the possibility of a new Renaissance mind.

In Chapter 5, the longest of the book, I discuss various forms of artificial intelligence (AI) technologies. My aim here is not to debunk them but rather to redirect our philosophical interest in them. According to the pragmatic approach defended in this chapter, the useful technological products and services that are going to be made available are only a subclass of those that are economically feasible, which are again only a subclass of those that are physically possible, which are in turn only a subclass of those that are logically possible. Take interfaces for example. We have stopped interacting audibly with our information systems sometime after Augustine. (He reported with admiration that his teacher Ambrose was able to read silently; this was indeed rather extraordinary if one recalls that manuscripts often lacked interword spacing, capitalisation and punctuation.) But sooner or later our computers may go "vocal", allowing us to talk and listen to our PC. The possibility in itself is not in question, but have you ever tried to give operating instructions orally to someone who cannot see what he is doing? Or to receive instructions via telephone about where to find an object you are looking for? Instead of transforming a simple task, like "save file x in format y in the directory z" into a "mission impossible", we may just reconsider the actual utility of a vocal interface (some readers may have had a similar experience with "smart" alarm clocks that can be switched off by shouting at them). A speech-recognition, hands-free application is not necessarily useful *per se*, especially if it is not mobile as well.

Chapter 5 begins with an analysis of the classic or strong AI programme, which is sometimes called GOFAI (Good Old Fashioned AI). First I discuss Turing's Test and show why GOFAI was unsuccessful. I then move on to consider the conditions of possibility of a more pragmatic and philosophically less ambitious programme in AI, which I call "light AI" (LAI). I argue that a LAI approach is the most promising strategy in many areas of AI application. The second half of the chapter is dedicated to the introductory analysis of these areas: fuzzy logic systems, artificial neural networks, parallel computing, quantum computing, expert systems, knowledge engineering, formal ontologies, robotics, cybernetics and artificial agents. I close the chapter by reminding the reader of the limits of LAI.

In the conclusion, I try to picture the kind of work that I believe a future philosophy of information will need to undertake. Philosophers constantly occupy themselves with conceptual problems and explanations. There are philosophers' problems, which people often find uninteresting and are glad to leave to the specialists, and there are philosophical problems, problems about which any educated person will usually feel the urge to know and understand more. The development of an information culture, a digital society and a knowledge economy poses problems of the second kind. They may not yet have gained their special place in the philosophers' syllabus, but this does not make them any less important. I suggest that they open up a whole new area of philosophical investigation, which I have labelled the "philosophy of information", and promote the development of a general new philosophical perspective, which I define as critical constructionism. It is only the sketch of a philosophical programme, though, and I do not attempt a full argument in favour of the views I present there.

One of the remarkable things about computer science and ICT is that they have provided and continue to contribute to a sort of metadisciplinary, unified language. Information-related concepts and powerful metaphors acting as "hermeneutic devices" through which we may more or less acritically interpret the world are now common currency in all academic subjects and I introduce some of the most widespread in the course of this book. I know that readers may be worried about ICT and mathematical terminology, and I must admit that some elementary working knowledge is assumed; but most of the technical terms are explained, often when I first use them, and sometimes when they occur in the right context. There are also a few mathematical and logical expressions. They are there only for those readers who will find them helpful to clarify the points I am discussing. I have tried to make them useful but not indispensable, transliterating them in plain English whenever possible, so I hope that leaving them aside will not affect the general understanding of the text. I have not fully "normalised" the text because *repetita iuvant*, so whenever I have thought a point required some redundancy I have preferred to say things twice rather than be too succinct.

To my knowledge, there is no other general introduction to ICT for philosophers. However, the amount of primary and secondary literature on the topics discussed in this book is simply formidable and it is constantly growing. To try to deal with it, I have adopted a radical approach. First, whenever possible I have avoided footnotes, in order to keep the text as uncluttered as possible. I must admit it gave me special pleasure to be able to avoid treating this text as a scholarly book on the history of ideas. Second, and more importantly, I have merged the printed and the electronic medium to make the most of both: all printed and electronic sources used or mentioned in the book, and all suggestions for further reading have been placed in a webliography, which is available free and online at http://www.wolfson.ox.ac.uk/~floridi/webliography.htm. I opted for this solution for a number of reasons. First, because it saves me from the embarrassment of publishing yet another printed book arguing in favour of the vital importance of digital information. This text may be seen as a printout of a more complex "webook". Second, because it would have been pointless to provide Web references on paper when the reader needs them online anyway. Third, because an online webliography enables me to include information about topics that, for reasons of space and the editorial orientation of the text, could not be included here, such as information and computer ethics, artificial life, genetic algorithms, or nonmonotonic reasoning. And finally, because a webliography can be corrected and updated easily and on a regular basis, thanks to interaction with the readers.

I have selected the materials in the webliography according to the following criteria:

1 bibliographical and Internet sources that I have used, or referred to, in the book;
2 documents and sites that provide information for further philosophical research in the field;

3   sites that provide tutorials online that are:
   • strictly relevant to the topics treated in the book;
   • of reliable scientific quality (usually university courses);
   • technically accessible for philosophy students with only a minimal background in mathematics and logic.

The references and sites are organised according to the chapters in the printed book.

There is a quotation from Goethe, in Chapter 4, that describes very well how this work developed: "If I had actually been aware of all the efforts made in the past centuries, I would never have written a line, but would have done something else." I embarked upon this ambitious project only because I thought I could simply build on a guide to ICT for philosophers I had written in Italian (Floridi 1996). When I discussed the idea of a substantially updated and slightly adapted English edition of that book with Adrian Driscoll, the philosophy editor at Routledge, I imagined I was simply going to do some editorial work and include a few new ideas that I had developed. The referees, however, suggested further expansions, and a virus destroyed part of the initial files. By rewriting, updating, reshaping, adapting and expanding the original text, I ended up writing what is in fact a new book. When I finally realised what I was doing, it was too late. I missed two deadlines and I carried on. What remains of the original text is little more than the general project and a few paragraphs.

Apart from relying on the earlier book in Italian, I have also made use of Floridi 1995, 1997a, 1997b and 1997c. Parts of a first draft of the book were discussed in a series of papers I gave in Italy from 1996 to 1998 at the Universities of Bari, Perugia, Rome ("La Sapienza" and III Università), Torino, at the "Luigi Pareyson" School of the Istituto di Studi Filosofici in Cuneo, and during three courses I taught in Bari, Trapani and Rome. Parts of the book, especially the parts that come from Floridi 1995, the section on the Church–Turing thesis in Chapter 2 and the whole of Chapter 5, have been available on the Internet as "call for comments" documents for a long time. As a result, many people, literally hundreds, have helped me to refine my ideas. It would be impossible to thank all of them. My explicit thanks go to Adrian Driscoll for his editorial suggestions, Anna Gerber, editorial assistant at Routledge, for her patience and editorial help, and also to Margherita Benzi, Giorgio Bertolotti, Andrew Boucher, Marco Celani, B. Jack Copeland, Peter Denley, Mauro Di Giandomenico, Gary Forbis, Marco Giunti, Frances S. Grodzinsky, Stephen Harris, Nicola Guarino, Roberto Miraglia, Marco Mondadori, Hugh Rice, Neil Rickert, Hava T. Siegelmann, Peter Suber, Leonardo Valcamonici, Catherine A. Womack for many technical and conceptual suggestions on previous drafts of this book or sections thereof, and to Paul Oldfield and Mary Dortch for their editorial revisions of the final draft. Some of the contents of the book were also discussed with my students in Oxford, during our tutorials on mathematical logic, epistemology and metaphysics, philosophy of logic, and ethics and I am grateful to them for their valuable comments.

Research on the various stages of this work was made possible by the generous support of many institutions over the years, and I wish to thank the CASPUR (Consorzio interuniversitario per le Applicazioni di Supercalcolo Per l'Università e la Ricerca) for two research grants, the Department of Philosophy of the University of Bari, for a visiting professorship during the academic year 1996–7 at the Centre of Epistemology and Informatics directed by Mauro Di Giandomenico, and the Department of Educational Studies of the University of Rome III for a visiting professorship during the academic year 1997–8 at the SFEC Centre (Scuola a fini speciali di ricerca e di applicazione per la Formazione di Educatori di Comunità) directed by Paolo Impara. Not only did the two Centres provide an extraordinary environment in which to develop my research, but the courses I taught there on philosophy and ICT gave me the opportunity to re-focus my thoughts on a number of topics, especially the possible role of a future philosophy of information. Throughout the past few years, my college in Oxford, Wolfson College, has always provided excellent ICT facilities for my research, while Jesus and St Anne's Colleges have given me the opportunity to enjoy important feedback from my classes. Finally, the usual disclaimer: I am the only person responsible for any mistakes in the pages that follow, much as I wish I were not.

Luciano.Floridi@philosophy.ox.ac.uk
www.wolfson.ox.ac.uk/~floridi

Chapter 1

Divide et computa: philosophy and the digital environment

The digital revolution

Information and communication technology (ICT) has shaped the second half of the twentieth century irreversibly and more profoundly than atomic energy or space exploration. We may well do without nuclear power stations or the space shuttle, but nobody can reasonably conceive of a future society in which there are no more computers, no matter what dangers may be inherent in such an ineluctable evolution of our habitat. Evidence of a digital destiny is everywhere. In 1971, Intel launched the world's first commercial microprocessor, the 4004 (Intel is to hardware as Microsoft is to software: its chips account for 80 per cent of world-wide sales of general-purpose microprocessors), and some twenty-five years later microprocessors are hidden in virtually any technological device supporting our social activities, financial operations, administrative tasks or scientific research. At the beginning of 1998, experts estimated that there were more than 15 billion chips operating all over the world. In advanced societies, computer chips have become as widely diffused as the engines they control and ICT is today a highly pervasive, infra-technology that will eventually cease to be noticed because it has become thoroughly trivial.[1] Of course, many past predictions were simplistic exaggerations: tele-democracy, the paperless office, the workerless factory, the digital classroom, the cashless society, the electronic cottage, tele-jobs, or a computer generation were either chimeras dreamed up by overenthusiastic high-tech prophets, or just smart marketing slogans, for technological changes require longer periods of time and have a more complex nature. Nevertheless, it is hard to deny that our reliance on computer systems is a macroscopic phenomenon, and constantly growing. Even in science fiction the only consistent scenarios we can imagine are those in which highly sophisticated and powerful computers have become imperceptible because completely transparent to their users, overfamiliar objects behaving as ordinary components of the environment. Cash and capital were the lifeblood of our economies, but now they are being replaced by information, and computers are the best tools we have to manage it. Unless we find something better, they are here to stay and will play an ever more important role in our lives.

The knowledge economy apart, the extraordinary pervasiveness of ICT has been a direct effect of the increasing user-friendliness, powerfulness, flexibility, reliability, and affordability (inexpensiveness in terms of price/performance ratio) of computing devices. The virtuous circle created by the mutual interaction between these five factors has caused the merging of the three Cs (computers, communications and consumer electronics). Contemporary microelectronics, the discovery and manufacture of new materials, the elaboration of better algorithms and software, and the design of more efficient architectures are some of the factors that have made possible the extraordinary development of computing devices with enormous and yet steadily increasing computational power, which can easily be adapted to a very wide variety of humble tasks, at a cost that is constantly decreasing, sometimes in absolute terms. In the 1960s, Gordon Moore, the co-founder of Intel, predicted that the number of transistors that could be placed on a single chip would double every eighteen months. If Moore's famous law is still true fifty years after he proposed it – and there is currently no reason to think that it will not be – then at the beginning of the 2020s microprocessors may well be as much as 1000 times computationally more powerful than the Pentium III chip we were so proud of only yesterday, yet a child will be able to use them efficiently.

What we call "the information society" has been brought about by the fastest growing technology in history. No previous generation has ever been exposed to such an extraordinary acceleration of technological power and corresponding social changes. No wonder that the computer has become a symbol of the second half of the twentieth century and even of the new millennium, playing a cultural role comparable to that of mills in the Middle Ages, mechanical clocks in the seventeenth century and the loom or the steam engine in the age of the Industrial Revolution. Total pervasiveness and high power have raised ICT to the status of the characteristic technology of our time, both rhetorically and iconographically (Pagels 1984; Bolter 1984 provides a cultural perspective; see Lyon 1988 for a sociological analysis). The computer is a defining technology.

Such profound transformations have been already interpreted in terms of a digital revolution. It is a rather extreme view, and its epochal overtones may perhaps be unjustified, but those who reject it should consider that computer science and ICT applications are nowadays the most strategic of all the factors governing the life of our society and its future. The most developed post-industrial societies now literally live by information, and digital ICT is what keeps them constantly oxygenated. I am not referring just to the world of entertainment – perhaps we can do without it, though its economy is becoming a dominating variable in developed societies – but to fields such as economics and international politics.

In advanced economies, computing is undoubtedly a crucial element, if not by far the leading factor determining the possibility of success (Dertouzos 1997; Tapscott 1996; Tapscott and Caston 1993). It is not that a fully computerised company will necessarily be successful, but rather that a non-computerised company will stand no chance of survival in a competitive market. If digital technology is causing unemployment among blue- and white-collar workers, eroding job opportunities in some manufacturing and service sectors, it is also true that it has created completely new fields of investment for human and financial resources. This is so much the case that it is still unclear whether, in the long run, the phenomenon may not be more accurately interpreted as a displacement and reallocation of the working force. Like other technological innovations, computers can certainly be used to make workforces redundant or de-skilled, reducing people to the condition of low-waged machine-minders, but at the same time they can be used to enhance the quality of working life, improve workers' job satisfaction and responsibility, and re-skill the workforce. The real point is that technological determinism is unjustified and that work organisation and the quality of working life depend much more on overall managerial philosophies and strategic decisions than on the simple introduction of a particular type of technology. It is obviously premature to talk of a cashless society, but although it is not yet a digital market, the market in the digital is a flourishing economic area, which can partially balance the negative effect that computerisation has on job opportunities. In 1997, 25 per cent of America's real economic growth was generated by the PC industry, while international sales of ICT amounted to $610 billion, making ICT the largest industrial sector in the world. As for the convergence and globalisation of regional economies, this is only a macroscopic effect of the more fundamental phenomenon represented by the development of a world-wide system of digital communication, through which information can be exchanged anywhere, in real time, constantly, cheaply and reliably.

In international politics, digital technology showed its muscle in the Gulf War. In less than two months (16 January to 28 February 1991) guided missiles, "smart" munitions, night vision equipment, infra-red sensors, Global Positioning Systems, cruise missiles, free-flight rockets with multiple warheads, anti-missile missiles, and modern data communications systems helped to destroy a 500,000-strong Iraqi army. It was the defeat of an "object-oriented" army by an information-based superpower. The digital revolution has brought about transformations in modern technological warfare comparable only to the industrial production of weapons, or the invention of tanks and military aircraft. No power will ever be an international superpower without an army of computer engineers, not least because of the unreliability of our machines, as the tragic killing of 290 innocent civilians in an Iranian airbus, mistakenly brought down by a US guided missile during the conflict, will remind us for ever.

The four areas of the digital revolution

Information has matured into an asset of growing value, with marketable quantities and prices. It is the new *digital gold* and is one of the most valuable resources at our disposal. We all know this and this is why we are ready to describe our society as the information society. In the information society, changes in social standards are ever more deeply and extensively ICT-driven or induced. Such modifications in the growth, the fruition and the management of information resources and services concern four main sectors: computation, automatic control, modelling, and information management. This sequence follows a conceptual order and only partially overlaps through time.

Computation

"Computation" seems to be a sufficiently intuitive concept, but as soon as we try to provide a clear and fully satisfactory definition of it we immediately realise how difficult the task is (Cutland 1980). According to different perspectives, computation may be described as a logical or physical process of generation of final states (outputs) from initial states (inputs), based on:

1   rule-governed state-transitions, or
2   discrete or digital rule-governed state-transitions, or
3   a series of rule-governed state-transitions for which the rule can be altered, or
4   rule-governed state-transitions between interpretable states.

There are some difficulties with these definitions. (1) is too loose, for it also applies to devices such as printers and washing machines, physical systems that we do not include in the class of computational systems; (2) is perhaps too strict, for it excludes forms of analogue computation (I shall discuss this point at greater length when talking about Super Turing machines); (3) is either vague or too strict, for there are computational systems, like pocket calculators, with embedded rules (non-programmable algorithms); (4) seems to be the most satisfactory. It makes the interpretable representation of a state a necessary condition for computation. However, even (4) is not uncontroversial because it is not altogether clear whether state-transitions of quantum computers (see Chapter 5) – which are computational systems that belong to the same class of Turing machines – are all *interpretable* representations in the same sense in which all states of a so-called Turing machine are, given the fact that it is impossible to gain complete knowledge of the state of a quantum register through measurement, as we shall see later (measuring or describing by direct inspection the states of a quantum register alters them, contrary to what happens in a "Newtonian" device). The same problem arises if we consider the brain a computational system. We shall see in the next chapter that it may be easier to explain the concept of "computability" by referring precisely to a Turing machine and its properties. For the time being, let us rely on our intuitive understanding of the concept.

That a computer is above all a computational system, in the sense of a straightforward number cruncher, is a trivial truth hardly worth mentioning. The earliest and most direct applications of computers concerned the elaboration and advancement of quantifiable information. The remarkable technological and scientific developments of the second half of the twentieth century owe a great deal to the possibility of solving a huge number of mathematical and computational problems practically (though not in principle) beyond the power of our finite, biological brains, and hence of carrying out operations which would not have been humanly sustainable either in terms of organisation or time-consumption, even if armies of assistants had been available. This has been true since the beginning of the history of computer science. One of the first high-speed electronic digital computers (EDC), known as ENIAC (Electronic Numerical Integrator and Computer) was built in 1945 by John W. Mauchly for the American army, in order to calculate complex ballistic firing tables. There was no human–computer interface, as we understand the concept nowadays, because the user was literally inside the computer, given its dimensions, and programming was performed with a screwdriver. ENIAC occupied 167.3 square metres, consisted of 17,469 vacuum tubes, had a speed of several hundred multiplications per minute, could perform 5,000 additions per second, and was extremely difficult to program, since its "software" was wired into the processor and had to be manually altered, a problem definitively solved only in the 1950s, with the construction of UNIVAC 1 (Universal Automatic Computer) and then IBM's first mainframes, which adopted more efficient architectures. In this respect, ENIAC, UNIVAC, pocket calculators or the latest personal computers all belong to the long history of computational devices which stretches from the abacus to Pascal's adding machine (1642), through Leibniz's multiplication machine (1671) to Babbage's analytical engine (1835), but I shall say more about this in the next chapter.

Automatic control

Although computation has remained a major area of application, it would be short-sighted to think that the impact of the technological innovations brought about by the diffusion of digital ICT has been limited just to straightforward numerical problems, and hence to important but quite specific sectors of mathematical applications. For not only have computers helped us to read some of the most complex chapters in the "mathematical book of nature", they also have put us in a position to control a large variety of physical and bureaucratic processes automatically (office automation and EDP, electronic data processing). Today, the complex functioning of an increasing number of manufacturing and administrative operations, including the manipulation of consumption, requires the constant intervention of microprocessors and other digital devices. Following on from the process of mechanisation, computers have caused a second industrial revolution through the implementation of massive automation. As industry has moved from a low-technology, unspecialised, and labour-intensive stage to a highly mechanised, automated (electronics), AT-intensive (advanced technology) and more specialised stage, it has become extensively information-based and hence more and more computer-dependent. Thus, we speak of

- computer-numerically-controlled (CNC) machines that are employed to repeat operations exactly as programmed, rapidly and accurately;
- computer-aided manufacturing (CAM), i.e. the use of computers in factories to control CNC machine tools, robots and whole production processes cheaply and virtually without operators;
- computer-aided design (CAD), i.e. the use of computers to design and model most, when not all, of the features of a particular product (such as its size, shape, the form of each of its component parts, its overall structure) by storing data as two- or three-dimensional drawings, and hence to simulate its performance and make it easier for large groups of designers and engineers to work on the same project even when they are in different locations;
- computer-controlled logistics (CCL);
- computer-integrated manufacturing (CIM) systems, i.e. methods of manufacturing resulting from the combination of CNC + CAM + CAD + CCL, that allow designers, engineers and managers to project, model, simulate, test and produce a particular product more efficiently and quickly, while also monitoring the whole process.

Computers are today so commonly used to plan whole manufacturing processes, to test finished parts, to activate, carry out, regulate and control whole phases in the production process, that virtually all aspects of the manufacturing of goods – including better working conditions and safety measures, constant progress in the implementation of cost-saving procedures, the improvement of the quality/price ratio of finished products and the semi-customisation of goods (*tailoring*) – are thoroughly dependent on the evolution, application and diffusion of computing in all its varieties. The possibility of the fully automated AT factory, in which human intervention is limited to overall control and decision-making, is only one more effect of the digital revolution.

Modelling and virtual reality

The mathematical description and the digital control of the physical environment have provided the solid premises for its potential replacement by mathematical models (systems of differential equations) in *scientific computing* (i.e. "the collection of tools, techniques and theories required to solve on a computer mathematical models of problems in science and engineering", Golub and Ortega 1993: 2) and virtual reality environments (Aukstakalnis and Blatner 1992; Rheingold 1991; Woolley 1992; Heim 1993 provides a "Techno-Taoist" [*sic*] approach; on the use of IT for philosophical modelling see Grim *et al.* 1998). Digital computing has become crucial whenever it is necessary to simulate real-life properties and forecast the behaviour of objects placed in contexts that are either not reproducible in laboratory situations or simply not testable at all, whether for safety reasons, for example, or because of the high cost of building and testing physical prototypes, or because we need non-invasive and non-destructive techniques of analysis, as in medical contexts. Bi- or tri-dimensional (2D and 3D) digital images are produced either by drawing them with a conventional paint program, as in many software games–we may call this the "imagist" approach – or by means of computer graphics (used by engineers, architects or interior designers, for example). In the latter, the computer is programmed to model the object in question, to describe its geometry, accurately render its colour, texture and surface features, depict its movements convincingly, and represent perspective views, shadows, reflections, and highlights – hence adopting an obviously "constructionist" approach. The results are synthetic entities and phenomena, software-generated objects and digital effects representing fully articulated, solid and photorealistic realities, which are capable of responding to the environment and interacting with other synthetic entities or external inputs, and which may not necessarily stand in for counterparts existing or experienceable in real life. The ultimate goal is authenticity, understood as a virtual hyper-realism. The possibility of modelling virtual objects, their properties and the phenomena they are involved in, has become an essential requirement not only in meteorology or nuclear physics, but also in biochemistry and computational molecular biology (where computers are essential to reconstruct the human genome), in tectonics, in economics, in architecture (e.g. to create realistic walkthroughs of proposed projects), in astrophysics, in surgical simulations (surgeons explore surgical procedures on computer-modelled patients), and in computerised axial tomography,[2] just to mention some of the most obvious applications. Indeed, every area of human knowledge whose models and entities – whether real or theoretical no longer matters – can be translated into the digital language of bits is, and will inevitably be, more and more dependent upon ICT capacity to let us perceive and handle the objects under investigation, as if they were everyday things, pieces on a chess board that can be automatically moved, rotated, mirrored, scaled, magnified, modified, combined and subjected to the most diverse transformations and tests.

It is true that, so far, digital technology has made swifter and deeper advancements in the reproduction of sound than of images and animation – technologically, digital sound and compact disks represent a reasonably mature sector – but it is sufficient to think of the potential offered by CAD and CG (computer graphics) programs, of the evolution of computer animation and sophisticated digital effects in films like *Star Wars*, *Independence Day*, *The Fifth Element*, *Titanic* (50 per cent of the film contains "digital realities") or of the total virtuality of *Toy Story* (a film with 500 Gb worth of pixels, made possible by 800,000 hours of computing time on Silicon Graphics workstations and Sun SparcStations) to realise that the diffusion of more or less rich forms of virtual reality environments (VRE) is only a matter of years away, and that in the future not only cartoons but actors too may never age.[3]

In a rich VRE, single or multiple users are immersed in an environment comprised of data and can interact and operate in real time with the aid of a dataglove, full body suit, 3D eyephones and a simulation of 360 degree sound (touch-feedback systems are also possible). After a long period in which there has been a prevailingly Cartesian view of knowledge and rational thinking as a series of intuitions enjoyed by a disembodied mind and chiefly brought about by a flow of algebraic equations and analytic steps, we are witnessing the revaluation of the sensorially-enriched (visual and tactile and synthetic) epistemology so dear to Greek and Renaissance philosophers (Barwise and Etchemendy 1998; Floridi 1997b). Seeing is believing and by means of digital technology we can recreate or, even more radically, generate the reality we deal with, first by codifying it into the language of bits and then by further translating the digital outcome into analogue entities easily manageable by our minds.

Information management

The computerised description and control of the physical environment, together with the digital construction of a synthetic world, are, finally, intertwined with a fourth area of application, represented by the transformation of the encyclopaedic macrocosm of data, information, ideas, knowledge, beliefs, codified experiences, memories, images, artistic interpretations and other mental creations into a global *infosphere*. The infosphere is the whole system of services and documents, encoded in any semiotic and physical media, whose contents include any sort of data, information and knowledge (for an analysis of the distinction between these three notions see Chapter 4), with no limitations either in size, typology or logical structure. Hence it ranges from alphanumeric texts (i.e. texts including letters, numbers and diacritic symbols) and multimedia products to statistical data, from films and hypertexts to whole text-banks and collections of pictures, from mathematical formulae to sounds and videoclips. As regards the infosphere, the symbolic-computational power of ICT tools is employed for ends that go beyond the solution of complex numerical problems, the control of a mechanical world or the creation of virtual models. Computer science and ICT provide the new means to generate, manufacture and control the flow of digital data and information (which is also being generated, in increasingly huge quantities, by the three areas of application just mentioned) thus managing its life cycle (creation, input, integration, correction, structuring and organisation, updating, storage, searching, querying, retrieval, dissemination, transmission, uploading, downloading, linking, etc.). This is the most recent development of ICT and deserves particular attention.

From the analogue to the digital: the new physics of knowledge

As one of the fundamental forces behind the digital revolution, the importance of the managerial functions exercised by ICT with respect to the whole domain of codified knowledge can hardly be overemphasised. The infosphere constitutes an intellectual space whose density and extent are constantly increasing, although at disparate rates in different ages and cultures. Here are a few indications. At the end of the 1970s, it was estimated that 200,000 theorems were proved in the various branches of mathematics every year. Data concerning the trends in 1997/8 show that 14,000 publishers released 50,000 new titles on to the market every year, and this was just in the USA. In the world as a whole, there are at least 40,000 scientific journals, accounting for more than 1 million new articles published every year, that is, about 3,000 scientific articles every day. The MIT Laboratory for Computer Science estimated the total quantity of digital data in the world at the beginning of 1998 to be around 10^{18} bytes (this is approximately an exabyte = one thousand million gigabytes, or more precisely 2^{60} bytes), meaning that each person living at the time had inherited 200 Mb of digital data from the past. In 1996, it was calculated that there were 100 billion photographic images in the world. Sociologists of knowledge reckon that our encyclopaedic space doubles every ten years. The reader will certainly have felt a similar sense of overwhelming dismay when considering the rate at which the already huge literature in her or his special field is constantly growing. It is not just the result of a "publish or perish" policy. The pace of change is bound to accelerate the larger the population of educated people becomes. Now, within each information system, be this a bank, a city council office, a school or even, as in our case, the universe of organised knowledge taken as a whole, the demand for further information increases in a way that interacts directly with the extent and the degree of complexity of the system in question. This is to say that, apart from human ingenuity, the relative extent to which any specific sector of the infosphere can expand, at any particular time in history, is a function of three variables:

- the quality and quantity of information stored until that time;
- the current degree of actual accessibility of the memory of the system;

- the level of efficiency with which the retrievable information can be further elaborated.

Naturally, effective management aims at establishing a satisfactory equilibrium between the increasing magnitude and complexity of the system, on the one hand, and the equally expanding amount of information constantly required by its functioning and growth, on the other, the actual level of accessibility representing the degree of success attained by such efforts at any particular moment. It follows that, in theory, each information system constantly strives to promote the creation of all management procedures that, being reasonably achievable and adoptable, may grant and improve economical access to, and satisfactory treatment of, the amount of information required by the system itself. A clear instance of this general law is the development of Erp (enterprise resource management) software, which allows a company to control, plan and organise the information resources of the system, and intranet products. An *intranet* is a bounded network that provides services similar to those provided by the Internet, but which is not necessarily connected to the latter. (If the intranet provides some external access to its contents or services it is known as *extranet*.) Having discovered the extraordinary utility, flexibility, efficiency and friendliness of Internet applications, companies have been quick to exploit the same concepts and applications for the management of their internal information and procedures, grasping, in a matter of months, the obvious similarities between the outside macrocosm of information, represented by the Internet, and the inside microcosm represented by each company's own database and information processes.

Since there is no constructive advancement of knowledge without an accurate memory of the past, so that the interminable process of constructing, recording and structuring the infosphere would be fruitless if efficient and economical methods were not concurrently devised to make past knowledge adequately available and processable, the capitalisation of information constantly regulates its own growth and the extension of the infosphere develops through a series of homeostatic stages,[4] more or less macroscopic in nature. Thus one could outline the comparatively brief history of western culture in terms of the evolution of the methods whereby organised knowledge has been made potentially available to the individual mind. Organised knowledge moved from the frail and volatile memory of oral transmission to the more stable memory of written texts, from papyrus *volumina*, capable of providing only linear access to their contents, to parchment *codices*, which made random access possible, from the appearance of the tables of contents to the elaboration of indexes, from the invention of printing to the establishment of public libraries and then the elaboration of a science of bibliography, from the appearance of scientific journals to reference texts such as companions, encyclopaedias or lexicons, from the publication of reviews to ever more specialised forms of literature such as dictionaries, thesauri, directories, guides and catalogues. Each invention and innovation has been the outcome not only of new cultural climates – the development of philosophical historiography since the Renaissance, or the diffusion of scholarly journals written in Latin during the seventeenth and the eighteenth century are two obvious examples – but also by the appearance of crucial technologies, thanks to which thought has been able to take the greatest advantage of its own past, thus making important advances in the scale of the full fruition of knowledge.

Within the process whereby knowledge promotes both its growth and the elaboration of the means for its own management, the invention of printing and of computers have usually been considered two turning points, and they certainly deserve special places in the history of culture, as long as their importance is not misunderstood, or obscured by superficial associations. At the beginning of modern times, the printed book represented a powerful new medium whereby a text, now mechanically fixed on paper, could be reproduced more quickly and cheaply, and hence be more safely stored and more widely diffused. Its innovative character consisted in the tremendous acceleration it brought in the recovery, conservation and dissemination of knowledge among an increasingly large number of people, now coming to be described as the public or readership. But such enlarged availability of knowledge did little to improve the degree to which an individual could take advantage of the entire infosphere, since the process of information retrieval remained largely unaffected by the appearance of printed paper. Wider consumption should not be confused with more efficient exploitation. Quite the contrary, in terms of the effective use of all the available printed resources, the publication of million of texts only made the problems of management more complex, while their solution became every day more crucial. The wider the extension of organised knowledge became, the higher and more specialised the hierarchy of the maps of the universe of knowledge had to be. In the end, the printed medium showed itself capable of coping with the extension of knowledge only vertically, by producing increasingly specialised guides and then further guides to guides, in an endless hierarchy. So much so that, soon after Gutenberg, the development of new, automatic methods to manipulate, access and control the encyclopaedic domain became first critical, then indispensable. As a consequence, the history of modern technology is full of attempts to reproduce, at the level of the automation of the information process, the same mechanical improvements already achieved by the press and movable type at the level of the reproduction of knowledge. Jonathan Swift's description of the work done in the grand Academy of Lagado, in *Gulliver's Travels*, is a classic parody of such efforts. The passage is entertaining and worth quoting in full:

> I was received very kindly by the Warden, and went for many days to the Academy. Every room has in it one or more projectors, and I believe I

could not be in fewer than five hundred rooms. . . . We crossed a walk to the other part of the Academy, where, as I have already said, the projectors in speculative learning resided.

The first professor I saw was in a very large room, with forty pupils about him. After salutation, observing me to look earnestly upon a frame, which took up the greatest part of both the length and breadth of the room, he said perhaps I might wonder to see him employed in a project for improving speculative knowledge by practical and mechanical operations. But the world would soon be sensible of its usefulness, and he flattered himself that a more noble exalted thought never sprang in any other man's head. Everyone knew how laborious the usual method is of attaining to arts and sciences; whereas by his contrivance the most ignorant person at a reasonable charge, and with a little bodily labour, may write books in philosophy, poetry, politics, law, mathematics, and theology, without the least assistance from genius or study. He then led me to the frame, about the sides whereof all his pupils stood in ranks. It was twenty feet square, placed in the middle of the room. The superficies was composed of several bits of wood, about the bigness of a die, but some larger than others. They were all linked together by slender wires. These bits of wood were covered on every square with paper pasted on them, and on these papers were written all the words of their language, in their several moods, tenses, and declensions, but without any order. The professor then desired me to observe, for he was going to set his engine at work. The pupils at his command took each of them hold of an iron handle, whereof there were forty fixed round the edges of the frame, and giving them a sudden turn, the whole disposition of the words was entirely changed. He then commanded six and thirty of the lads to read the several lines softly as they appeared upon the frame; and where they found three or four words together that might make part of a sentence, they dictated to the four remaining boys who were scribes. This work was repeated three or four times, and at every turn the engine was so contrived that the words shifted into new places, as the square bits of wood moved upside down.

Six hours a day the young students were employed in this labour, and the professor showed me several volumes in large folio already collected, of broken sentences, which he intended to piece together, and out of those rich materials to give the world a complete body of all arts and sciences; which however might be still improved, and much expedited, if the public would raise a fund for making and employing five hundred such frames in Lagado, and oblige the managers to contribute in common their several collections.

He assured me, that this invention had employed all his thoughts from his youth, that he had emptied the whole vocabulary into his frame, and made the strictest computation of the general proportion there is in books between the numbers of particles, nouns, and verbs, and other parts of speech.

I made my humblest acknowledgements to this illustrious person for his great communicativeness, and promised, if ever I had the good fortune to return to my native country, that I would do him justice, as the sole inventor of this wonderful machine; the form and contrivance of which I desired leave to delineate upon paper, as in the figure here annexed. I told him, although it were the custom of our learned in Europe to steal inventions from each other, who had thereby at least this advantage, that it became a controversy which was the right owner, yet I would take such caution, that he should have the honour entire without a rival.

The ironic tone of the passage should not mislead us. The construction of a Borgesian library *ante litteram* was indeed ridiculous, but the mechanical idea behind it was far from being silly. Swift's masterpiece was published anonymously in 1726. In 1801, after becoming bankrupt, the French textile manufacturer Joseph-Marie Jacquard invented a system of punched cards to control looms and to allow patterns to be woven without the intervention of the weaver. In 1833, Charles Babbage, the English mathematician rightly considered the most important precursor of modern information technology, borrowed Jacquard's idea to design his analytical engine, a general-purpose computing machine for mechanically performing different calculations according to a program input on punched cards. The analytical engine was never constructed, and only later re-discovered. It would have required some 50,000 moving components. However, around 1880 the US inventor Herman Hollerith applied the same technology to construct the first data-processing machine, using punched cards for the US census, and Jacquard-style punched cards were widely used in the early computers of the 1940s–1970s. Early efforts to construct merely mechanical devices to process information efficiently all failed, but the reason why they failed is not that punched cards or other similar devices were unpractical, but that such an enterprise required a much more radical approach than the simple extension of a mechanical solution to the problem of semiotic management. A modification both in the language of the infosphere – binary logic – and in its physical nature – the electronic implementation of such a logic via the microprocessor – was necessary. Only a new physics of knowledge, the passage from printed paper to digital-electronic data, finally made possible a thoroughly satisfactory way of managing information, and hence much more efficient control over the system of knowledge. Punched cards acquired their great value only as input devices of a binary and electronic machine. Once this step was made, ICT, as the long-awaited response to the invention of printing, quickly became the most pervasive of all the technologies of our time. The lesson to be learnt from such a process is clear. If on the one hand the appearance and spread of computer technology has caused the expansion of knowledge, already begun with the invention of printing, to accelerate – thus equally helping to promote the impressive growth of scientific specialisation – on the other hand ICT has also begun to provide at least a partial solution to the organisational problems arising from the immense domain of codified knowledge.

The digitisation of the infosphere: three steps

The press mechanically enlarged and strengthened our intellectual space; the computer has made it electronically modifiable, orderable, retrievable and processable. We have seen that the appearance of ICT in the second half of the twentieth century in an attempt to solve our problems of infosphere management can be interpreted, conceptually, as a perfectly coherent out-come of the self-regulating process governing the growth of the infosphere itself. The necessary process of converting the entire domain of organised knowledge into a new, digital macrocosm began slowly in the 1950s and, since then, has followed three fundamental directions:

(1) *Extension*: from numeric data to multimedia information and virtual reality

Formal and natural languages, all intrinsically discrete and well structured, have been the first to become digitised. The next step has concerned the domain of sounds, images and motion, three kinds of phenomena that, being reproducible in analogue fashion, could also be subject to digital encoding (a multimedia document consists of a seamless synthesis of alphanumeric texts, sounds, images and motions). The result has been a steady increase in the kinds of digital information available, which in turn has made possible the construction of a digital domain that has come to encompass not only num-bers and texts but also sounds, images and then animation.

(2) *Visualisation and manipulation*: from punched cards to 3D graphic interfaces

The growing extent of the binary domain soon required forms of access far more congenial to the human mind than the digital. The invention and improvement of VDU (visual display units, the screen of the computer), together with the development of GUI (graphic user interface, i.e. interfaces such as Windows) and WYSIWYG software ("what you see is what you get" applications, such as word processors) and WIMP systems (the Windows, Icon, Menu, Pointer system made popular by Apple) have made possible a spectacular return of the analogue, as the fundamental threshold between the binary, intersubjective macrocosm of information and the mental microcosm of each individual's understanding. As a result, we have moved from being inside a real computer to being inside a computerised reality: visual interfaces have first enabled us to keep some distance from the system, as images to see and then "images to read" (e.g. the Web), and have ended up generating images to inhabit.

(3) *Convergence and integration*: from the mainframe to the Internet

Finally, the translation of alphanumeric texts, images, sounds and animation into the language of bytes has made possible an increasing integration of the various domains of the infosphere into an ever wider and more complex digital universe. The process has further developed in two directions: the qualitative integration of the various types of digitised information by means of virtual reality; and the quantitative integration of the local domains into a more and more extended environment of networks, which tends towards a global, multimedia, hypertextual, unified macrocosm of digitised documents.

The global network is only a stage in the endless self-regulating process through which the infosphere constantly strives to respond to its own growth. As a consequence of the three processes of extension, visualisation/ manipulation and convergence/integration, we shall see, in Chapter 3, that the Internet has made possible a management of knowledge that is faster, wider in scope, more complete in terms of types of information and easier to exercise than ever before. Finally, as a stage in the life cycle of the encyclopaedia, the network has already given rise to unprecedented innovations and to fundamental new problems, some of which are especially relevant to the future of scholarship and organised knowledge. The convergence of the three fundamental trends analysed in this section was already evident in the United States by the end of the 1980s and overcame its critical stage at the beginning of the 1990s, when the Internet finally became a widely-diffused technology, bringing about the third information age (see Chapter 3).

The relations between philosophy and computing

Having established that human society is at a stage in which issues arising from the management of information are as crucial and rich in consequences as problems caused by its generation, it is legitimate to ask now how far this macrocultural phenomenon may concern philosophy, both as a discipline which provides the conceptual means necessary to explain and understand such significant phenomena, and as an area itself deeply affected by the recent technological transformations. For the sake of simplicity, the different relations between philosophical studies and computer science with its ICT applications can be organised into four, often overlapping, areas.

Sociology of the information society

We may consider under a single heading the great variety of investigations that have occupied philosophers and scientists since they have attempted to interpret and understand the cultural and intellectual transformations brought about by the diffusion of digital technology. Typical examples are provided by the works of Baudrillard (1972, 1981, 1991), Bolter (1984), De Kerkhove (1991), Lévy (1990), Machlup (1980–4), Machlup and Leeson

(1978), Machlup and Mansfield (1983), and Weizenbaum (1976). This is still a rather new sector of scientific research, and one that will probably require more work in the future. Unfortunately, it still suffers from a lack of specific academic recognition (journals, associations, undergraduate courses, a market for basic introductory literature on the topic, etc.) and from the often over-influential presence of a previous well-established tradition of mass media studies. The same holds true for the following field.

The philosophy of information

Owing to the emergence of the information society, there has in recent times been an increasing interest in what I shall call the philosophy of information (Bynum and Moor 1998; Deutsch 1997; Dretske 1981; Mitcham and Huning 1986; Sloman 1978; Winograd and Flores 1987). Some examples of this area of contact between philosophy, computing and OCT applications are:

Information and Management Systems Methodology: Harry 1990 is a good conceptual introduction; see also Dahlbom and Mathiassen 1993, Winder *et al.* 1997;

Formal Ontology: Burkhardt and Smith 1991;

The Metaphysics of Virtual Reality: see Heim 1993 for a bibliography;

The Epistemology of Computing (methodological investigations concerning computer science): Thagard 1988; Vamos 1991;

The Philosophy of Artificial Intelligence: Feigenbaum and Feldman 1963; Weizenbaum 1976 is an early criticism; Haugeland 1985 is a good and critical philosophical introduction; see also Minsky 1987; Boden 1987 and 1990, which is a useful collection; Dreyfus and Dreyfus 1986 and 1988; Dreyfus 1992 and 1998 offer interesting criticisms of AI from a phenomenological perspective, on which Chapter 5 is based, but also a questionable, if influential, Heidegerrian reconstruction of AI's conceptual roots in the history of philosophy; Copeland 1993 is one of the best philosophical introductions; Gillies 1996 analyses AI in connection with methodological issues; see also Simon 1996; Shapiro 1992 is a useful reference; Rich and Knight 1991, Russell and Norvik 1995 are two technical introductions; Partridge and Wilks 1990 is a sourcebook that includes reprints of seminal papers, some new essays and a fifty-page annotated bibliography;

Computer Ethics: Johnson 1994; Moor 1985;

The Philosophy of Artificial Life: Boden 1996; Emmeche 1991; artificial life abstracts the details of a range of lifelike systems, e.g. ecologies, immune systems, autonomously evolving social groups, identifies the essential properties that unify and explain them, synthesises the latter in computationally implemented models and simulations, and then seeks to understand the essential processes shared by broad classes of lifelike systems, such as bottom-up, emergent generation of order, spontaneous self-organisation, co-operation, self-reproduction, metabolisation, learning, adaptation and evolution;

The Philosophy of CMC (computer-mediated communication): Ess 1996;

Artificial Morality (the use of computerised models for the study of rational choice in ethical contexts).

In all these cases, we are presented with studies that investigate computer science and its technological applications both as an autonomous body of knowledge and as the constitutive source of the new environment of modern life, the infosphere.

It is not the task of this book to develop even a sketch of what a philosophy of information may be like in detail. Much work still needs to be done before a unified theory may emerge. Currently, one may only suggest that the specific nature of the philosophy of information is probably comparable to that of other special branches, such as the philosophy of mathematics or the philosophy of logic: they are old philosophical subjects which nevertheless have acquired their salient features only relatively late in the history of thought.

All "philosophies of . . ." show a tendency to converge towards two poles, one *phenomenological* and the other *metatheoretical*. The philosophy of language or the philosophy of knowledge are two examples of "phenomenologies" or philosophies of a phenomenon: their subjects are semiotic codes, not linguistic theories, and epistemic capacities, practices and contents, not cognitive sciences. The philosophy of physics and the philosophy of social sciences, on the other hand, are obvious instances of "metatheories": they investigate philosophical problems arising from organised systems of knowledge, which only in their turn investigate natural or human phenomena.

Some specific "philosophies of . . .", however, show only a tension between the two poles, often combining both phenomenological and metatheoretical interests. This is the case with the philosophy of mathematics and the philosophy of logic, for example, and it may also apply to the philosophy of information itself. These special philosophies caught in the middle, as it were, show a tendency to work on specific classes of phenomena – as is the case with other phenomenologies – but they also address such phenomena through metatheoretical approaches, that is, by starting from an interest in specific classes of theoretical statements, technical concepts or scientific issues concerning those very same classes of phenomena – as is the case with other philosophies of theories.

In the end, the tension pulls each specific "philosophy of . . ." more towards one or other pole. Hence the philosophy of logic shows a constant tendency to concentrate mainly on problems arising from logic understood as a specific mathematical theory of deductive inferences that are formally valid, whereas it pays comparatively marginal attention to problems concerning logic as a field of phenomena, or what, for want of a better description, one may call the expression of the human rational logos. In other words, the philosophy of logic is metatheoretically biased. Conversely, the philosophy of information is primarily concerned with the whole domain of phenomena represented by the world of information, and inclines towards a metatheoretical approach only in so far as it addresses the philosophical problems implicit in the world of information by starting from the vantage point represented by information science, computer science and ICT. The philosophy of information is therefore phenomenologically biased, and is more a philosophy of the infosphere than a philosophy of computer science or ICT *tout court*.

This metatheoretical interest in the sciences of information and computation is justifiable. If the scientific revolution in the seventeenth century made philosophers redirect their attention from the nature of things to the epistemic relation that human beings have with them, the subsequent growth of the information society and the appearance of the artificial infosphere, as the true environment in which people now spend most of their intentional lives as conscious beings, have led contemporary philosophy to privilege, rather than epistemological investigations *tout court*, critical reflection first on the domain represented by the memory and languages of organised knowledge and then on the instruments whereby the infosphere is managed.

Both the last two sections show what philosophy could do for the interpretation of the digital revolution and the information society, but neither area constitutes the central topic of this book, in which we shall rather concentrate on the next two fields.

The philosophy of AI (artificial intelligence)

The study of artificial intelligence (AI), in strict relation to psychological and physiological investigations of the nature of biological intelligence and the philosophy of mind, represents the oldest area of contact between philosophy and computer science. Given the aim of this book, however, we shall concentrate on AI understood as a chapter in the history of ICT, rather than on the philosophy of AI, e.g. arguments concerning the possibility of artificial intelligence based on Searle's Chinese room or Gödel's theorem. I trust the distinction will become fully clear by the end of Chapter 5. What seems worth anticipating here is that, in the past, the heated debate on the analogies, or even the potential identity, between minds/brains and computers appears to have had the unfortunate counter-effect of keeping a number of philosophers away from other aspects of the digital revolution of equally profound philosophical interest.

Philosophy and aided intelligence

This last field, which is sometimes described, with a wordplay, as that of aided or augmented intelligence ("Augmented Intelligence" was coined in the

1960s by Douglas Engelbart, one of the fathers of hypermedia), is the one to which I have tried to call the reader's attention in the foregoing pages, and it belongs to the wider subject known as humanities computing (Hockey 1980; Kenny 1992; Lancashire 1988; Miall 1990; Tannenbaum 1988, 1991). In such a context, wondering what is implicit in the relation between computing, ICT and philosophy means to ask not only whether philosophers may be able to exploit recent technological innovations for their work, and if so, to what extent, but also what it means for a philosopher to be abreast of the technology of our time (Burkholder 1992; Bynum and Moor 1998). As regards the first issue, we need to become acquainted with, and understand how to use the main instruments and services provided by ICT, including personal computers, software applications, the Internet, databases and electronic texts. I shall not dwell on this topic here because this is the task of the following chapters. However, a few more words may be said on the second issue. Today, to be up to date with the most advanced ICT developments means

- to be able to understand and make use of computer technology in an everyday context (computer literacy);
- to use to the full the digital products already available, both in order to carry out one's own tasks as a student, teacher or researcher more quickly and efficiently, and to combat sectorial specialisation, which is suffocating philosophy, in favour of a more fruitful interdisciplinarity;
- to enlarge the range of projects which are theoretically feasible. As elementary examples, one may think of the opportunity of editing hypermedia versions of the classics in combination with the relevant secondary literature, or producing interactive logic textbooks on the Web;
- to present oneself not only as a philosopher but also as an informed and intelligent user, who can enter into dialogue with the industry and promote the production of new technological solutions in order to obtain increasingly adequate and flexible services from the ICT market.

In summary, philosophers should be able to make the most of what has been made easier by ICT, get the best out of what has been made possible for the first time by ICT, and finally suggest new ICT applications for future needs. One of the aims of this book is to provide sufficient background for the fulfilment of these goals. We shall begin by looking at the computational nature of the instruments in question, the tools of our digital workshop.

Chapter 2

The digital workshop

From the laboratory to the house

At the end of 1993 there were about 300 million users of personal computers (PCs) and in 1997 their number was estimated at almost 2 billion. The mass diffusion of the PC since the middle of the 1970s has spread the need for computer literacy, supermarkets list computers as ordinary commodities, and nowadays everyone is supposed to be able to choose and work with a computer, without having any special competence. A PC is just slightly more difficult to use than a car, or domestic white or brown goods, not least because the latter too have become computerised. Of course, each device has a number of features that one should be informed about if one aims to distinguish between the different models, choose more wisely according to one's own needs and employ them to their best. Nevertheless, it is also true that the products on sale are all subject to the same marketing strategies, so the price/performance ratio is hardly ever a source of big surprises. Consequently, if one buys a PC of a decent brand in the nearest shop, with a dash of common sense and an eye to one's wallet rather than to the latest advertisements, one is unlikely to make a big mistake. All this is to reassure the computer-terrified. On the other hand, if you wish to buy a better machine, obtain more for less, get the most from your PC and aim at high performance you need some essential information about its basic features. Moreover, and more importantly, if you are interested in the philosophical issues arising from the information revolution you cannot avoid having some elementary knowledge of the technology in question. The task of the present chapter is to provide this minimal background. It is far from being a technical introduction to computing, which would require a whole volume by itself (see for example Boolos and Jeffrey 1989; Brookshear 1989 and 1997; Cohen 1997; Dewdney 1996; Hopcroft and Ullman 1979; Lewis and Papadimitriou 1998; Minsky 1967; Moret 1998; Savage 1998; Sipser 1997; Taylor 1997). It is only a guide to what one needs to know to be able to take advantage of the technology in question and understand more critically some of the points I shall make in the following chapters.

What is a computer?

Assuming that the computers we shall mostly be concerned with have a classic structure (for some non-classic machines see Chapter 5), answers to this question can be of two kinds: epistemological or commercial. We shall begin with the former and end with the latter, though with a proviso. In the history of science and technology it is often the case that, when people eventually achieve significant results, this is more because they have been chipping away from different angles at what is later discovered to be the same problem, rather than because they have systematically hacked through it inch by inch, so to speak. The history of computing (Goldstine 1972; Metropolis *et al.* 1980; Shurkin 1984; Williams 1997) is a typical example and in the following pages I do not mean to review all the steps, some of which were apparently lost for long periods of time, but only to sketch the major conceptual breakthroughs that can help us to understand what computers are and can do for us.

Before the computer: two semantic distinctions

Human beings rarely wish to think, and whenever thinking requires either repetitive or difficult mental processes we positively dislike the practice, so efforts to devise "intelligent" mechanisms that may help, when not replace altogether, the minds of their owners as well as their muscles, are as old as human history.

For a long time, the only widespread tool for performing calculations was the abacus, usually a frame with balls strung on wires. It was no small advance. A good abacist is capable of making arithmetical calculations at great speed, as Kiyoshu Matzukai, a Japanese abacist, showed in 1946, when he won a two-day contest against an electronic calculator.

It was only after the Renaissance that the number of projects and the variety of calculating machines actually devised began to grow steadily, in connection with the new computational demands brought about by geographical and astronomic discoveries, the scientific revolution, the mathematisation of physics and the emergence of ever more complex forms of conflict (the need for precise ballistic calculations has been behind the history of computing ever since the invention of gun powder), of economic processes (e.g. financial mathematics) and of social organisation (e.g. statistics). The more demanding the intellectual tasks, the more pressing the search became for machines that could take care of them instead of reluctant and unreliable human beings. Some devices, such as Leonardo's, were never built; others, such as Napier's multiplication machine ("Napier's bones"), the slide rule, in which multiplication and subtraction are computed by relying on physical distances, Pascal's adding machine (1642), or Leibniz's multiplication machine (1671), enjoyed some success. Specific mechanical devices were still in widespread use for specialised calculations in several fields as late as the

1960s, and only in the 1970s did their economic value and computational power become uncompetitive compared to that of digital computers.

Mechanical calculators have long been out of fashion, so why mention them at all? Because, from a conceptual point of view, and using our present terminology, calculating machines helped to disseminate two fundamental ideas. The first is the distinction between the following three processes.

1   *data input*, constituting the raw material elaborated by the machine;
2   *the process of elaboration of the data input*, mechanically carried out by the device, following pre-determined patterns or sets of rules. Computing machines are mechanical not in the sense of (a) not being electrical, since there are mechanical machines operated by electrical engines, but in the positive sense of (b) including operational stages requiring no human operator or a human operator with no knowledge of the meaning of the operations performed, and, more often, in the negative sense of (c) not being digital (see below); and
3   *information output*, constituting the result of the process.

The other distinction concerns the semantic system adopted and hence the further distinction between analogue and digital computers.

An analogue computer performs calculations through the interaction of continuously varying physical phenomena, such as the shadow cast by the gnomon on the dial of a sundial, the approximately regular flow of sand in an hourglass or of water in a water clock, and the mathematically constant swing of a pendulum, exploited since the seventeenth century to make the first really accurate clocks and then, in terms of spring-controlled balance wheels, to construct watches. Clearly, it is not the use of a specific substance or reliance on a specific physical phenomenon that makes a computer analogue, but the fact that operations are directly determined by the measurement of continuous physical transformations of whatever solid, liquid or gaseous matter is employed. There are analogue computers that use continuously varying voltages and a Turing machine, as we shall see in a moment, is a digital computer but may not be electrical.

Given their physical nature, analogue computers operate in real time (i.e. time corresponding to time in the real world) and therefore can be used to monitor and control events as they happen, in a 1:1 relation between the time of the event and the time of computation (think of the hourglass). However, because of their nature, analogue computers cannot be general-purpose machines but can only perform as necessarily specialised devices. As far as analogue signals can be subject to substantial interference and physical distortion (think of the scratches on a vinyl record, or the background noise in a radio programme), they are easily prone to malfunctioning, though, conversely, they have a high degree of resilience (fault tolerance), being subject to graceful degradation (you can play a vinyl record almost forever) and able to deal successfully with noisy or damaged input data.

Now, old calculating devices, such as the abacus and the slide rule, are the precursors of analogue computers, with which they share a fundamentally geometrical and topological semantics: they deal with the continuum of physical variations, and perform calculations by relying on mechanical rotations, circular movements, reallocations, distances, contiguities, ratios, etc. For this reason, they may all be considered machines based on the geometrical management of a Euclidean space of information.

In contrast, our computers handle only digital signals in series of distinct steps, and they are the outcome of an algebraic treatment of information. Digital signals are binary (i.e. encoded by means of combinations of only two symbols called *bits*, *b*inary dig*its*) strings of 0/1 comparable to the dots and dashes in the Morse code. For example, in binary notation the number three is written 11. Since the value of any position in a binary number increases by the power of 2 (doubles) with each move from right to left (i.e. . . . . 16, 8, 4, 2, 1; note that it could have been 1, 2, 4, 8, 16, and so on, but the binary system pays due homage to the Arabic language) 11 means $[(1 \times 2) + (1 \times 1)]$, which adds up to 3 in the decimal system. Likewise, if you calculate the binary version of 6, equivalent to $[(1 \times 4) + (1 \times 2) + (0 \times 1)]$ you will see that it can only be 110. A *bit* is the smallest semantic unity, nothing more than the presence or absence of a signal, a 1 or a 0. A *nibble* is a series of four bits, and a series of 8 bits forms a *byte* (*by* eigh*t*), a semantic molecule through which it becomes possible to generate a table of 256 (2^8) alphanumeric characters (a *word* is used to represent multiple bytes). Each character of data can then be stored as a pattern of 8 bits. The most widely used of such codes is the ASCII (American Standard Code for Information Interchange), which relies on only 7 bits out of 8 and therefore consists of a table of 128 characters. Thus in ASCII representation, each digit of a number is coded into its own byte. Here is how a computer spells "GOD" in binary: 010001110100111101000100, that is

G	off = 0	on = 1	off = 0	off = 0	off = 0	on = 1	on = 1	on = 1
O	off = 0	on = 1	off = 0	off = 0	on = 1	on = 1	on = 1	on = 1
D	off = 0	on = 1	off = 0	off = 0	off = 0	on = 1	off = 0	off = 0

Quantities of bytes are calculated according to the binary system:

- 1 Kilobyte (Kbytes or Kb) = 2^{10} = 1,024 bytes
- 1 Megabyte (Mbytes or Mb) = 2^{20} = 1,048,576 bytes
- 1 Gigabyte (Gbytes or Gb) = 2^{30} = 1,073,741,824 bytes
- 1 Terabyte (Tbytes or Tb) = 2^{40} = 1,099,511,627,776 bytes

As will become clearer in a moment, such economical semantics has at least three extraordinary advantages.

To begin with, bits can equally well be represented logically (true/false), mathematically (1/0) and physically (transistor = on/off, switch = open/ closed, electric circuit = high/low voltage, disc or tape = magnetised/ unmagnetised, CD = presence/absence of pits, etc.), and hence provide the common ground where mathematical logic, the logic of circuits and the physics of information can converge. This means that it is possible to construct machines that are able to recognise bits physically and behave logically on the basis of such recognition. This is a crucial fact. The only glimpse of intelligence everyone is ready to attribute to a computer uncontroversially concerns the capacity of its devices and circuits to discriminate between binary differences. If a computer can be said to perceive anything at all, it is the difference between a high and a low voltage according to which its circuits are then programmed to behave. Finally, digital signals can have only two states, thus they can be either present or absent, and such *discrete variation* means that a computer will hardly ever get confused about what needs to be processed, unlike an analogue machine, which can often perform unsatisfactorily. Above all, a digital machine can recognise if a signal is incomplete and hence recover, through mathematical calculations, data that may have become lost if there is something literally odd about the quantity of bits it is handling.

A computer can handle operations involving terabytes of information only because it is capable of processing series of bits (billions of 0s and 1s specially ordered into patterns to represent whatever needs to be symbolised either as retrievable data or as executable instructions) at extraordinary speed, something a mechanical device could never achieve. Thus a digital computer, as we know it today, could not be constructed as long as three other fundamental elements were missing:

1   a clear distinction between the fixed hardware of the machine and its replaceable instructions, and hence a theory of algorithms (the programmed instructions implementing the algorithm are known as software, and the machine that executes the instructions is known as hardware);
2   the harmonisation of data and instructions by means of the same binary notation;
3   the transformation of the string of binary data and list of instructions into a flow of electric pulses that could travel easily and safely at very high speed (the speed of light is 30 cm/nanosecond, but electricity travelling through copper wire has a limit of 9 cm/nanosecond).

By itself, the binary codification of data and the following logic of bits was already known to Leibniz (see Leibniz 1968). Nevertheless, even at the end of the nineteenth century, it would have been extremely counterintuitive to pursue the project of the automation of computations and data management by multiplying the number of elements to be processed. Suppose you wish to construct a simple device, with gears and cogs, which could automatically calculate additions and subtractions of whole numbers. The last thing you would begin with would be a digital codification of numbers from 0 to 9 and of the corresponding instructions, a process that would enormously increase the quantity of data to be taken into consideration by the machine. Yet this is precisely what happens in a computer, which does not recognise the capital letter A as such, for example, and instead of processing only one datum must process the 7 positions of the 0s and 1s in the unique binary string 1000001 standing for "A" in the ASCII table. Although both Leibniz and, later on, Ferdinand de Saussure (Saussure 1983), had made it quite clear that meaningfulness is achievable by the simple presence or absence of one signal, for a long time (roughly until Alan Turing's theoretical achievements) the most promising programme of research for the automatic elaboration of information was thought to be a mechanical *ars combinatoria*. It was hoped that this would enable macroscopic blocks of simplified information such as letters, numbers, words or even whole concepts to be usefully combined following predetermined routes. The speed of the mechanical process was left to the mechanical engine, but the correct management of the necessary instructions remained dependent on human understanding. We have already encountered Swift's ironic description of such a programme of research.

Babbage's analytical engine

It is on the conceptual basis provided by mechanical analogue computers that Charles Babbage, later helped by his associate Augusta Ada Byron (Countess of Lovelace), the daughter of Byron, designed the Difference Engine and then the much more ambitious Analytical Engine (1835), the first true precursor of the modern digital computer (Hyman 1982; Morrison and Morrison 1961). Again, our interest in the device is conceptual rather than technical. The actual engine was never constructed, was fully mechanical, and relied on the ten digits to carry on its calculations, but its blueprint contained a number of brilliant new ideas, some of which we still find applied in the construction of our computers. Four deserve to be mentioned here:

1 The computing process was based on the rule of finite differences for solving complex equations by repeated addition without dividing or multiplying.
2 Instructions for the engine were programmed using conditional algorithms, i.e. branching instructions with loop-back clauses (the pattern is "if such and such is the case then go back to the previous step number n and re-start from there, if such and such is not the case then go to the next step number m") made possible by the punched card system.
3 Both data and instructions came from outside, as input encoded on punched cards.
4 The engine itself implemented only a basic logic and consisted of an

input device, a memory called the Store, a central processing unit called the Mill, and a printer used as an output device.

Since the analytic engine was capable of performing different operations by following different programs, it could qualify as a general-purpose machine, and in 1991 the National Museum of Science and Technology in London created a working example, using Babbage's plans and parts available to him in his time, that turned out to be perfectly efficient.

Turing machines

For centuries, human ingenuity addressed the problem of devising a conceptual and discrete language that would make it possible to assemble and disassemble ever larger semantic molecules according to a compositional logic. Today, we know that this was the wrong approach. Data had to be fragmented into digital atoms, yet the very idea that the quantity of elements to be processed had to be multiplied to become truly manageable was almost inconceivable, not least because nobody then knew how such huge amounts of data could be processed at a reasonable speed. The road leading to semantic atomism was blocked and the analytical engine was probably as close as one could get to constructing a computer without modifying the very physics and logic implemented by the machine. This fundamental step was first taken, if only conceptually, by Alan Turing (Carpenter and Doran 1986; Herken 1988; Hodges 1992; Millican and Clark 1996; on the conceptual and logical issues concerning computability see Boolos and Jeffrey 1989; Minsky 1967; Montague 1962).

Alan Turing's contributions to computer science are so outstanding that two of his seminal papers, "On Computable Numbers, with an Application to the Entscheidungsproblem" (Turing 1936) and "Computing Machinery and Intelligence" (Turing 1950), have provided the foundations for the development of the theory of computability, recursion functions and artificial intelligence. In Chapter 5, we shall analyse Turing's work on the latter topic in detail. In what follows, I shall merely sketch what is now known as a Turing machine and some of the conceptual problems it raises in computation theory. In both cases, the scope of the discussion will be limited by the principal aim of introducing and understanding particular technologies. (Barwise and Etchemendy 1993 is a standard text and software application for the study of Turing machines.)

A simple Turing machine (TM) is not a real device, nor a blueprint intended to be implemented as hardware, but an abstract model of a hypothetical computing system that Turing devised as a mental experiment in order to answer in the negative a famous mathematical question (Herken 1988). In 1928, David Hilbert had posed three questions:

1   Is mathematics complete (can every mathematical statement be either proved or disproved)?

2   Is mathematics consistent (is it true that contradictory statements such as "1 = 2" cannot be proved by apparently correct methods)?

3   Is mathematics decidable (is it possible to find a completely mechanical method whereby, given any expression *s* in the logico-mathematical system *S*, we can determine whether or not *s* is provable in *S*)?

The last question came to be known as the *Entscheidungsproblem*. In 1931, Kurt Gödel proved that every formal system sufficiently powerful to express arithmetic is either incomplete or inconsistent, and that, if an axiom system is consistent, its consistency cannot be proved within itself (Davis 1965). In 1936, Turing offered a solution to the *Entscheidungsproblem*. He showed that, given the rigorous representation of a mechanical process by means of TM, there are *decision problems* (problems that admit Yes or No answers) that are demonstrably unsolvable by TM.

To understand what a Turing machine is it may help to think of it graphically, as a flowchart (a stylised diagram showing the various instructions constituting the algorithm and their relationship to one another), a matrix, or just a program. For our present purposes, we can describe a TM as a (possibly fully mechanical) elementary tape recorder/player consisting of:

1   a control unit that can be in only one of two internal states s, usually symbolised by 0/1 (s $\in$ {0,1}), operating

2   a read/write head that can move to the right or to the left (m $\in$ {R, L}), to scan

3   an unlimited tape, divided into symmetric squares, each bearing at most one symbol α or β (where both α and $\beta \in$ {0,1} and there is a finite number of squares bearing a 1). The tape holds the finite input for the machine (the string of 0s and 1s), stores all partial results during the execution of the instructions followed by the control unit (the new string of 0s and 1s generated by the head), and provides the medium for the output of the final result of the computation.

The computational transitions of TM are then regulated by the partial function: f: (α, s) → (β, m, s') (a function f: S → T is an operation that maps strings of symbols over some finite alphabet S to other strings of symbols over some possibly different finite alphabet T; a partial function holds only for a proper subset of S) and the machine can be fully described by a sequence of ordered quintuples: for example, <0, α, β, R, 1> can be read as the instruction "in state 0, if the tape square contains an α, then write β, move one cell right and go into state 1". Note that we have already simplified the finite alphabet of TM by limiting it to only two symbols and that we have also limited the number of tapes that TM can use to only one. The number of types of operations that TM can perform is very limited. In each cycle of activity TM may:

- read a symbol at a time from the current square of the tape (the active square);
- write a symbol on the active square;
- change the internal state of the control unit into a (possibly) different state;
- move the head one space to the right or to the left (whether it is the tape or the head that moves is irrelevant here);
- halt (i.e. carry out no further operations).

TM begins its computation by being in a specified internal state, it scans a square, reads its symbol, writes a 0 or 1, moves to an adjacent square, and then assumes a new state by following instructions such as "if the internal state = 0 and the read symbol on the active square = 1 then write 1, move left, and go into internal state = 1". The logical sequence of TM operations is fully determined at all times by TM's internal state (the first kind of input), the symbol on the active square (the second kind of input) and the elementary instructions provided by the quintuples. The machine can be only in a finite number of states ("functional states"), each of which is defined by the quintuples. All this means that a standard TM qualifies as *at least* a deterministic finite state machine (FSM, also known as finite automaton or transducer. Note that I say "at least" because a TM can do anything a simple FSM can do but not vice versa) in that it consists of:

- a set of states, including the initial one;
- a set of input events;
- a set of output events;
- a state transition function that takes the current state and an input event and returns as values the new set of output events and the next state.

TM is deterministic because each new state is uniquely determined by a single input event. At any particular moment in time, TM is always in a fully describable state and something that I shall later analyse in terms of algorithmic design ensures a very high level of control over the computational process. Any particular TM provided with a specific list of instructions could be described in diagrammatic form by a flow chart, and this helps to explain why TM is better understood as a program or software, and therefore as a whole algorithm, than as a mechanical device. After all, the mechanical nature of the tape recorder is irrelevant, and any similar device would do.

Despite the apparent simplicity of a TM, it is possible to specify lists of instructions that allow specific TMs to compute an extraordinary number of functions (more precisely, if a function is computable by a TM this means that its computation can be transformed into a series of quintuples that constitute the TM in question). How extended is this class of functions? To answer this question we need to distinguish between two fundamental results achieved by Turing, which are usually known as Turing's theorem (TT) and the Church–Turing thesis (CTT), and a number of other corollaries and hypotheses, including Church's thesis (for a more detailed discussion see Copeland 1997. Some of the following remarks are partly based on an excellent article by B. J. Copeland in the *Stanford Encyclopaedia of Philosophy*, available on the Internet, see webliography).

The theorem proved by Turing was that there is a Universal Turing machine (UTM) that can emulate the behaviour of any special-purpose TM. There are different ways of formulating this result, but the one which is most useful in this context, in order to distinguish TT from other hypotheses, refers to the class of functions that are computable by a machine. Turing's theorem says that there is a UTM that computes (C) any function f that is computable by a TM (TMC):

$$(TT) \quad \forall f \exists x \, (TMC(f) \to (UTM(x) \land C(x, f)))$$

TT means that, given any TM, there is a UTM whose tape contains the complete description of TM's data and instructions and can mechanically reproduce it or, more briefly, that can be programmed to imitate TM. The smallest UTM, devised by Minsky in 1967, can use as little as only 4 symbols and 28 instructions. TT is a crucial result in computation theory: to say that a UTM is a TM that can encompass any other TM is like saying that, given m specific flow charts, drawn in a standard and regimented symbolism, which describe the execution of as many specific tasks, there is a universal flow chart n, written with the same symbols, that can reproduce any of them and thus perform the same tasks. This "super flow chart", UTM, is a general-purpose programmable computing device that provides the logical foundation for the construction of the PC on our desk. Its universality is granted by the distinction between the elementary operations, performed by the hardware, and the instructions, which are specified by a given program and are contained in the software. Unlike the abacus, an analogue calculator or a special-purpose TM, the same UTM can perform an unlimited number of different tasks, i.e. it can become as many TMs as we wish. Change the software and the machine will carry out a different job. In a way that will become clearer in a moment, the variety of its functions is limited only by the ingenuity of the programmer. The importance of such a crucial feature in the field of computation and information theory can be grasped by imagining what it would be like to have a universal electric engine in the field of energy production, an engine that could work as a drill, a vacuum cleaner, a mixer, a motor bike, and so forth, depending on the program that managed it. Note that sometimes UTMs may generically and very misleadingly (see below) be called Super Turing machines.

Turing's fundamental theorem brings us to a second important result, a corollary of his theorem:

(U) a UTM can compute anything a computer can compute.

This corollary may be the source of some serious misunderstandings. If by U one means roughly that

(U.a)   a UTM can be physically implemented on many different types of hardware

or, similarly, that

(U.b)   every conventional computer is logically (not physically) equivalent to a UTM

then U is uncontroversial: all computer instruction sets, high-level languages and computer architectures, including multi-processor parallel computers, can be shown to be functionally UTM-equivalent. Since they belong to the same class of machines, in principle any problem that one can solve can also be solved by any other, given sufficient time and space resources (e.g. tape or electronic memory), while anything that is in principle beyond the capacities of a UTM will not be computable by other traditional computers. All conventional computers are UTM-compatible, as it were. However, on the basis of a more careful analysis of the concept of computability, the corollary U is at best incorrectly formulated, and at worst completely mistaken. To understand why we need to introduce the Church–Turing thesis.

There are many contexts in which Turing presents this thesis (it is originally formulated in Turing 1936; for a survey of the problems concerning the thesis see Galton 1996). In 1948, for example, Turing wrote that "[TMs] can do anything that could be described as 'rule of thumb' or 'purely mechanical', so that 'calculable by means of a [TM]' is the correct accurate rendering of such phrases" (Turing 1948:7). A similar suggestion was also put forward by Alonzo Church (Church 1936) and nowadays this is known as the Church–Turing thesis: if a function f is effectively computable (EC) then f is computable by an appropriate TM, hence by a UTM (UTMC: henceforth I shall allow myself to speak of TMC or UTMC indifferently, whenever the context does not generate any ambiguity), or more formally

$$(CTT)\ \ \forall f(EC(f) \rightarrow TMC(f))$$

Broadly speaking, CTT suggests that the intuitive but informal notion of "effectively computable function" can be replaced by the more precise notion of "TM-computable function". CTT implies that we shall never be able to provide a formalism F that both captures the former notion *and* is more powerful than a Turing machine, where "more powerful" means that all TM-computable functions are F-computable but not vice versa. What does it mean for a function f to be effectively computable? That is, what are the characteristics of the concept we are trying to clarify? Following Turing's approach, we say that f is EC if and only if there is a method m that qualifies as a procedure of computation (P) that effectively computes (C) f:

$$\text{(a)} \quad \forall f\,(EC(f) \leftrightarrow \exists m\,(P(m) \wedge C(m, f)))$$

A method m qualifies as a procedure that effectively computes f if and only if m satisfies all the following four conditions:

(1) m is finite in length and time.

m is set out in terms of a finite list of discrete, exact and possibly repeatable instructions, which, after a given time (after a given number of steps), begins to produce the desired output. To understand the finite nature of m in length and time recall that in a TM the set of instructions is constituted by a finite series of quintuples (more precisely, we say that a TM is a particular set of quintuples), while in an ordinary computer the set of instructions is represented by a stored program, whose application is performed through a fetch–execute cycle (obtaining and executing an instruction). A consequence of (1) is the halting problem that we shall analyse at the end of this section.

(2) m is fully explicit and non-ambiguous.

Each instruction in m is expressed by means of a finite number of discrete symbols belonging to a language L and is completely and uniquely interpretable by any system capable of reading L.

(3) m is faultless and infallible.

m contains no error and, when carried out, always obtains the same desired output in a finite number of steps.

(4) m can be carried out by an idiot savant.

m can (in practice or in principle) be carried out by a meticulous and patient human being, without any insight, ingenuity or the help of any instrument, by using only a potentially unlimited quantity of stationery and time (it is better to specify "potentially unlimited" rather than "infinite" in order to clarify the fact that any computational procedure that necessarily requires an actually infinite amount of space and time to begin producing its output never ends and is not effectively computable; see below). Condition (4) makes explicit that m requires no intelligence. A consequence of (4) is that whatever a UTM can compute is also computable *in principle* by a human being. I shall return to this point in Chapter 5. At the moment, it is sufficient to notice that, to become acceptable, the converse of CTT requires some provisos, hidden by the "in principle" clause, for the human being in question would have to live an arbitrarily long time, be infinitely patient and precise, and use the same kind of stationery resources used by UTM. I suppose it is easier to imagine such a Sisyphus in Hell than in a computer room, but in its most intuitive sense, the one endorsed by Turing himself (see Chapter 5), the thesis is easily acceptable as true by definition.

More briefly, we can now write that:

$$\text{(b)} \quad \forall m\,(((P(m) \wedge C(m, f)) \leftrightarrow (\{1,2,3,4\}(m))))$$

When a TM satisfies $\{1,2,3,4\}$ we can say that it represents a particular algorithm, if a UTM implements $\{1,2,3,4\}$ then it is a *programmable system* and it is not by chance that the set of conditions {1,2,3,4} resembles very closely the set of conditions describing a good algorithm for a classical Von Neumann machine (see below). The main difference lies in the fact that condition (4) is going to be replaced by a condition indicating the *deterministic* and *sequential* nature of an algorithm for VNM. Since the criteria are less stringent, any good algorithm satisfies {1,2,3,4}, and the three expressions "programmable system", "system that satisfies the algorithmic criterion" and "system that satisfies conditions {1,2,3,4}" can be used interchangeably, as roughly synonymous.

CTT holds that if a computational problem cannot be solved by a TM then it cannot be solved by an algorithmic system. Typical cases of computational procedures satisfying the algorithmic criterion are provided by truth tables (Galton 1990; Schagrin *et al.* 1985) and tableaux (Hodges 1977; Jeffrey 1994; Smullyan 1968) in propositional logic, and the elementary operations in arithmetic, such as the multiplication of two integers. It takes only a few moments to establish that $a = 149 \times b = 193 = c = 28757$, although, since in this example both a and b are prime numbers (integers greater than 1 divisible only by 1 and themselves), it is interesting to anticipate here the fact that there is no efficient algorithm to compute the reverse equation, i.e. to discover the values of a and b given c, and that the computation involved in the prime factorisation of 28757 could take us more than an hour using present methods. This is a question concerning the complexity of algorithms that we shall discuss in more detail in Chapter 5. Here, it is worth remarking that the clause "in principle", to be found in condition (4) above, is important because, together with the unbounded resources available to the idiot savant, it means that huge elementary calculations, such as $7^{98876} \times 3^{8737}$, do not force us to consider the multiplication of integers a procedure that fails the test, no matter how "lengthy" the computation involved is.

Clearly, conditions {1,2,3,4} are sufficiently precise to provide us with a criterion of discrimination, but they are not rigorous and formal enough to permit a logical proof. This seems to be precisely the point of CTT, which is perhaps best understood as an attempt to provide a more satisfactory interpretation of the intuitive concept of effective computation, in terms of TM-computability. From this explanatory perspective, wondering whether it is possible to falsify CTT means asking whether it is possible to show that CTT does not fully succeed in capturing our concept of effective computation in its entirety. To show that CTT is no longer satisfactory we would have to prove that there is a class of functions that qualifies as effectively computable but is demonstrably not computable by TM, that is

$$(\text{NOT-CTT}) \quad \exists f (\text{EC}(f) \wedge \neg \, \text{TMC}(f))$$

The difficulty in proving NOT-CTT lies in the fact that, while it is relatively easy to discover functions that are not TM-computable but can be calculated by other mathematical models of virtual machines – all non-recursive functions would qualify (see below) – it is open to discussion whether these functions can also count as functions that are effectively computable in the rather precise, though neither sufficiently rigorous nor fully formal sense, adopted in (a) and (b) and specified by the algorithmic criterion. The problem of proving whether NOT-CTT is the case can be reformulated in the following terms: does the existence of Super Turing machines (STMs) falsify CTT? STMs are a class of theoretical models that can obtain the values of functions that are demonstrably not TM-computable. These include the ARNN (analogue recurrent neural network) model of Siegelmann and Sontag (1994; Siegelmann 1995, 1998).

ARNNs consist of a structure of n interconnected, parallel processing elements. Each element receives certain signals as inputs and transforms them through a scalar – real-valued, not binary – function. The real-valued function represents the graded response of each element to the sum of excitatory and inhibitory inputs. The activation of the function generates a signal as output, which is in turn sent to the next element involved in a given transformation. The initial signals originate from outside the network, and act as inputs to the whole system. Feedback loops transform the network into a dynamical system. The final output signals are used to encode the end result of the transformation and communicate it to the environment. Recurrent ANNs are mathematical models of graphs not subject to any constraints. We shall discuss the general class of artificial neural networks at greater length in Chapter 5, where we see some of their structural properties, their application-areas and the kind of philosophical mistakes that can be made when interpreting their operations. Note that neural networks may represent dynamic systems, but the latter can also be discrete models. The question concerning the computational significance of such models is perfectly reasonable, and trying to answer it will help us to understand better the meaning of CTT, and the power of UTM (recall that we began this section by asking how large the class of functions that are UTM-computable is).

Let us begin by presenting a second hypothesis – sometimes simply mistaken for CTT and sometimes understood as a "strong" version of it – which is plainly falsified by the existence of STM. Following the literature on the topic, I shall label it M:

$$\text{(M)} \quad \forall f\,(\text{M/C}\,(f) \to \text{TMC}(f))$$

M says that if f is a *mechanically calculable* (M/C) function $-f$ can be computed by a machine working on finite data in accordance with a finite set of instructions – then f is TM-computable (for a recent restatement of M see for example Bynum and Moor 1998: 2). M is irrecoverably false. It may never be possible to implement and control actual STMs – depending on the model, STMs may require an actually infinite number of processing elements or, if this number is finite, an infinite degree of precision in the computational capacity of each processing element – but this is irrelevant here. A TM is also a virtual machine, and the demonstration of the existence of a class of Super Turing (virtual) machines is sufficient to prove, at the mathematical level, that not every function that can *in principle* be *calculated* by any machine is also *computable* by a TM, that is

$$(\text{STM}) \quad \exists f (\text{M/C} (f) \wedge \neg \, \text{TMC}(f))$$

Since we can prove STM, this falsifies M:

$$(\text{NOT-M}) \quad \text{STM} \rightarrow \neg \, \text{M}$$

The first consequence of what has been said so far is that, while CTT does not support any substantial philosophical conclusion about the possibility of strong AI, NOT-M undermines any interpretation of the feasibility of strong AI based on M. The brain may well be working as a computational engine running mechanically computable functions without necessarily being a UTM ("brain functions" may be TM-uncomputable), in which case it would not be programmable nor "reproducible" by a UTM-equivalent system. But more on the strong AI programme in Chapter 5. A second consequence of NOT-M is that the concept of calculability and the weaker concept of input–output transformation must be distinguished from that of effective computability in such a way as to make room for the possibility that the behaviour of a system of state-transitions may be determined (i.e. obtained or describable in terms of calculations or transformations) without necessarily being, for that reason alone, effectively computable and therefore fully predictable (this applies to microsystems such as ANNs as well as to macrosystems such as weather conditions).

We may now wonder whether NOT-M implies that CTT is also falsified, that is, whether we should also infer that

$$(\text{CTT}) \quad \text{STM} \rightarrow (\text{NOT-CTT})$$

Some computer scientists and philosophers seem to hold that CTT is the case (Bringsjord 1998; note that, although Siegelmann 1995 is typically interpreted as a defence of CTT and indeed it has been used as an important source in favour of CTT, she has later clarified that her actual position is not in contrast with the one presented here. See also Siegelmann 1998.). They interpret the existence of STMs as ultimate evidence that CTT is no longer tenable and needs to be revised. They may in fact be referring to M, in which case they are demonstrably right, that is CTT = NOT-M. However, if we refer more accurately to NOT-CTT, CTT is incorrect, for STMs do not satisfy the first half of the conjunction. They are theoretical machines that can compute classes of TM-uncomputable functions, but they do not qualify as machines in the sense specified by the algorithmic criterion, that is STMs implement *computational processes* but not rule-based, *computational procedures* that *effectively compute f* in the sense specified by {1,2,3,4}. In Bringsjord 1998, for example, we find that the argument in favour of CTT requires the class of real numbers to be effectively decidable, something that Bringsjord himself acknowledges to be doubtful, and that is definitely untenable if "effectively" is correctly specified by {1,2,3,4}. In STMs we gain more computational power at the expense of a complete *decoupling*[5] between programming and computation (we have calculation as an input-output transformation phenomenon determined by the structure of the hardware, without having computational programmability as a rule-based procedure), while in UTM-compatible systems we gain complete *coupling* between the programmable algorithmic procedure and the computational process of which it is a specification (in terms of computer programs, the process takes place when the algorithm begins its fetch-execute cycle) at the expense of computational power.

A likely criticism of the previous analysis is that it may end up making the defensibility of CTT depend on a mere stipulation, or definitional criterion. There is some truth in this objection, and by spelling it out we reach the second important result inferable from the existence of STMs (the first is NOT-M).

A purely definitional position with respect to CTT may hold that all computable functions are TM-computable and vice versa:

$$(\text{CTT}^{\text{def}}) \quad \forall f (C(f) \leftrightarrow \text{TMC}(f))$$

Obviously, if $(\text{CTT}^{\text{def}})$ is the case under discussion, since M follows from it, defenders of ~~CTT~~ may really be referring to $(\text{CTT}^{\text{def}})$ when they seem to move objections against CTT. In which case, it is possible to show that they are arguably right in evaluating the significance of STMs for CTT. For the existence of STMs proves that $(\text{CTT}^{\text{def}})$ is either incorrect and hence untenable, or that it is tenable but then only as a matter of terminological convention, i.e. it should actually be rewritten thus:

$$(\text{Def.}) \quad (\forall f (C(f) =_{\text{def.}} \text{TMC}(f)))$$

My suggestion is that the possibility of STMs is sufficient to let us abandon (Def.). This is the second interesting contribution to our understanding of the validity of CTT, made by defenders of the computational significance of STMs. If we adopt (Def.), it becomes thoroughly unclear precisely what kinds of operation STMs perform when they obtain the values of TM-uncomputable functions. The acceptance of (Def.) would force us to conclude that STMs are not computing and, although this remains a viable option, it is certainly a most counterintuitive one, which also has the major flaw of transforming the whole problem of the verification/falsification of CTT into a mere question of vocabulary or axiomatic choice. As a result, it is more useful to acknowledge that STMs should be described as *computing* the values of f. We have seen, however, that they do not *effectively compute f*, in the sense specified by the algorithmic criterion, although they *calculate* its values. Given the differences between TMs and STMs, the class of calculable functions is therefore a superclass of the class of effectively computable functions. This is the strictly set-theoretic sense in which Super Turing machines are *super*: whatever can be computed by a TM can be calculated by a STM but not vice versa.

Up to Turing power, all computations are describable by suitable algorithms that, in the end, can be shown to be equivalent to a series of instructions executable by a Turing machine. This is the Church–Turing thesis. From Turing power up, computations are no longer describable by algorithms, and the process of calculation is detached from the computational procedure implementing and hence controllable via instructions. This is the significance of STMs. Since there are discrete dynamical systems (including parallel systems, see below) that can have super-Turing capacities, the distinction between *effective computability* and *calculability* cannot be reduced to the analogue/digital or continuous/discrete systems distinction; the key concept is rather that of general-purpose, rule-based transformation.

It turns out that Turing's model of algorithmic computation does not provide a complete picture of all the types of computational processes that are possible. Some types of artificial neural networks are computing models that offer an approach to computational phenomena that is complementary and potentially superior to the one provided by conventional algorithmic systems. In terms of computational power, digital computers are only a particular class of computers, though they may be the only physically implementable, general-purpose devices. However, even if STMs enlarge our understanding of what can be computed, it should be clear that this has no direct bearing on the validity of CTT. The fact that there are STMs demonstrates that M is false and shows that CTT^{def} is either provably incorrect or trivially true but unhelpful, but STMs do not prove that CTT is in need of revision in any significant sense, because the latter concerns the meaning of *effective computation*, not the extent of what can be generally calculated by a system. CTT remains a "working hypothesis", still falsifiable if it is possible to prove that there is a class of functions that are effectively computable in the sense of {1,2,3,4} but are not TM-computable.

So far, any attempt to give an exact analysis of the intuitive notion of an effectively computable function – the list includes Post Systems, Markov Algorithms, λ-calculus, Gödel–Herbrand–Kleene Equational Calculus, Horn Clause Logic, Unlimited Register machines, ADA programs on unlimited memory machines – has been proved either to have the same computational power as a Universal Turing machine (the classes of functions computable by these systems are all TM-computable and vice versa) or to fail to satisfy the required algorithmic criterion, so the Church–Turing thesis remains a very plausible interpretation of the concept of effective computation. This holds true for classical parallel processing computers (PPC) and non-classical quantum computers (QC) as well (but see Deutsch 1985 for a modified version of CTT). As I hope will become clearer in Chapter 5, either PPCs and

QCs are implementable machines that perform *effective* computations, in which case they can only compute recursive functions that are in principle TM-computable and CTT is not under discussion, or PPCs and QCs are used to model *virtual* machines that can calculate TM-uncomputable functions, but then these idealised parallel or quantum STMs could not be said to compute their functions effectively, so CTT would still hold.

From the point of view of what is technologically achievable, not just mathematically possible, PPCs and QCs are better understood as "super" Turing machines only in the *generic* sense of being machines that are exponentially more efficient than ordinary TMs, so rather than "super" they should be described as *richer* under time constraints (i.e. they can do more in less time). The "richness" of PPCs and QCs lets us improve our conception of the tractability of algorithms in the theory of complexity, but does not influence our understanding of the decidability and computability of problems in the theory of computation. Since they are not in principle more powerful than the classical model, *richer* computers do not pose any challenge to CTT.

At this point, we can view a UTM as the ancestor of our personal computers, no matter what processors the latter are using and what software they can run. The computational power of a UTM does not derive from its hardware (in theory a TM and a UTM can share the same elementary hardware) but depends on

- the use of algorithms;
- the intelligence and skills of whoever writes them;
- the introduction of a binary language to codify both data and instructions, no longer as actual numbers but as symbols;
- the potentially unlimited amount of space provided by the tape to encode the whole list of instructions, the input, the partial steps of computation and the final output; and finally
- the potentially unlimited amount of time the machine may take to complete the huge amounts of very simple instructions provided by the algorithms in order to achieve its task.

Despite their impressive capabilities, UTMs are really able to perform only the simplest of tasks, based on recursive functions. A recursive function is, broadly speaking, any function f that is defined in terms of the repeated application of a number of simpler functions to their own values, by specifying a recursion formula and a base clause. More specifically, the class of recursive functions includes all functions generated from the four operations of addition, multiplication, selection of one element from an ordered n-tuple (an ordered n-tuple is an ordered set of n elements) and determination of whether a < b by the following two rules: if F and $G_1, \ldots, G_n$ are recursive, then so is $F(G_1, \ldots, G_n)$; and if H is a recursive function such that for each a there is an x with $(Ha, x) = 0$, then the least such x is recursively obtainable.

We can now state the last general result of this section. According to Church's thesis, every function that is effectively computable is also recursive (R) and vice versa:

$$(CT) \; \forall f \, (EC(f) \leftrightarrow R(f))$$

CT should not be confused with, but can be proved to be logically equivalent to, CTT since it can be proved that the class of recursive functions and the class of TM-computable functions are identical. Like CTT then, CT is not a theorem but a reasonable conjecture that is supported by a number of facts and nowadays results widely accepted as correct. If we assume the validity of CT, then we can describe a function f from set A to set B as recursive if and only if there is an algorithm that effectively computes $f(x)$, for $x \in A$. This is the shortest answer we can give to our original question concerning the extension of the class of functions computable by a UTM. We still have to clarify what it means for a problem to be provably uncomputable by a Turing machine.

Recall clause (1) above: m is finite in length and time. A computer is a discrete-and-finite states machine that can deal only with a finite number of digits, these being data or instructions. Now this indicates that it is both a fallible and a limited machine. Its basic arithmetic (see below) can never treat real numbers that require an infinite list of digits to be represented, but only finite approximations, and this may then give rise to rounding errors, which may occur when real numbers are represented as finite numbers (thus the same program running on two different computers may not always produce the same answers because of different conventions for handling rounding errors implemented by hardware manufacturers; this unsatisfactory situation is bound to be eliminated thanks to the adoption of common standards of approximation, not because approximations will no longer be necessary), discretisation errors, which may occur when a continuous problem is translated into a discrete problem, or convergence errors, which may occur when iterative methods are used to approximate a solution. Of course, if the task in question is endless, such as the generation of the infinite expansion of a computable real number, then there is a sense in which the algorithm cannot terminate, but it would still be a correct algorithm. This is a different case from that represented by problems that cannot be solved by any TM because there is no way of predicting in advance whether or when the machine will ever stop. In the former case, we know that the machine will never stop. Likewise, given sufficient resources and a record of the complete functional state of the execution of the algorithm at each step, it is possible to establish that, if the current state is ever identical to some previous state, the algorithm is in a loop. Problems are provably TM-unsolvable when it is possible to demonstrate that, in principle, it is impossible to determine in advance whether TM will ever stop or not. The best-known member of this class is the halting problem (HP). Here is a simple proof by contradiction of its undecidability (a direct demonstration of the existence of undecidable problems can be achieved by using Gödel numbers; see Brookshear 1997: 411–15 for a very clear illustration):

1   Let us assume that HP can be solved.
2   If (1) then, for any algorithm N, there is an algorithm P such that P solves HP for N.
3   Let us code N so that it takes another algorithm Q as input, i.e. $Q \Rightarrow N$.
4   Make a copy of Q and code it so that $Q \Rightarrow Q$.
5   Let P evaluate whether $Q \Rightarrow Q$ halts (i.e. whether Q will halt with Q as an input) and let the algorithm N be coded depending on the output of P.
6   If the output of P indicates that $Q \Rightarrow Q$ will halt, then let N be coded so that, when it is executed, it goes into an endless loop.
7   If the output of P indicates that $Q \Rightarrow Q$ will not halt, then let N be coded so that, when it is executed, it halts. In other words, let N be coded in such a way that it does exactly the opposite of what the output of P indicates that $Q \Rightarrow Q$ will do. It is now easy to generate a self-referential loop and then a contradiction by assuming $N = Q$. For when we use algorithm N as input to algorithm N:
8   if the output of P indicates that $N \Rightarrow N$ will halt, then because of (7) when N is executed it will enter into an endless loop and it will not halt.
9   If the output of P indicates that $N \Rightarrow N$ will not halt, then, because of (8) when N is executed it will halt. So, according to (8), if $N \Rightarrow N$ halts then it does not halt, but if it does not halt then according to (9) it does halt, but then it does not halt and so forth. This is a contradiction: N does and does not halt at the same time. Therefore:
10 there is at least one algorithm N such that P cannot solve HP for it, but (2) is true, so (1) must be false: HP cannot be solved.

Sometimes, a simple way to show that a computational problem is undecidable is to prove that its solution would be equivalent to a solution of HP.

After Turing, we have a more precise idea of the concepts of "mechanical procedure", "effective computation" and "algorithm". This was a major step, soon followed by a wealth of mathematical and computational results. Nevertheless, a UTM leaves unsolved a number of practical problems, above all the unlimited resources (space and time) it may require to complete even very simple computations. To become a reliable and useful device, a UTM needs to be provided with a more economical logic, which may take care of the most elementary operations by implementing them in the hardware (some hardware can be regarded as a rigid but highly optimised form of software), and a more efficient architecture (HSA, hardware system architecture, that is, the structure of the system, its components and their interconnections). In summary, one may say that Boole and Shannon provided the former, and Von Neumann, with many others including Turing himself, the latter (Von

Neumann's work was the epilogue to prior innovative ideas, hence, when I refer to a Von Neumann machine I shall do so only for the sake of simplicity).

Boolean logic

Boolean algebra is named after George Boole, who first formulated it in his *An Investigation into the Laws of Thought, on which are founded the Mathematical Theories of Logic and Probabilities* (1854). Boole's work went largely ignored (Peirce was one of the few exceptions) until Claude Shannon, the father of the mathematical theory of information, rediscovered it when working on telephone circuits, thus laying the groundwork for the internal logic of our computers. In 1930, when writing his doctoral thesis, and then in 1938 in a classic paper entitled "A Symbolic Analysis of Relay and Switching Circuits", Shannon showed that, once propositional logic – with its two alethic values T (true) and F (false), their truth tables and proof system – is translated into a Boolean algebra (Boolean logic), it can be implemented electronically by means of high and low voltage impulses passing through switching circuits capable of discriminating between on and off states (Shannon 1993).

In modern notation, a Boolean algebra is any 6-tuple $\{B, \oplus, \otimes, \neg, 0, 1\}$ that satisfies the following conditions:

1   B is a set of elements.
2    $\oplus$ and $\otimes$ are two binary operations on B (a binary operation on a set B is a function from $B \times B$ to $\oplus$, for example the truth tables for "OR" and "AND") that are
   (a) *commutative*, a binary operation, *, on B is said to be commutative if and only if
      $\forall x \, \forall y \, (((x \in B) \wedge (y \in B)) \rightarrow (x * y = y * x))$
   (b) *associative*, a binary operation, *, on B is said to be associative if and only if
      $\forall x \, \forall y \, \forall z \, ((((x \in B) \wedge (y \in B)) \wedge (z \in B)) \rightarrow (x * (y * z) = (x * y) * z))$
   (c) *idempotent*, a binary operation, *, on B is said to be idempotent if and only if
      $\forall x \, ((x \in B) \rightarrow (x * x = x))$.
3   Each binary operation is *distributive* over the other; a binary operation $\otimes$ is said to be distributive over a binary operation $\oplus$ on a set B if and only if
    $\forall x \, \forall y \, \forall z \, ((((x \in B) \wedge (y \in B)) \wedge (z \in B)) \rightarrow (w \otimes (y \oplus z) = (w \otimes y) \oplus (w \otimes z)))$.
4   The constant 0 is the identity for $\oplus$ and the constant 1 is the identity for $\otimes$. An identity for a binary operation, *, on B is an element e in B for which
    $\forall x \, ((x \in B) \rightarrow (x * e = x = e * x))$.

5   The *complement operation* ¬ is a unary operation satisfying the condition

$$\forall x\,(x \in B \rightarrow ((x \oplus \neg\, x = 1) \wedge (x \otimes \neg\, x = 0))).$$

Since propositional logic, interpreted as a 6-tuple {{F, T }, ∨, ∧, ¬, T, F}, can be shown to satisfy such conditions it qualifies as a Boolean algebra, and this holds true in set theory as well, where B is the set of subsets of a given set, the operations of intersection (∩) and union (∪) replace ∧ and ∨ respectively, and the set complement plays the role of Boolean algebra complement. The question then becomes how we implement a Boolean algebra electronically. We need electronic switches arranged into logical gates, which can be assembled as components of larger functional units. Once this is achieved, it becomes a matter of technological progress to construct increasingly efficient logic gates that are smaller and faster. We have seen that the basic Boolean operators are AND, OR and NOT. The three operators can be constructed as as many gates that assess their inputs, consisting of high or low voltages, and produce a single output, still consisting of a high or low voltage, as their "logical" conclusions:

1   The AND gate yields an output = T/1/On/High (depending on the language we wish to use: mathematical logic, Boolean logic, switch logic or electric voltage) only if both its inputs are high voltages, otherwise the output = F/0/Off/Low.
2   The OR gate yields an output = T/1/On/High whenever it is not the case that both its inputs are low voltages, otherwise the output = F/0/Off/Low.
3   The NOT gate yields an output = T/1/On/High if its input = F/0/Off/Low, and vice versa.

We can then combine such elementary gates in more complex gates to obtain:

4   the XOR gate = exclusive OR, which yields an output = T/1/On/High only if its inputs are different, otherwise the output = F/0/Off/Low;
5   the NAND gate = NOT + AND, which yields an output = T/1/On/High whenever it is not the case that both its inputs are high voltages, otherwise the output = F/0/Off/Low; and
6   the NOR gate = NOT + OR, which yields an output = T/1/On/High only if both its inputs are low voltages, otherwise the output = F/0/Off/Low.

And since combinations of several NAND gates, or OR gates, are sufficient to yield any possible output obtainable from the combination of the set {AND, OR, NOT} (in propositional calculus all 16 two-place truth-functions can be expressed by means of either NAND or NOR, the only two "universal" functions), the logic circuits of a UTM can be constructed by using only one kind of logic gate, taking advantage of the fact that to design circuits built with negative logic gates takes fewer transistors.

Once classic (i.e. two-value) propositional logic, Boolean algebra, the algebra of set theory and switching algebra become interchangeable, electronic technology can be used to build high-speed logical switching circuits such as adders, multipliers, etc. from simple logical units, and a real UTM can be physically implemented by assembling gates together. For example, by adjusting the sequence of the combinations of gates, we obtain adders that make it possible for a UTM to execute its list of instructions for addition of two binary digits rapidly and reliably. Depending on the technology we use, physical switchers may be huge or very small, slow or incredibly fast, more or less efficient, robust and power-consuming. Logically speaking there is no real difference, although it may be convenient to classify computers by generation depending on their type of hardware.

Generations

We are used to the speed with which computers evolve. A new model has an average life of four to six months, after which a newer and better model supersedes it. This is a life-span that seems to be determined more by financial and marketing factors than by technological improvements, which sometimes occur even faster. As a result, the history of computing has moved so fast through so many technological stages that in fifty years it has accumulated a full archaeological past and four time scales, based on the three macro revolutions, represented by the appearance of the first computers, PCs, and the Internet – the third age of ICT; the evolution of programming languages (see below), the evolution of interfaces (the latter time scale was suggested by John Walker, founder of Autodesk); and finally the improvements in the structure of hardware, which we shall see in this section.

The first generation of machines, developed in the 1940s and 1950s, had gates constructed with valves and wire circuits. In 1940, John Atanasoff and Clifford Berry used 300 vacuum tubes as switches to construct their device, and so did John Mauchly and J. P. Eckert when they developed the ENIAC at the University of Pennsylvania Moore School. A vacuum tube works as a switch by heating a filament inside the tube. When the filament is very hot, it releases electrons into the tube whose flow can be controlled by the tube itself, so that the absence or presence of a small but detectable current can stand for the required 0 and 1. Given the great inefficiency of vacuum tubes, they were soon replaced by more manageable, reliable and less energy-consuming transistors. Invented in 1947 by William Shockley, John Bardeen, and Walter Brattain of Bell Labs, a standard transistor is a semiconductor amplifying device with three terminals attached to as many electrodes. Current flows between two electrodes and is modified depending on the electrical variations affecting the third electrode, thus implementing the standard 0/1 logic. The semiconductor constituting the transistor is usually a crystalline material such as silicon (but germanium or gallium arsenide, though more expensive, can also be employed to increase the quality of the performance), that can be modified to allow current to flow under specific circumstances.

Second-generation computers, emerging in the late 1950s and early 1960s, incorporated the new technology of smaller, faster and more versatile transistors and printed circuits. Once devised, however, transistors posed a problem of complexity of structure that was solved in 1958 by Jack St Clair Kilby of Texas Instruments: he first suggested how to assemble together a large collection of interconnected transistors by manufacturing an integrated circuit (chip).

The third generation, from the late 1960s onwards, used integrated circuits, which resulted in the further reduction of size (hence increase in speed), and in reduced failure rate, production costs and hence sale prices. The chip became a microprocessor in 1971, when Intel constructed its 4004, the first commercial member of a successful family, which could process 4 bits at a time. The commercial PC as we know it today was born. There followed the 8080, the 8086, then the 8088 (8 and 16 bit, 10Mhz) and the 80186 (8 bit). In 1982, the 80286 (16 bit and 16Mhz) was launched, in 1985 there appeared the 80386 (32 bit), then in 1990 the 80486, and in 1993 the 80586, known as the Pentium. The difference between the 8080 and the Pentium in terms of velocity of execution was 1/300, and after 1993 such an evolution led to talk of fourth-generation computers, based on microprocessors, sophisticated programming languages and ultra-large scale integration.

The scale-integration parameter refers to the fabrication technology that allows the integration of transistors on a single chip:

- in the 1960s, MSI (moderate-scale integration) allowed the integration of $10^2/10^3$ transistors per chip;
- in the 1970s, with LSI (large-scale integration) it became possible to integrate $10^4/10^5$ transistors;
- in the 1980s, VLSI (very LSI) allowed the integration of $10^5/10^7$ transistors;
- in the 1990s, ULSI (ultra LSI) made possible the integration of $10^7/10^9$ transistors.

For a general perspective on the corresponding evolution of computing speed one may compare the following figures. To multiply together two 10-digit numbers,

- a first generation computer (vacuum tubes and wire circuits) took approx. 1/2000 second;
- a second generation computer (transistors and printed circuits) took approx. 1/100,000 second;
- a third generation computer (integrated circuit) took 1/2,400,000 second;
- a fourth generation computer (LSI and higher) took approx. 1/2,000,000,000 second.

During the mid-1980s there was much talk about a fifth generation of computers, with a ten-year project, sponsored by the Japanese Ministry of International Trade and Industry, and initiated in 1981, aimed at the construction of intelligent systems. It was an interesting failure, whose consequences will be discussed in Chapter 5. The first half of the 1990s was dominated by the partly unexpected revolution caused by the Internet, not by artificial intelligence machines.

Von Neumann machine

In a famous paper, entitled "Preliminary Discussion of the Logical Design of an Electronic Computing Instrument" (1946; see Neumann 1961–3), John von Neumann, also relying on a wealth of work done in the area, suggested the essential architecture of a UTM that became universally accepted as standard in the following decades. A Von Neumann machine (VNM) is any UTM that satisfies the following criteria:

- It is a stored-program computer.
  Instructions and data (including partial data generated by the computer during the process) are all stored in a single memory unit rather than separately.
- It is a random-access machine.
  "Random-access" is a conventional, but rather misleading, term referring to the ability of a VNM to access an arbitrarily chosen (not really random) memory location at each step. The memory of the machine can be accessed "randomly", that is, directly, by using data addresses (think of them as telephone numbers for a group of individuals), rather than sequentially, that is by scanning the whole memory space every time, as happens with the ideal tape of a UTM (using the same analogy, one may compare this to the home addresses of the same individuals). The address system allows the re-usability of subroutine processes – roughly chunks of instructions, specifically dedicated to the execution of basic and common tasks – that can be "called into action" within the main program, whenever needed, as a single line of instructions (something like "now go to this address, execute the subroutine you will find there and come back to the present address when you are ready").
- It is a sequential machine.
  The central processing unit (CPU) of a VNM carries out instructions sequentially, i.e. one after the other in time, and never performs two operations simultaneously.
- It is a single path machine.
  There is a single path between the memory unit and the CPU, although this "von Neumann bottleneck" may be just logical.

For all these reasons, it is sometimes suggested that a good definition of a

VNM would be "control-flow machine". Given the previous model, the construction of a VNM requires three basic hardware components:

1   a main memory unit working as storage medium, partly comparable to a UTM's unlimited tape. It is worth recalling that, in the 1970s, personal computers commonly stored programs on an everyday audio-cassette recorder;
2   a CPU, comparable to a UTM's control unit and head;
3   an input/output (I/O) system, again comparable to a UTM's tape.

The I/O system provides data and instructions to the memory unit from the outside. The memory unit stores programs and initial, intermediate and final data. The control unit (CU) of the CPU interprets the instructions provided by the program and causes them to be executed one after the other, performing a specified sequence of read and write operations on the memory itself. The arithmetic and logic unit (ALU) of the CPU, where we find the logic gates introduced above, performs the arithmetic and logic operations. When the process is complete, the output system provides the result.

To achieve its goals a VNM repeatedly performs the following series of actions:

1   Start.
2   Check instructions.
    (a) If there is any unexecuted instruction to be executed then go to (3).
    (b) Else (i.e. if there are no unexecuted instructions then) go to (9).
3   Retrieve the first unexecuted instruction to be executed from memory.
4   Decode the retrieved instruction.
5   Retrieve from memory all data required by the instruction decoded in (4).
6   Execute the instruction decoded in (4) by processing the data retrieved in (5).
7   Store results obtained in (6) in memory.
8   Go to (2).
9   Stop processing.
10   Transmit the output.

In 1951, UNIVAC 1, the first American computer available on the market, already had a Von Neumann architecture and nowadays VNMs are the most common example of UTMs, although we shall see in the next chapter that there are computers (the web computers) which are neither UTM nor VNM and, in Chapter 5, that there are also several types of computers that are still instances of UTMs but are not VNMs.

The physical problems faced by a UTM are partially solved in a VNM by implementing the most basic logical operations in the hardware (logic gates working as Boolean operators) and improving the execution time of the instructions. The latter strategy is simple but very efficient. Suppose our UTM takes one hour to execute all its instructions because it must read/write a tape 1 km long. To shorten the process one can speed up its movements in several ways (better materials, better algorithms, better structure, better organisation of tasks, etc.), but the most elementary solution is to make the spaces occupied by each square of the tape half their size. The string of 1s and 0s remains the same and so does the logic implemented, but the machine can now move from one to the other in approximately half the time. Decrease their size more than a thousand times and exactly the same machine will need less than a second to perform the same task. Consider now that the circuits of a personal computer are much more than a thousand times smaller than those of a machine like UNIVAC and you will start to understand why, though they are both VNM, the former is orders of magnitude more powerful than the latter. By means of microscopic circuits and chips built through photochemical processes, a PC takes only a fraction of the time required by UNIVAC to achieve the same results, so it can do much more in much less time. This is why microprocessors have become constantly smaller since their first appearance.

At the beginning of 1998, nanotechnology produced ordinary chips with up to 5.5 million transistors measuring 0.25 micrometre each (1 micrometre = 1 millionth of a metre; in the past it was known as a micron; a micron = 1 thousandth of a millimetre; the width of a human hair is approximately 1 millimetre), small enough to pass very easily through the narrowest eye of a needle; 0.15 micron transistors and chips hosting more than 10 million transistors were physically realisable, if very expensive; and transistors as small as 0.1 micron (sailing on one of these through the eye of the same needle we would not be able to see the latter's circumference), with chips hosting up to 50 million of them, were expected to be realisable soon. Theoretically, it was possible to store hundreds of gigabytes of data in an area no larger than the head of a pin. All this made the construction of SOCs (whole computational systems realised on a single chip) perfectly possible in 1998. Unfortunately, there are obvious limits to such "micro-strategy". The ultimate speed of a chip is fixed by the rate at which electronic on/off switches can be flicked. This, in turn, depends on the time it takes for individual electrons, the ultimate "data-carriers", to move across the device. The execution time can be decreased by increasing the speed of the operations, and the latter can be increased dramatically by reducing the space required by the data and their movements, but one cannot increase the data storage density, the superconductivity and the microminiaturisation of circuits indefinitely, and this is not just because of diminishing returns, which are in any case relevant for actual production, but also mathematically, because of subatomic physical properties and quantum noise. The travelling speed of a signal cannot be increased indefinitely. Thus, the more demanding a computational problem is, the more evident the original physical limits of a UTM turn out to be. We must now leave this question on one side, but in Chapter 5 we shall see that there are problems whose computational complexity is so great as to overcome all possible resources physically available to any Von Neumann machine and to require new solutions.

Programming languages and software

As physical realisations of UTM, the computational power of computers depends entirely on the design of their instructions and the physical speed at which they can execute them. The amount of time–space resources available and the quality of the algorithms are therefore crucial (Harel 1992). Software is the soul and blood of our machine but, to change our metaphor, "she loves me, she loves me not . . ." is roughly all a computer is really capable of doing. One may say that computers have very little intelligence of their own, for they can only recognise high and low voltages, or the presence or absence of love, if you prefer, and manage their flux. A binary code is all they can reliably understand (likewise, clocks can record particular movements, but they do not understand time). A computer's operations are invoked by internal instructions that are unintentionally (blindly) triggered by external inputs. This is the sense in which a computer can do only what it is explicitly programmed to do, unlike an organism like a dog, for example, which is naturally structured to respond to the environment in a way that is interactively open. Computer instructions are therefore vital. Take the software away and a computer is just a useless lump of plastic, silicon and metal. Programming is the practical art of writing instructions for a specific instance of a Universal Turing machine. The better the programming, the better the machine will perform, and it should not be surprising that a machine using good software may be better at doing something than its programmer. After all, our cars do run faster than our engineers. But more on this in Chapter 5.

We have seen that to accomplish a task, a computer must perform a detailed sequence of operations that are indicated by an algorithm in terms of a finite list of instructions, expressed by a finite number of symbols. Now, a correct algorithm for a classical computer needs to satisfy a number of properties that I have already partly outlined when discussing the Church–Turing thesis. An algorithm must be

1 *explicit* and *non-ambiguous*; it is completely and uniquely interpretable by any computing device capable of reading the symbols of its language;
2 *faultless* and *infallible*; it contains no error and, when carried out, it obtains always the same output (this is also known as *reliability*);
3 *finite*; it consists of a finite list of (repeatable) instructions that after a given time (begin to) produce the desired output;
4 *deterministic* and *sequential*; it prescribes one operation to be performed at a time, which operation is to be performed at a given time t_1, and which step is to be taken at the following time t_2, once the operation at time t_1 has been performed.

To write a good algorithm for a computing system we need an appropriate language, but when we analyse the "language" of a computer, it is important to distinguish between several levels of representation. At the most basic level we find the *physical system*, made up of a structure of integrated circuits, wires, etc., where there is not yet any explicit representation but rather physical phenomena. Physical phenomena acquire a logical meaning only at the higher level of the *logical system*, where we find OR-gates for example, or the interpretation of a high/low voltage as 1/0. The logical system is a first abstraction made possible by the physical system. A third level is then constituted by the *abstract system*, where the logical patterns, occurring at the second level, acquire a more complex meaning: for example patterns of 0/1 can now represent alphanumeric characters, while commands may stand for whole sets of logical instructions. We then reach the higher-level *conceptual system*, represented by software applications and the programming languages used to write them. Clearly, software is written using programming languages that in the end must result in a series of bits interpretable by the gates of the CPU, the so-called machine code at the level of the logical system, which in turn must correspond to physical patterns interpretable by the physical system at the physical level.

What now seems a long time ago, programmers were as close as possible to the physical level and used to write instructions in *machine language*, that is actual strings of 0s and 1s. When the 0s and 1s were physical vacuum-tube ON–OFF switches, the latter had to be set manually and programming a simple task such as sorting an array of names could take a team of programmers days of hard work. Later on, more intuitive, symbolic representations of machine languages were devised, known as *assembly languages*; they assigned short, mnemonic codes, usually of three letters each, to each machine language instruction, which therefore became easier to handle. Programming started to distance itself from the physical implementation of the software. Assembly languages are converted to machine code by an assembler that translates the source code, i.e. the whole list of mnemonic codes and symbolic operands, into objective (i.e. machine) code. There followed easier and much more intuitive high-level languages, such as FORTRAN (Formula Translating System, a *de facto* standard in scientific computing), ADA (a language especially suitable for parallel computing, named after Augusta Ada Byron), ALGOL, COBOL, BASIC (Beginner's All-purpose Symbolic Instruction Code), which make programming far more intuitive. Two of these programming languages that have been very popular for AI applications are LISP (LISt Processor) and PROLOG (PROrogramming in LOGic). LISP was developed in the 1950s and it was specifically designed for processing heterogeneous lists of symbols. PROLOG was developed in the 1970s and is based on first order logic. OOL (object-oriented languages, see Chapter 4), such as Smalltalk, Objective C, C++ and OO extensions to LISP (CLOS: Common LISP Object System) and PROLOG (L&O: Logic & Objects), are also used for AI programming.

In high-level languages, English words, such as OPEN or PRINT, are used as commands standing for whole sequences of hundreds of machine language instructions. They are translated into machine code by the computer itself thanks to *compilers* or *interpreters*. Compilers are programs that convert other programs, written in a programming language and known as the *source programs*, into programs written in machine language (executable machine code) known as the *object programs*, or into programs written in assembly language, which are then converted into object programs by a separate assembler. The translation is performed before the program is run. Interpreters are programs that directly execute other programs written in a programming language. The conversion of each part of the program is performed as it is being executed.

The development of programming language design has essentially been determined by four factors:

- *Naturalisation*: Programming languages have become increasingly user-friendly by moving away from the machine language and acquiring more intuitive symbolic interfaces.
- *Problem-orientation*: New programming languages have tended to make the structure of resulting programs fit more closely the structure of the problems that they deal with rather than the machine language.
- *Portability*: New programming languages have considered the ease with which the resulting program can be "ported", i.e. made to run on a new platform and/or compiled with a new compiler reliably and with a minimum effort.
- *Maintainability*: New programming languages have considered the ease with which the resulting program can be changed through time to make corrections or add enhancements.

The direction is evident: languages and applications have been steadily moving away from the physical system towards the conceptual system.

If we look now at the resulting software, it is common to distinguish three main categories: operating systems (OS), utilities and applications. Commercially, the distinction is becoming increasingly blurred, but it is still useful to make it. The OS constitutes the environment within which we can manage the computer and run other programs. In the past, the best-known OS was MS-DOS (Microsoft Disk OS) and today it is MS-Windows in its various versions (note that before Win95, MS-Windows was not an OS but a GUI, since it required MS-DOS in the background to run), a multi-tasking software (i.e. it allows you to run more than one program at a time). However, Unix, a multi-user general-purpose OS available in many versions, some of which are free, is also widely used, especially since it is very popular for scientific computing and Internet service providers. Without an OS, a PC is practically useless. The best OS have plug and play facilities that allow the user to connect the PC to other peripherals without too many difficulties (though sometimes it is more a case of "plug and pray"). Some versions of MS-Windows offer the possibility to run 16-bit (backward compatibility) as well 32-bit applications. Utilities are special software designed to make the management of the computerised system easier and more efficient. Applications are complete, self-contained programs designed to perform specific tasks, such as *word-processing*, an expression coined by IBM in 1964 to describe the function of a brand of electronic typewriter, and cannot be used unless they are installed via the OS.

Types of commercial computers

So far we have described a computer as an electronic, general-purpose, programmable, digital data-processing device that can store, retrieve, process and output data according to programmed instructions. Let us now turn to what a computer is from a commercial perspective.

Computers available on the market are often classified into five groups according to their size, power and intended use:

(1) *Palmtops or notepads*: These are very small devices, similar to pocket calculators. They can have word-processing functions and work as personal organisers. Their processing power and memory are very limited but increasing, and the best models can dialogue with a PC and use the Internet.

(2) *PCs (personal computers,* also known as *microcomputers* or *home computers)*: These can be separated into laptops (also known as notebooks), when they are portable, or desktops and towers, depending on the structure of the case, the main part of the machine. We shall analyse the structure of a PC in a moment.

(3) *Workstations*: These are a more powerful variety of PC, usually with larger screens for more complex graphic applications, and provided with fast connections for communication. They are multi-user (can support many users simultaneously) and multi-tasking, and can be very expensive. As a general rule, the most powerful workstations have the same overall computing power (100 megaflops, 1 megaflop = 1 million floating-point operations per second, a common unit of measurement of performance of computers) as the previous generation supercomputers.

(4) *Minicomputers*: This is a rather old-fashioned term, mainly used to refer to computers built between about 1960 and 1985, that were smaller and less powerful than a mainframe but more powerful than the ordinary PC. They were explicitly designed for multiple users and to be connected to many terminals, but they were replaced by workstations.

(5) *Mainframes*: The heavy-weight players of the family, they can process millions of instructions per second and are the fastest and most powerful stations available. These are used for any high-volume data processing, such as the high performance computing (HPC) necessary, for example, for worldwide weather forecasting, the management of huge company databases,

military centres, scientific laboratories or the administration of very large networks. Supercomputers belong to the top class of mainframes, can process billions of instructions per second and are approximately 50,000 times faster than personal computers.

The dividing lines between the five groups are getting less and less clear the more powerful and the smaller their hardware becomes. In Chapter 5, we shall encounter other types of computers, but for our present purposes we can now safely limit our attention to the standard PC to be found in a shop or a university lab.

The personal computer

The PC is a typical Von Neumann machine and represents the most common class of computers available today, dominating the Soho (small office and home computing) and educational markets. It is normally a single-user machine, of moderate price, capable of increasingly good performance (multi-tasking, the possibility of running more than one program at a time, is now standard) and can easily be connected to other computers to form a network and thus share resources (data, software, peripherals).

The typical hardware configuration of a PC includes eight types of components. In the same system box, the case, we find, among other things, the three usual components of all VNMs: the CPU, the hard disk and at least one drive for the operations of input and output (I/O) of data.

(1) The CPU (central processing unit)

This is the microprocessor that makes the whole machine work, consisting of five principal components: the ALU, the registers, the internal clock, the program counter (PC) and the CU (control unit). These can be found on the motherboard, also known as system board, a fibreglass and copper platform bearing all the principal components of the machine and possibly a number of slots for expansion cards, small circuit boards necessary to perform specialised tasks such as sound reproduction (sound card), video-graphics or communication (ethernet cards). The ALU (arithmetic and logic unit) is the component of the CPU responsible for the logic and arithmetic operations. The registers provide a limited storage for immediate data and results during the computer's operation, the CU is responsible for performing the machine cycle (fetch, decode, execute, store), and the program counter is the register that contains the address of the next instruction to be executed sequentially by the CPU. The CPU communicates with internal and external devices by means of a set of conductors, called buses, which carry data between the various types of memory (internal buses) and to and from the ports (external buses) to which are attached peripherals, such as the keyboard, the mouse, the monitor or a printer. The width of the bus (data path) represents the largest data item that the bus can carry, and is expressed in bits (remember 8 bits = 1 byte). We have already encountered the Intel 4004, a processor that could work with only 4 bits of data at a time. Today, current microprocessors have 32-bit and 64-bit buses (they can process 4 or 8 bytes simultaneously), both internally and externally, although internal buses tend to be wider (usually twice the width) since their size affects the speed of all operations. The clock is an electronic device, normally a stable oscillator, that generates a repetitive series of signals whose constant frequency, expressed in hertz (MHz, 1 MHz = 1 million cycles of electrical pulses per second) is used to synchronise the activities of the system. *Ceteris paribus* (we are comparing the same type of CPU), the higher the MHz of the clock, the faster the computer performs its most basic operations such as adding two numbers. To get some idea of the speed of a clock, consider that in 1981 the original IBM PC had a clock rate of 4.77 MHz, and that during the first half of 1998 systems with a 266 MHz microprocessor were entry-level, while a Pentium II processor ran at 400 MHz. Instructions and data are stored in the memory of the system, but contrary to what happens in the simplified model of a VNM, the CPU of a PC is supported by at least four types of memory:

(a) *The ROM (read only memory):* This is the permanent (non-volatile and non-modifiable) memory, embedded in the microprocessor. It can only be read and is used for storage of the lowest level instructions (firmware, a list of about a hundred primitive machine language operations wired into the chip) required by the system to begin to work (bootstrap)

(b) *The RAM (random access memory)*, also known as SRAM (static RAM) or DRAM (dynamic RAM) depending on specific features: This is a volatile, modifiable, internal and electronic memory, built from semi-conductor integrated circuits. To perform its tasks, the CPU needs to retrieve data and instructions from a memory unit, but to speed up the process the CPU does not access external memories such as the hard disk directly. Instead, data are transferred to faster internal memory before they can be used. The RAM is the logical space directly accessed by the CPU, where relevant instructions and data are temporarily stored for as long as they are needed, but are lost when the computer is switched off. Data in a RAM can be accessed very quickly by the CPU because the order of access to different locations does not affect the speed of access. Without a large RAM, the PC cannot run most of the latest versions of software, so new computers are provided with increasingly large memories, and if a PC with 2 Mb of RAM was standard at the beginning of the 1990s, at the beginning of 1998 entry-level machines had 32 or 64 Mb of RAM.

(c) *Different types of external, magnetic or optical, memory units*: These are represented by hard disks, floppy disks, magnetic tapes or CD-ROMs (see below), which work as high-capacity, non-volatile but much slower storage mediums. In this case too, storage capacity has been constantly increasing.

(d) *Cache memory*: This is a limited memory, built from very fast chips (they can be accessed in less than $1/1^{12}$ seconds). The cache memory, rather than the main memory, is used to hold the most recently and often accessed data, and hence speed up their subsequent access.

(2) The hard disk (HD)
This is the non-volatile magnetic memory of the machine that is kept when the computer is switched off. In 1995 the standard PC could have 500 Mb of memory; at the beginning of 1998, a 2 Gb disk was ordinary.

(3) At least one drive for the operations of input and output (I/O) of data
This is usually the floppy disk drive (FDD), but for the operations of input CD-ROM players are becoming the standard device (see below).

(4) One peripheral for the input operations, the CD drive
A CD-ROM (a compact disk read only memory; a WORM is a "write once read many times" CD) is identical to an audio compact disk, an optical medium that takes advantage not of magnetic fields but of laser light phenomena. Digital data are stored not electronically but as microscopic pits, whose presence or absence can be read by a laser beam. CDs are therefore pressed, are much more durable and economical than magnetic disks (HD), but their lower speed of access and the fact that, because of their technology, they cannot be easily transformed into reusable (erase/write many times) memories, make them suitable chiefly for permanent data storage. More technically, CDs have a very high degree of *coercivity* (strictly speaking, this a measure of how difficult it is to rewrite the encoded information on a *magnetic* support). A CD can hold over 550 megabytes, that is about 80 million words, approximately equivalent to 1,000 books of 200 pages each. During the first half of 1998 the velocity of a CD drive ranged between 24 and 32-speed.

(5) More and more often, the standard configuration of a PC may include a modem, an essential piece of hardware for any Internet service via telephone.
A modem is an electronic device, managed by a software package, that allows a computer to transmit data over a telephone line to and from other computers. There are two basic methods whereby bytes can be transferred: either one bit at a time (serial communication) or all eight bits at the same time (parallel communication). A printer, for example, is a parallel device, but a modem is a serial device that converts (MOdulates) digital data (series of bits) into audible tones (analogue signals) and sends them as serial frequencies over dial-up phone lines to another modem, which then re-converts (DEModulates) them back into digital data again. The speed at which a modem transfers data is expressed in BPS (i.e. multiple of 8 bits per second, such as 9,600, 14,400 or 57,600) and is also often referred to as the baud rate. Built-in error correction and data compression algorithms allow modems to communicate more reliably and two or three times faster than the rated speed.

Outside the system box there are two peripherals for the data input:

(6) the keyboard,
(7) the mouse,

and a single peripheral for the data output,

(8) the VDU (video display unit), that is, a monitor.

The computer revolution began precisely when it became possible, in the 1970s, to interact with a computer in a user-friendly environment constituted by visual aids, keyboard and mouse. Standard keyboards are known as QWERTY from their top-left six letters, and represent a very powerful interface between the user and the machine. We work with letters, numbers and symbols that the computer immediately translates into strings of bits. The other essential input device is the mouse, a point-click-drag little box made popular by the graphical user interface (GUI) invented at Xerox PARC and popularised by Apple for the management of the icons, buttons and windows of WIMP (Windows, Icons, Menus and Pointers) applications. Virtually all commercial software requires the use of a mouse and many applications are WYSIWYG ("what you see (on the screen) is what you get (out of the printer)"). The monitors – often 14″ or 15″ screens, but 17″, 19″ or 21″ screens are easily available at higher prices – have resolution expressed in number of pixels (PICtures ELement, the smallest resolvable rectangular area of an image) or DPI (dot per inch) that can be displayed, and are commonly capable of displaying about 800×600 pixels in any of 256 colours (8-bit colour), although for "photorealistic" images one needs over 65,000 colours (16-bit colour) and, preferably, many millions (24-bit colour). When discussing UTMs and Von Neumann machines, I have never mentioned the presence of a VDU and this is because, strictly speaking, the monitor is not an essential part of the computer. In theory, one can use a PC perfectly well even if the screen is not working at all since the latter is there only to make the user's life easier for the I/O operations. This is why it is not necessary to buy a new screen every time one buys a new computer.

Peripheral devices, such as printers or modems, are plugged into the computer through sockets, called ports, which allow them to communicate with the computer by giving them access to the computer's main data lines. Input and output devices, e.g. the modem, commonly plugs into a serial port, also known as Comm port. Printers and other devices that require faster data communication often plug into parallel ports. SCSI (small computer system interface) ports can handle multiple devices concurrently and they are extremely fast and versatile. They can be used for more "demanding" devices such as scanners.

Clearly, among the main variables to be taken into account to evaluate a PC we find

- the speed of the CPU. This is determined by the clock speed, the number of bits it can process internally and the data path. MIPS (million instructions per second) are often used to measure the absolute speed of a CPU, but the indication of how fast a CPU can run may be misleading when used to compare different CPUs;
- the size of the various memories;
- the quality of the monitor (at least size and resolution);
- the speed of the CD drive;
- the presence and speed of the modem.

At this point, it is worth recalling a well-known fact. The world of personal computers is unfortunately divided into two: on the one hand there is a niche of Apple Macintosh (Mac) users (between 1994 and 1998 Apple's share of the global market decreased from 9.4 per cent to 2.6 per cent) and, on the other hand, the vast majority of PC users. There are more than a thousand manufacturers of PCs and, as one may guess, such competition favourably affects the price of the products, if not necessarily the quality. It would be tedious to list the arguments in favour of one or the other type of machine, though, and I would advise the novice to familiarise him- or herself with both types of machines anyway, since their basic software is now the same and differences in use are becoming negligible; what may be a little more interesting is to understand why, given the fact that both a Mac and a PC are VNMs, they are not compatible.

A computer can be described at three different levels of analysis: computational power, types of algorithms used by the system and implementation architecture. The same architecture can have different hardware (HSA) implementations. If such implementations share the same or similar information structure architecture (ISA, this is the programmer-visible portion of a processor's architecture, such as the machine language instructions and registers) of their components, then they all belong to the same family capable of operating with the same software (at least in principle), even if they have a different internal organisation (as in the case of cloned chips). Thus, we speak of IBM-compatible, DOS-compatible or Windows-compatible computers to mean that the machines in question can all work with the same software. On the other hand, since each type of CPU recognises a certain set of instructions, if two microprocessors implement different ISA then their software will not be compatible. This is why we cannot use software written for a Macintosh with an IBM-compatible and vice versa, although both are VNMs. It is like saying that a whale and a dog are both mammals but cannot eat the same food.

Chapter 3

A revolution called Internet

The Internet as a basic technological change

The Internet is the most revolutionary phenomenon in the history of ICT since the diffusion of personal computers in the 1970s. It is a basic technological change not in the sense that it is simple or independent of other previous technology, as the wheel was, but because it lays the foundation for a number of other economic, technological and social transformations, as the steam engine or the telephone did. By so describing it, not only do we acknowledge the fact that the Internet has become the centre of a technological whirlpool that is rapidly affecting most aspects of advanced societies, we also make it possible to apply to its evolution Schumpeter's classic model of the three stages in the development of a technology: invention, innovation and diffusion.

The invention stage (1968–84): the Internet as a Cartesian network

In 1963, Arthur C. Clarke published a story called *Dial F for Frankenstein*, in which he imagined the following scenario. On 31 January 1974 the last communications satellite is launched in order to achieve, at last, full interconnection of the whole international telephone system. The day after, all the telephones in the world ring at once. It is the horrible cry of an artificial supermind, born out of the global network of 80 billion individual switches in the world's automatic exchanges.

Of course, the story was a piece of science fiction, and nobody remembered it in 1975, when Apple launched its first models of personal computer. We were at the beginning of the second age of information technology: during the following ten years personal computers achieved mass diffusion, and became an indispensable commodity. In 1982 *Time* declared the computer "Man of the Year", and even the space age started to be seen as an episode in the computer age.

In 1984 Intel and Microsoft were still building their empires when the newspapers suddenly rediscovered George Orwell's dystopia (Orwell 1949). In *Nineteen Eighty-four* he had imagined a world dominated by propaganda and lies, without a language in which to express critical thought, and controlled by a Big Brother. In search of understanding, many intellectuals reached for their copies of McLuhan's classic, *Understanding Media* (McLuhan 1964). Most people were confident that Big Brother could be identified with television. The global village was going to be the effect of a TV culture.

Few people seemed to recollect *War Games*, a very popular film that had been showing the year before. The plot was very simple: a clever teenager plays with the mainframe of the Pentagon by means of a personal computer and a modem, and in so doing he runs the risk of starting the third world war. One could simply dismiss *War Games* as one more way of pointing up the gap between the two generations. And one would have misunderstood what the real novelty was: the remote control of a computer, the interactive play across the network, the exciting adventure of navigating into a virtual reality.

This time *War Games* was a piece of science fiction only for Europeans. Since 1968, the Department of Defence of the USA had supported the Advanced Research Projects Agency (ARPA) for the construction of a network, known as ARPANET, which could still provide a system of communication after a nuclear attack. ARPANET was a completely decentralised network in which different sites could share information and computing facilities placed elsewhere, even in war conditions, thanks to a highly distributed (i.e. non-hierarchical and non-centralised) structure that could allow easy rerouting. It was, in more philosophical terms, a Cartesian network in which the intelligence of the system (software, services, documents, communication and processing functions) was as independent as possible of the extended hardware and could survive even if the latter was heavily damaged. As Descartes put it in *Meditation VI*:

> For when I consider the mind, or myself in so far as I am merely a thinking thing, I am unable to distinguish any parts within myself; I understand myself to be something quite single and complete. Although the whole mind seems to be united to the whole body, I recognise that, if a foot or arm or any other part of the body is cut off, nothing has thereby been taken away from the mind. As for the faculties of willing, of understanding, of sensory perception and so on, these cannot be formed parts of the mind, since it is one and the same mind that wills and understands and has sensory perceptions.
>
> (1984: vol. II, 59)

More technically, ARPANET's Cartesian dualism meant that each packet of information could travel in the direction of its final destination through any nodes that were still functioning, no matter which particular route was still available (think of an underground system in which every station can be reached from any other station).

Since nobody dropped an atomic bomb on the States, ARPANET soon became a popular means for government contractors and researchers to exchange mails and data, providing the first fundamental model of the Internet. The growth of ARPANET and many other networks throughout the USA, such as USENET, were so successful that in 1981 another grandparent of the Internet appeared, BITNET, which provided electronic mail and servers to distribute information. As a result, in 1983 *War Games* was for the American public just an imaginary treatment of a rather commonplace reality.

Several background conditions made the increasing success of the project possible during the initial two decades:

- the availability and spread of ever-increasing and ever-cheaper computing power;
- the constant growth of the number of digital resources available online;
- the development and improvement of national and international telephone lines allowing faster, more reliable and cheaper ways of communication;
- the construction, all over the world but especially in the United States, of national, broadband, backbone networks for digital transmission;
- a growing mass of users that made it more convenient to provide further services and resources.

Three technological factors were critical in determining the genesis of the Internet:

(1) The packet switching technology, first implemented in 1968

This is a simple, robust and very efficient system for sharing expensive, long-distance communication circuits. The information stream is divided into small amounts of digital data, known as information packets, which bear a destination address and an order of composition. Packets are put in line by the source system, with packets from other computers online, and sent in turn down a network. The network only knows where to deliver the packet, and it is its responsibility to deliver each packet to the specified destination. When the destination system receives the packets, it reassembles them into the original information stream, according to their order of composition.

(2) The adoption, in 1982, of the Transmission Control Protocol (TCP) and Internet Protocol (IP), as the standard protocols for communication over the network

TCP/IP are still the two fundamental standards defining the characteristics of information packets, the procedures for setting up a connection to exchange data, error procedures, etc. Through TCP/IP different networks can exchange data irrespective of local equipment type (hardware or software); thus the protocols constitute a sort of lingua franca for the entire network. The new, anarchic state of the Internet was "virtually" born when TCP/IP was adopted.

(3) The implementation, in 1984, of a strictly hierarchical Internet naming system, known as DNS (Domain Name-server System)

The DNS is a unique international catalogue of addresses of Internet locations, each one consisting of a sequence of abbreviated names (either alphabetically or numerically), separated by dots, listed left to right from the most specific to the most general. A host computer or end node – a reachable, connected computer "hosting" services or documents – counts as part of the Internet if and only if:

(a) It implements the required protocols, including at least the TCP/IP standards.
(b) It has its own Internet address ("Sitename" or "Internet Host Address"), a network number known in the routing tables in the Internet routers. This numeric address, known as the IP address, is a 32-bit number, but to make it more readable it is commonly written as four digits separated by periods (dotted decimal notation) or transformed into a name, which is then used as a short-hand notation for it. The IP address is what can be found for example *after* the @ in an e-mail address. A computer can have several hostnames (aliases), but only one is designated as its canonical name.
(c) It has a communication connection that enables it to exchange packets of information (IP packets) with any other machine on the Internet.

A domain consists of a set of computers whose hostnames share a common suffix, called the domain name. Countries, for example, have domain names such as ".uk" standing for United Kingdom, and ".cl" for Chile, while commercial hosts' addresses in the USA usually end with ".com." Within each domain, there are further subdomains.

The innovation stage (1984–95)

Evolving background conditions and critical factors led the Internet to enter the innovation stage. In the late 1980s commercial services started to use the network, offering access and further applications. After 1988, the number of host machines with direct TCP/IP connections begun to double every year. In 1989 the RIPE (Reseaux IP Europeens) was established in order to co-ordinate the development of the Internet in Europe. By then, several national networks were fully developed and interconnected, while linking more and more sites each day. The escalation reached its critical stage in the early 1990s. During the 1970s and 1980s the Internet had grown across the world mainly as a military and then academic international network, but now it gradually assumed a more commercial nature and began to be exploited economically. The end of the cold war opened up the Internet to Eastern European countries. In 1993, there were 176 million computers in the world, and theoretically each of them could have been connected to the Internet. In fact many of them were. The Internet finally appeared to the public as the most revolutionary phenomenon since the invention of the telephone, though in this case *Time* missed the opportunity to elect the Internet "Man of the Year".

During this stage of development major improvements were represented by the appearance of user-friendly interfaces, new NIM (networked information management) and NIR (networked information retrieval) systems and corresponding protocols such as the Internet Relay Chat (IRC, 1988), Hytelnet (1990), the Wide Area Information Servers (WAIS, 1991), Gopher (1991), the World Wide Web (WWW, first implemented in 1990), VERONICA (1992) and NCSA-Mosaic (1993). I shall describe some of these in the following pages. Cyberspace became an increasingly busy and friendly environment and at the beginning of the 1990s the Internet had already begun to approach the third stage of technological change, that of general diffusion among an increasing population of "lay" users.

The diffusion stage (1995–)

In 1990, ARPANET ceased to exist and the first commercial providers of Internet dial-up access came online. Between the end of 1993 and the beginning of 1994 the number of commercial hosts (DNS = .com, see below) surpassed the number of educational and research hosts (DNS = .edu, see below), becoming the driving force behind the growth of the network. But the year which really signalled the end of the innovation stage was 1995, when the NSFNet (the network run by the National Science Foundation in the USA) reverted to being a research network, thus allowing the main USA backbone traffic to be routed through commercial interconnected network providers. In September 1995, the US Federal Government stopped subsidising, through the NSF, the administration of the domain names at the second level of the five world-wide, top-level, generic domains known as .com (commercial), .org (organisation), .net (network operations), .edu (educational), and .gov (government). Since then, Network Solutions, the InterNIC Registrar, has charged an annual fee for the registration and maintenance of root-level domains within the previous five domains, although NSF continues to pay for .edu registration and, on an interim basis, for .gov. In the end, Internet users pay the costs of domain name registration services.

Some thirty years after the first exchange of email on ARPANET, the technology had become well established and widely used. Every country in the world is online, there are tens of thousands of nodes providing entire libraries of any sort of digitised information, the Internet is still growing at an extraordinary rate (in its early stages it was 450 per cent per year), and it has become a vital instrument for the development of research, communication, business and education activities. In 1993, there were 1.5 million domains; five years later there were 30 million. A total population of perhaps 100 million people interacts by means of the global network. It is the most educated community that has ever appeared on earth, from a philosophical perspective a global academy that thinks, always, like a single Leibnizian mind.

The Internet is still a new world, however, about which most people seem to have many doubts and few certainties. Despite Clarke, McLuhan, Orwell or films like *War Games*, it seems that its appearance found most of us, and especially the intellectual community, thoroughly unprepared. In the 1994, the first eight months of the *New York Times On-Disc* contained 240 occurrences of the word "Internet", while there was none in the *Philosopher's Index on CD-ROM*. We do not know what to think of this new phenomenon, or how to deal with it. What is the Internet exactly? What can it be used for? And what will be the effects of such a radical revolution in the way we handle the world of information? These are some of the fundamental questions that will determine the future of organised knowledge; three questions that, in this chapter, I shall attempt to answer only with an increasing degree of imprecision.

What is the Internet?

The Internet has been described in many ways, some of which are rather amusing, like "infernet". The word "Internet" refers to the INTERnational NETwork of digital communication, emerging from the agglomerate of thousands of networks (LAN = Local Area Network, CWIS = Campus Wide Information System, MAN = Metropolitan Area Network, WAN = Wide Area Network, regional or national) that interact through a number of common protocols all over the world. In this chapter, we shall analyse the Internet more technically as the totality of three different spaces:

- the infrastructure (the physical dimension)
- the memory platform (the digital dimension)
- the semantic space (the cyberspace dimension).

Internet as a physical infrastructure

The Internet is an *information carriage*, consisting of a global mesh of computer networks. In 1998, this amounted to more than 10^5 government, university and corporate networks situated in more than 170 countries. What makes a network part of the same structure is its capacity for interactive communication, thanks to a number of shared telecommunications protocols, including the essential TCP/IP suite. Thus, non-interactive,

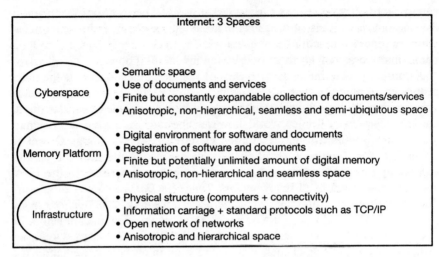

Internet: 3 Spaces	
Cyberspace	• Semantic space • Use of documents and services • Finite but constantly expandable collection of documents/services • Anisotropic, non-hierarchical, seamless and semi-ubiquitous space
Memory Platform	• Digital environment for software and documents • Registration of software and documents • Finite but potentially unlimited amount of digital memory • Anisotropic, non-hierarchical and seamless space
Infrastructure	• Physical structure (computers + connectivity) • Information carriage + standard protocols such as TCP/IP • Open network of networks • Anisotropic and hierarchical space

asynchronous communication services, usually providing only email facilities, tend to be considered as lying outside the Internet, as part of the so-called *Matrix* (communications are asynchronous if the information can be stored for later retrieval thus becoming time-independent). The Internet is an open network of independent networks, in which each sub-network (backbone, mid-level and stub networks) operates and is administered autonomously. Such modularity grants that any individual or organisation can become (or stop being) part of it as long as connectivity and protocols are implemented, with practically no limitations on the purposes for which the connection may be used. The Internet currently represents only part of the infosphere – the world's information system that also includes many other channels of communication and dissemination of information such as libraries and bookshops, radio, television or newspaper networks – but it is likely that the increasing digitisation of classic mass media will progressively blur this difference in the future. The Internet as a physical infrastructure has the typical configuration of all network graphs, with central and peripheral nodes and more or less important links among them, from backbones to online dial-up systems. The nodes are actual computers located in the physical space. Likewise, though wireless and satellite connections are diffuse, the global connectivity of the network is largely ensured by physical links, in terms of fibre optic cables (hair-thin glass fibre which allows light beams to be sent very fast and reflected with low levels of loss and interference), coaxial cables and twisted copper telephone wires.

Internet as a memory platform

The physical infrastructure implementing the common protocols makes possible a global *memory platform*, which results from the cohesion of all the memories of all the computers in the network. The memory platform inherits from the physical network a number of features. Above all, the extent of the memory space is constantly increasing, so it is potentially unlimited, but it is finite, and does not have a uniform distribution (this absence is called "anisotropy"), as in the case of the physical infrastructure. That is to say that, at any given time, the memory platform has a particular extension, to be calculated in terabytes, which makes up an anisotropic space, where the amount of memory fully available to a user depends on his or her location. The memory platform has the structure of a continuous and seamless domain, which constitutes the digital environment both for software – middleware services, such as file systems or name servers; applications, such as ftp and remote control; GUI interfaces, and so forth – and for all sorts of digital documents.

Internet as cyberspace

The totality of all documents, services and resources constitutes a semantic or conceptual space commonly called *cyberspace*. Cyberspace inherits from the memory platform a discrete, anisotropic, seamless nature, to which it adds two further features:

- *semi-ubiquity*: any site or document x provided with an URL (uniform resource locator, a standard notation for specifying an object on the Internet by protocol or access scheme and location, e.g. ftp://address, http://address, news://address, mailto://address, telnet://address, and so forth) is closest to, and can be immediately accessed from, any other site or document y, i.e. without necessarily going through a third site or document z.
- *Cartesian saturation*: cyberspace is only potentially infinite, and contains no "empty space" within itself; that is, a region R in cyberspace which is utterly empty of any information (a white page counts as information) is not just undetectable but does not exist by definition.

Formally speaking, cyberspace can then be defined thus:
$$\forall x \forall y \, (((URL\,(x) \rightarrow (x \in S) \wedge URL\,(y) \rightarrow (y \in S)) \wedge C\,(x, y)) \rightarrow (S = cyberspace)) \wedge \neg \exists r \, ((r \in S) \wedge (Er)),$$ where $C\,(x, y) = x$ is maximally close to (immediately reachable from) y and $E(r) = r$ is devoid of information. It should not surprise us that such a definition of cyberspace also applies to the telephone system, for example, which can be described as a purely acoustic cyberspace, where any user can reach any other user without intermediation (note, however, that in cyberspace we may have $x = y$, whereas this is not possible within the telephone system). The two features of semi-ubiquity and saturation are what make possible the interactive dissemination of information as opposed to broadcasting. Finally, semi-ubiquity should not be confused with a phenomenon that is made possible by it, namely the hypertextual

structure of documents such as Web pages, where links are fixed in order to help navigation from one document to another *within* a pre-selected area of the cyberspace.

Since cyberspace lacks full ubiquity, sites and documents are not simply accessed but reached, starting from other sites or documents. This syntactic jump is made possible by the physical infrastructure (channels of communication) and the memory platform (software environment), which create a space with no empty regions, and generates traffic that is obviously more intense around areas where documents are in high demand. Traffic can then be interpreted as a function of at least four variables:

- connectivity;
- the type of software environment employed (for example, a non-graphic browser such as Lynx is obviously much faster than Netscape and its use could be compared to that of a motorbike as opposed to a car in a busy city centre; likewise, it makes a substantial difference whether one is using compression procedures);
- the popularity of sites/documents;
- the size of the files transferred.

Traffic causes a natural configuration of the semantic space into centres and peripheries, but contrary to the physical lack of uniformity, this lack of isotropism at the semantic level is never stable, for patterns of congestion vary according to the ever-changing nature of each of the four factors mentioned above. Since traffic is not perceived spatially, e.g. in terms of an overcrowded area or a queue, but chronologically, in terms of the amount of time required to access a particular site/document (e.g. thirty seconds can be perceived as a very long time to wait when using a computer), distances in the microcosm of our semantic space not only cannot be metric by definition (in a metric space semi-ubiquity is impossible) but are also relative to the point of departure and that of arrival, non-symmetric (it may take a different time to move from x to y than vice versa), variable (two point-documents x and y can be closer at a particular time and further apart at another) and calculated by reference to the amount of time required to reach y from x, as in the macrocosm of astrophysics, where light-years are employed. From this epistemological perspective, the demand for a more powerful infrastructure, i.e. ever larger broadband capacity (quantified in Mbps, Gbps or even Tbps, i.e. bytes per second) and more efficient NIR applications, can be interpreted as a demand for an improvement in the semi-ubiquity of cyberspace, a demand driven by the regulative ideal of full ubiquity, i.e. of immediate access to any available document instantaneously. Finally, like the memory platform, cyberspace undergoes a constant expansion and transformation, but at any given time it occupies a finite space, whose extension is provided by the sum of all documents stored in the global memory platform at that particular time.

Cyberspace is the new environment in which we spend more and more time as virtual entities. An empirically minded philosopher will question whether cyberspace is a space at all, but it seems difficult to deny the reasonableness of this view, given the fact that we can provide a mathematical definition of it and that very mundane events actually take place in such a space.

We shall see in Chapter 5 that, once the fundamental process of structuring and de-materialising the world has taken place, it is reasonable to expect that forms of artificial intelligence will find cyberspace a suitable place in which to operate, and that it is not by chance that Webbots and digital agents are among the most successful applications of AI. The mind, which tends to be ontologically creative, constructs a world for the machine and the machine can help the mind to live comfortably in this new space. The more synthetic or digital a world is the more easily AI creatures will be able to live in it. Of course, as a supervening entity, cyberspace is an epiphenomenon that cannot be physically perceived, or meaningfully located *in* space and time, over and above the set of interacting networks that constitute it. Moreover, although it is created artificially, nobody is finally responsible for it as a single enterprise. It is a collaborative initiative, a set of documents, services and resources, and each region that is part of it is accountable only for its own proper functioning. Nobody is earning money from the whole service either, because cyberspace is free, in the same way as one would expect the information in a public library to be free. There are many commercial services on the Internet, like shops in a city but, again, the streets are free and one can walk wherever one wishes. One may have to spend money to reach the place and stay there, as one may need to pay a telephone bill or a fee to a commercial company that gives access to the service, but then a lot of resources are there at one's disposal, free of charge. Nobody is running the system or will ever be able to control it in the future. When Bill Gates speaks of his plans to dominate the Internet, what he really means is that he wants to make sure that the new version of Microsoft Windows and its network will become the most popular interface and route for single users who wish to manage their own access to cyberspace through their personal computer. In other words, he would like to run the main bus line in the city, not the city itself. It is already a very ambitious project.

How to characterise the growth of the Internet

Depending on which space we are analysing, the growth of the Internet can be studied on the basis of many suitable parameters. Here are the most important.

(1) *The number of documents*: Consider query-engines such as AltaVista, Lycos, WebCrawler or Yahoo (the last name represents an entertaining coincidence; in *Gulliver's Travels* Swift describes not only the mechanical "computer" but also a land in which a race of sensible and noble horses, the

Houyhnhnms, embody reason and virtue, and their savages, the human Yahoos, have only the worst human qualities; the Yahoos have become digital agents). They automatically keep track of the number of various types of documents that are constantly available on the network. Data concerning AltaVista, for example, indicates that in May 1996 the service gave access to 30 million Web pages, found on 225,000 servers, and 3 million articles from 14,000 Usenet news groups, while being accessed over 10 million times daily. In 1997/8 AltaVista had a 60 Gigabyte index, while it was forecasted that in the following two/three years the number of Web pages available was going to reach 1.5 billion. Of course, it would be possible to study the growth of the Internet by focusing on such data.

(2) *The extension of use*: It is possible to register and study the increase in the volume of traffic, e.g. the number of messages, the number of connections implemented per given time, country or domain, the number of files or the quantity of bytes transmitted during a particular period of time.

(3) *The growth of population*: The study of this variable would refer to the size of user population and the quantity of time that on average users spend on the network (at the beginning of 1998, it was estimated that the number of users world-wide was 100 million).

(4) *The evolution of the software environment*: a study of the number, types, sophistication and efficiency of interfaces and services such as the NIR tools.

(5) *The growth of the physical network*: This may refer either to connectivity variables, such as the number of countries connected and of domains and hosts present on the network, or to channel variables, such as the nature, typology and extension of the physical global network.

The first four groups of parameters are less indicative than the last for the obvious reason that they refer to the growth of cyberspace and the evolution of the software environment, two phenomena which are made possible by the growth of the infrastructure and of the memory platform. No matter how far the growth of the infrastructure may be *sufficiently* justified by the demand for a better cyberspace, it is only the existence of the latter which *necessarily* requires the presence of the former. This is why statistics usually concentrate only on the last group of parameters, that is, the conditions of possibility of any future expansion of the memory platform and of cyberspace. Counting hosts means accepting the view that the client–server architecture (the software required by the operations is installed on the user's computer system, known as the *client*, which accesses, through a network connection, data and services located on another computer system, known as the *server*) will be further implemented, and that the trend towards the decentralisation of software running on users' end-node equipment will maintain its momentum. It would be interesting to take into consideration how the computers connected to the Internet have changed, but of course no sufficiently detailed data can be gathered about this particular aspect of the physical infrastructure. There remains the number of countries and domains, which can be employed to test the projections obtained from the analysis of the number of hosts, the only parameter which gives a reliable indication of the extension of the memory platform, the true environment within which cyberspace can expand.

What can the Internet be used for?

Our second question – what one can do with the Internet – must be left slightly more open, though for a different reason. Through the Internet we can share computational and information resources, exchange private messages with a friend, create an electronic club to discuss a particular topic with other people on the network, publish an electronic journal, set up a so-called slow reading group on Voltaire's *Candide*, run programs or access and control other computers in other places and so acquire data in all possible forms, from free software to millions of bibliographic records, from thousands of electronic texts (all the works of the major philosophers are online) to the splendid images of the Louvre's paintings, from statistical graphs, to musical pieces and whole data banks concerning an enormous variety of subjects. Any exchange and manipulation of digital texts, images and sounds is already possible on the Internet, or soon will be, so a brief presentation of such possibilities must necessarily be selective. It is not simply that we do not know how to use the system; it is rather that the variety of things that one can do through the Internet increases literally every single day, and cannot be finally fixed. Let us therefore concentrate our attention on five *typologies* of communication that can be implemented through the network. Three can be briefly described at once:

(1) *Remote control of other computers via telnet*: Telnet is a client–server system that allows a user to "log-in/log-out" to a remote computer (the command is "telnet + IP address") and transforms the local client into a terminal of the host computer, thus enabling one to use the remote machine as if one were physically there. For example, one can connect to a university mail account from home and use it via telnet.

(2) *File transfers*: FTP (file transfer protocol) is a client–server protocol that allows a user on one local computer to transfer files from (download) or to (upload) another remote computer over the Internet. It is used especially for the dissemination of beta software (non-commercial versions of commercial software, distributed for testing), demos (demonstration software, often only partially working or working until a given date), shareware (working software one can try for a specified time, after which, if one wishes to keep on using it, one must register) and freeware (free software). There are thousands of public distribution sites, known as anonymous ftp sites, with many terabytes of public domain, downloadable material (when downloading software via ftp, one should make sure that the obtained files are virus-free). Ftp sites usually contain files that have been compressed (reduced in size) to occupy less memory space. Compressed files are often known as "zipped",

after the most common software for compressing/decompressing procedures. Each ftp site will contain also information about how to unzip the material one wishes to transfer. Finally, those who wish to create a Web page need an ftp-client to upload their files.

(3) *Running applications over the Web*: It is possible to use or make available programs that run online. The language most commonly used to write these programs is called Java. Java is an OOL suitable for developing micro-applications that can work as interactive components of Web pages (Java applets). A Java virtual machine simulates a computer within a computer, and can adapt any Java program to run on any system. This makes it possible, at least in theory, for software developers to write their programs only once and expect them to run on any kind of OS.

(4) *Various forms of electronic mail exchange.*

(5) *Publication and consultation of Web pages and other information services available online.*

The last two typologies are the topics of the next two sections.

Email, the silent dialogue

Practically speaking, electronic mail is binary like the telegraph, fast, interactive and usually linguistic like the telephone, works a bit like an answering machine, and is often textual like a fax. To be able to write/read or send/receive emails one needs an email account (EA), that is, an individual electronic address-access comparable to one's own telephone number, consisting of a user-id or user-name and a password. More precisely, an email account can be:

- a simple shell account, which provides text-based access to the Internet, or
- a SLIP (serial line internet protocol) or PPP (point to point protocol) account, which provides full graphical Internet access and requires a fast modem.

Accounts can be provided by institutions (e.g. a university) or private services (e.g. an Internet provider in town). Since the connection from home requires a telephone call through a modem, one usually makes sure that the service provider offers local connectivity, otherwise, depending on local regulations, connectivity may be slow and bills very expensive. Once on the net, we can send messages everywhere and navigate as we wish, and costs will always refer to the telephone call that allows us to be connected, never to the "distances" we are covering on the network.

Let us now suppose that Mary has obtained an account from her university computing service. Her address has the following topographical structure mailto://username@hostname, based on the DNS (domain name server system). My own address, for example, is mailto://

luciano.floridi@philosophy.ox.ac.uk. First comes the kind of service/ protocol employed by the resource mentioned (mailto://), hence the address on the Internet where the resource is located. Before the @ there is the user mailbox name, and after it there is the host name, usually a hierarchical list of locations, more or less immediately connected with the relevant IP number. In the example just given, mail sent to me is sent to the "philosophy" address of the OXford node, on the ACademic network in the UK (note that depending on the software one is using URLs may or may not be case sensitive). Note also that mailto://luciano.floridi@philosophy.ox.ac.uk is in fact an alias: the real, original address is mailto://floridi@ermine.ox.ac.uk, where ermine is the server managing my email. Aliases are useful because they are easier to interpret, remember and locate. Once Mary is online, the easiest thing she can do is to correspond with other people. It is possible to manage one's own e-correspondence through some user-friendly interface. There are free email programs such as *Pine*, produced by the University of Washington, or commercial ones, like *Eudora* (there is a free version) or the one to be found enclosed in the last version of the Web browser one is using. As with an answering machine, Mary will find messages that have been sent to her stored into her account. The amount of memory space will be limited, so good administration of files will be essential. Suppose Peter has sent Mary a reading list. She can now read it, reply to him acknowledging receipt of his mail, download the file on to her hard disk, modify it, upload it into her account again and send it to a list of other students at a stroke. Depending on the email system, sending binary files containing software or special formats (word processed texts, spreadsheets or graphics) may be more or less elementary. In the past, formatted files had to be transformed into plain ASCII files first or encoded, and then decoded (uuencode/decode is still popular software); however, nowadays the standard method is to enclose them in an attachment (the file is automatically encoded), although this works only if the service implements a MIME (Multi-purpose Internet Mail Exchange) protocol. Files received in attachment cannot be read or run online, but need to be downloaded and read with the proper software for which they have been produced.

Let us now concentrate on some more conceptual features. Email is the morphologically and technologically poorest form of CMC (computer mediated communication) on the net and hence also the cheapest. Most of the time, through email one exchanges brief online-typed messages with other users, but it would be misleading to limit the importance of an EA (Email Account), for it has in fact three functions:

1   An EA allows a user to manage his or her private email correspondence.
2   An EA is a channel of communication.
3   An EA constitutes the user's identity as a virtual person, a second self.

Function (2) specifies that it is possible to consider an EA a gate to cyberspace, since it offers the possibility of linking a PC to the net via SLIP or PPP from home, obtaining the same kinds of services obtainable from a *public access* offered by a library, for example. One can then communicate with other computers online using TCP/IP and run dedicated software to consult Web pages, transfer files and control remote computers locally. Function (3) clarifies that an EA represents the *principium individuationis* of the owner on the cyberspace, exactly as every point in a 3D Cartesian space not only requires three co-ordinates (x, y, z) to be identified, but is *identical* with the three values of such variables. One exists in cyberspace only as a particular EA or, to paraphrase Quine, in cyberspace to be is to be the reference of a URL (uniform resource locator), and in this case one's URL is one's EA (knowing someone's email address, one can check whether it is active through the command "Ping + address" or get information about the owner through "Finger + address"). This may be highly misleading. Because of the kind of disembodied interaction implemented on the Internet, people often feel less "real" in cyberspace and may allow themselves to behave more freely and hence, unfortunately, less correctly. I shall come back to this point in a moment, but the importance of true anonymity on the Internet – a trivial example may be a student who wishes to write an email to her tutor commenting on the lecture – is shown by the ongoing heated debate concerning the legality and social acceptability of anonymous posting.

The relation physical person vs. virtual person can also generate confusion: there is usually one EA per physical user and vice versa (bijection), but it is not uncommon to find many physical users accessing the same EA, e.g. when an account is set up for a whole group of researchers to share information. If, for the sake of simplicity, we limit our attention to the bijection case, then the various forms of dialogue implementable via email can be organised on the basis of the kinds of relations between the virtual interlocutors into four typologies.

(1) *The asynchronous (occurring at a different time) dialogue one-to-one*: This is what is most commonly understood by email. We shall analyse it in a moment.

(2) *The asynchronous dialogue one-to-many*: This is the very common phenomenon of virtual communities based on mailing lists, newsgroups on USENET (the largest BBS, bulletin board system, on the net), electronic journals, newsletters and so forth. I shall come back to the topic of mailing lists in a moment.

(3) *The synchronous (occurring at the same time) dialogue one-to-one*: This is not a telephone call implemented via the network, as one might guess at first, but the possibility of "talking", via written messages in real time, with a user logged in on another Internet computer. The two users create a talk session by logging in at the same time so that the screen is divided into two parts, one presenting the incoming message and the other showing the outcoming one.

(4) *The synchronous dialogue one-to-many*: This is the so-called IRC (Internet Relay Chat), a *multi-user* and *multi-channel* service comparable to a telephone chat line. The user connects to a channel known to be active at a certain time and exchanges messages with whomever is online at that moment. Through an IRC service one can organise conferences at distance. Other similar tools are the MUD (multiple users dimensions) and the MOO (MUD object oriented), which provide multi-user environments, usually employed for role-playing games. Recall that, in principle, the exchange of data through the Internet can be extremely fast, for the Earth's circumference is 6378.4 km and, without traffic, a message could take much less than a second to cover the whole distance.

Let us now concentrate on the classic form of email, exemplified by (1) and (2). The desire to communicate is often an asymmetric one – people appear to be more likely to wish to speak than to listen – but the tool in itself is symmetric. A single email message, or simply a mail, has a beginning (incipit) a main body and an end (explicit). The incipit may contain data that are largely independent of the sender and, consequentially, that are also disregarded by the user as noise, i.e. uninformative strings of symbols. Some of the information provided there may be redundant, yet at least four indications are of interest: sender, subject, date and possible cc, i.e. a "carbon copy" (*sic*) of the message sent to someone else as well. In the body of the mail we find whatever message has been sent. Its syntax tends to be more paratactic (clauses or phrases appear one after another without connecting words) than hypotactic (clauses and phrases are subordinated). The style is often colloquial, telegraphic, rich in acronyms (e.g. Internet, Modem, IBM, but also ASAP = as soon as possible; BTW = by the way; OTOH = on the other hand; OIC = oh, I see!; ROF,L = rolling on floor, laughing; RTFM = read the F. manual, all words formed from the initial letters of other words), in technical words from the ICT vocabulary (input/output, interface, hardware/software, etc.) and in logograms (symbols that have a universal meaning independently of the language employed, such as mathematical symbols, &, #, $) that may initially baffle the uninitiated. The new *koinē* of the electronic *agora* is a kind of American English, often variously adapted depending on the nationality and education of the users. The words "information" and "knowledge", for example, can be seen more and more commonly used as countable nouns, with plural forms "informations" and "knowledges", while confusion between Latin and English may give rise to funny combinations such as "out ... out" standing for the Latin "aut ... aut" (either ... or). The peculiar style of email messages cannot be explained only in terms of "energetics", by referring to the need to optimise the ratio between resources (time and memory space) and effective communication. Informality often depends on the use of jargon for initiates, the implicit acceptance of a rhetoric of immediateness and rapid communication, confidence in the overwhelming importance of content rather than form, or even gestures of liberation from linguistic standards and conventions (e.g. people will often tend to write the first person singular pronoun as "i" instead of "I"). This introduces us to the analysis of some dialogical features that often occur in a email message: *emoticons*, *indexicals* and *citations*.

If your friend has enclosed in her message something like 8-) do not be surprised. It is an emoticon (EMOTion + ICON), a pictographic element obtained by using a standard keyboard. In this case its meaning is that the writer wears glasses and is smiling (try to see it by bending your head to the left). Emoticons can be of many different types and they are interesting in that they show that an email is clearly perceived as something half way between a written and an oral communication. To the textual model inherited from the former the writer feels the necessity of adding further graphical indications of the mood or "voice intonation" that is to be associated with a specific phrase. Thus the emoticons make up a semiotic system of their own, whose function is not metalinguistic but metacommunicative, since their role is not to "speak about what is said" but to modify its meaning. As far as they try to reproduce extralinguistic factors occurring in any oral communication, they are comparable to prosodic features accompanying spoken words, such as nasalization, voice pitch, intonation, etc.

Another clear sign of the peculiarly dialogical nature of email communications is the occurrence of indexicals, expressions such as "now", "there", "tomorrow" and so forth, which require full knowledge of the locutory situation to be properly interpreted. Someone writing from an EA showing to the receiver the DNS of the University of Oxford should make clear that she is connected via telnet to her EA while being in Paris, otherwise every "here" will constantly be misunderstood by her interlocutor.

Finally, the easy and automatic use of "citations" to reply to a previous message by reproducing portions of it in one's own new message as quoted text, provides further evidence of the dialogical nature of emails. It is a way of overcoming the chronological gap separating the various stages of the conversation. The result is a commented text, with marginalia that may grow beyond the limit of readability after a few exchanges, if they are not kept under control.

When we deal with paper correspondence, personalised features include the handwriting (or whether the letter has been word processed), headed paper, the weight and nature of the paper used, the visual format of the letter, the kind of postage, the type of envelope and many other physical aspects. All this is inevitably absent in an email message. On the net there is still no tradition of message encoding decipherable in terms of social or communication codes, only cues to be found in the electronic signature that is devised by each user and automatically enclosed at the end of each mail.

The signature usually consists of a few lines with the sender's data (check how people refer to their telephone number and address; do they call the former "voice" mail, in contrast to email's textual nature? Do they use

"Snail" for the latter, making fun of the slowness of the "US mail" service compared with email messages?), but there are no real limits to what one can put in it: profession, qualifications and academic titles, especially if ICT-related, URLs of home pages, a motto or even some decoration known as ASCII ART are very common. Such data in the signature may have three functions. They may just be *informative*; they often provide a way to *personalise* an otherwise very anonymous message (you may have noticed a similar need for personalisation affecting the nature of welcome messages on many answering machines or industrial objects such as cars); but sometimes they also have a *performative* role, i.e. they are meant to show the receiver the technological level of the sender, with the aim of establishing a relation of superiority with a novice, or of understanding with an adept.

Electronic communication clearly represents a secondary orality, one step beyond literacy but dependent upon it. So far, we have seen several features that assimilate email communication to an oral conversation. There are others that show the originality of the electronic "silent dialogue" in full. An email conversation is virtually endless and takes place on the basis of a delayed feedback that replaces the continuous process of instant adjustment in a direct dialogue (including one via telephone), where such a delay can even be perceived sometimes as a form of suspense (how many times do you check your email every day?). Second, there is no way to "refresh" the contact with the interlocutor while the conversation is open, by using expressions such as "Yes", "I see", "Ah!", "Really?" and so on (this is the absence of Jakobson's "fatica" function). There is no shared "situation" within which the communication act takes place and introductory procedures, which we may define as the *hand-shaking* process, borrowing the expression from the jargon of modem communication, become less common. This shows the difference between email communication and paper correspondence. It is normal to receive very informal mails in which the sender spends less than a couple of lines introducing herself and gets straight to the point. The phenomenon of a "message in an electronic bottle" never occurs in oral dialogue, and when something similar happens via telephone it is usually anonymous and has a negative character (sexual harassment, advertising, propaganda, etc.). There are several reasons. To begin with, there is a widespread sense of technological community, and among adepts it is easier to communicate without too many formalities. Secondly, the receiver is often perceived by the sender not only as a virtual person, but also as a *public* virtual person, to whom she can write in the same way as one can ask a policeman in the street for some information. In other words, one writes/talks to the social figure or the virtual reference of an EA, not to the real individual behind. Finally, the sender often feels a sense of detachment from her or his own virtual identity that helps the conversation to be less constrained by formal rules. One feels anonymous behind an EA (Turing would certainly have appreciated the popular comic strip in which a dog, typing his email on a computer, confesses to another dog that when you are on the Internet nobody can guess who you are) and hence slightly less responsible, socially speaking. Writing an email to someone you do not know is a bit like asking your secretary to write to Mr Smith on your behalf. This phenomenon of detachment can be further analysed by discussing another remarkable aspect of email conversation known as "flaming".

Argumentative discussion requires a long process of training: most untrained people will find it difficult to have a discussion without "arguing" and "flaming" their interlocutors. "Flaming" is unjustified aggression in reply to a previous mail. One may be flamed even for a silly question or for a request for trivial information sent to a mailing list. Like "spamming" (a form of aggressive advertising or broadcasting which consists of sending copies of the same commercial email to large numbers of newsgroups or users on the Internet), the phenomenon is a clear transgression of any "netiquette". The speed of communication leads one to mail inappropriate messages too hastily, and somebody sends Mr Spock to hell with the same speed, ease and carelessness as he or she would have done in the street, while driving in Rome for example. The phenomenon shows the dialogical nature of email once again, and clearly indicates the tension that email generates between personal individuality and anonymity, since flaming is not a bad habit restricted to undergraduates and SIDs (Sunday Internet Drivers), but occurs even among senior academics, who seem to be ready to shout via email what they would never whisper in public. The lack of immediate feedback or sense of the communication situation (you do not see the other hundreds of members of the mailing list while you are "shouting" electronically at someone else) makes the relation between interlocutors very indirect. One's feeling of detachment is greatest with respect to the receiver, and this may lead the sender to perceive her mail more as a monologue with the computer than a public dialogue. This perception is reinforced by the neutral character of the electronic message on the screen and by the fact that, when we use an EA to talk to other EAs, is hard not to feel less like ourselves and more like characters. The silent dialogue does not take place within the ordinary spatio-temporal conditions we have been so well acquainted with since childhood, but within a logical space, the cyberspace, to which one may apply the unities of time, place, and action that, according to some interpretations, represented Aristotle's view of classical tragedy. As virtual entities we operate within a space that is not metric but rather a single logical environment constituted by the relations occurring between the several subjects involved; it is an environment whose time is not the transient time experienced in real life, but the unitary time of the communication performance, enacted in a virtual agora, which in turn is not only the market square but also the square where plays are performed, as in a Renaissance travelling theatre. Ironically, we are really "persons" only in a virtual context (the Latin word *persona* originally meant "mask" and was used to refer to a specific character in a play, the *dramatis persona*), and our identity is all in that string of symbols that we call an email address. The physical individual, like a homunculus inside the virtual subject, can then take liberties he or she would never dream of IRL (in real life). This is the phenomenon of detachment referred to above. If an EA is sufficiently anonymous to motivate the creation of personal signatures it appears much more so when flaming is in question.

BBS and mailing lists: the electronic learned societies

Email makes possible not only dialogues but also "multilogues" and hence multiloguing through a BBS (Bulletin Board System, by analogy with a physical notice board where people place paper documents for public consumption) and mailing lists. A BBS consists of a computer that operates with an archive program and a modem to allow other computers with modems to communicate with it, leaving/submitting and retrieving/reading messages in a public space on a round the clock basis. Messages can form threads, series of computer-generated communications that generate a topic of open-ended discussion. There is an enormous number of BBS offering a wealth of information, including libraries of downloadable shareware programs, although today users are more inclined to set up interactive Web pages. The less technical BBS are also the most chatty and generic, and since philosophy is the chatty and generic subject *par excellence* one should be careful not to waste too much time discussing via a BBS or a mailing list how many angels can dance on the head of a pin, whether computers can think, or the best definition of realism. USENET is the greatest BBS on the network, consisting of thousands of areas of interest, known as newsgroups. Each newsgroup automatically records, indexes, and updates its files whenever someone sends a new message. To consult USENET newsgroups one needs a newsreader (try the command "news" when using your email).

A mailing list (ML) may have a similar function to a BBS but works differently and is much less "public". With USENET one needs to make an active check on the interest groups, while a mailing list automatically sends messages in one's mailbox. It consists of a computer running software (usually Majordomo or Listserv) designed to make group communication easier by automatically redistributing messages among a list of subscribers/ contributors via a common email-address of the form mailto:// listname@domain. People sharing some interest can then form a forum and communicate with each other by sending mail to the specified address. Any acceptable ("acceptable" either syntactically, if the system is run only by a computer, or also semantically, if the list is moderated by an individual) mail posted to the list eventually appears in the e-mailbox of every subscriber. A ML can be manually maintained or automatic. To join a manual ML one needs to subscribe by writing to the list administrator (the form of the address is mailto://listname-request@domain), while for an automated list one needs to write to the address of the software managing the list, the mailserver. To subscribe to the lists one is interested in it is usually sufficient to send a mail to the relevant address with the following command in the body of the message: "SUBSCRIBE listname Yourname Yoursurname [sometimes one needs to specify the email address as well]", without quotes, and substituting whichever list one wishes to get on for listname. To unsubscribe it is usually sufficient to send the following message "UNSUBSCRIBE [or alternatively SIGNOFF] listname Yourname Yoursurname". To find out more about mailserver commands, one can send to the mailserver address an empty message with "HELP" in the subject line. Note that it is important to distinguish carefully between the address of the list (think of it as a broadcasting address; whatever is posted to it is automatically distributed to all subscribers) the software address (to which one sends commands, such as the initial subscription) and the address of the list owner, the person who acts as organiser, co-ordinator and "referee" if there are any problems among subscribers. Likewise, when replying to messages coming from a list one should probably think twice and consider whether one wishes to correspond only with the sender of the message one is replying to.

Many MLs have a brief life, others very low traffic; one ML may be more "chatty", while another is more "information-only" oriented, and yet another may be organised as a reading group (for up-to-date information about which MLs are available see the guides listed in the webliography). Owing to their free-flowing, conversational and ephemeral nature, MLs are not meant to construct a stable and constantly accessible domain of information. This is a task for the Web.

The Web

Some people often equate the Internet with the World Wide Web (also known as W^3, WWW or more simply the Web), thus generating a remarkable degree of confusion. We have seen that the Internet is a combination of three spaces, while the Web is simply a way of organising cyberspace, albeit the most efficient and revolutionary one devised so far. Its story begins at the end of the 1980s, when the growth of cyberspace gave rise to the need for more efficient NIR (networked information retrieval) systems. Among the various solutions devised, two became especially popular, Gophers and Webs. Only the latter have survived.

The University of Minnesota originally developed Gopher in 1991 as a public domain, client-server based, distributed document search and retrieval system. It allowed users to organise, disseminate, browse, search and retrieve alphanumeric information through sites all over cyberspace, in a geographically oriented way. Each gopher had a root page (what we now call a home page) referring to other pages or implementing connections with, or gateways to, other gopher servers, ftp sites, telnet servers, whois address servers, WAIS (wide area information system) databases and other NIR systems. VERONICA (very easy rodent-oriented net-wide index to computerised archives) and JUGHEAD (Jonzy's universal gopher hierarchy excavation and display) were two typical gopher-oriented search engines that allowed the creation of personalised "gopher spaces" based on key-word queries. As usual, to access a gopher one needed a specific gopher client. If you are curious to see what a gopher looked like, try typing "gopher" at your email prompt to check whether your server still has a gopher client installed.

In June 1993, there were 4,800 gophers and only 50 Web sites on the Internet, but in a short time the latter replaced the former, and nowadays nobody would open a gopher service. A gopher was user-friendly, but it was text-based only (it had no multimedia features), was neither elementary enough nor sufficiently visual and, despite its menu-directed approach, its hypertextual features were strictly limited by a rigidly hierarchical structure. In other words, the gopher represented the Internet for an MS-DOS-based culture. Once the extraordinary potential of a hypermedia (hypertextual logic + multimedia contents) map of cyberspace had been grasped, the next step was the World Wide Web.

The World Wide Web originated from CERN, the High-Energy Physics Laboratory in Geneva, where it was designed as a very powerful tool with which to disseminate and share constantly updatable, hypermedia information within internationally dispersed teams and support groups. For once, it was the indirect result of scientific needs, not of a military research project. The Web was aimed at the high-energy physics community, but its potential soon made it a popular vehicle for all sorts of information. Its use quickly spread to other areas of information management, generating, in a matter of months, a critical mass of users and such a volume of traffic as to attract commercial investment. Today, the Web is the most advanced NIR deployed on the Internet.

Technically speaking, the Web is an Internet client-server (you need to run on your computer a client program, known as a browser, to connect to a server), wide-area, hypermedia, distributed NIR system. In a Web site every element (texts, images, sounds, menus, indices, video clips, programs, etc.) appears to the user as part of a hypermedia object in HTML (HyperText mark-up language) format or, more simply, part of a document with an .htm (DOS-based notation) or .html (UNIX-based notation) extension.

HTML was developed from a more powerful and elaborate computer language called "Standard generalised mark-up language" (SGML). There are now different versions of HTML but all of them consist of a standard set of plain ASCII control codes, known as hypertext markers, tags or tokens, which specify how the plain ASCII text file is to be displayed by the browser on the local computer, and hence what kind of formatting and interactive features and links to other documents are available. It is worth remembering that HTML does not indicate the exact typographical layout of the text on screen, since this depends largely on the local hardware and how the local browser is set up. Although both text and its markers are in ASCII, and therefore could be created with a simple text editor (this also explains why the same documents can be displayed on any type of computer), few sites contain "hand-made" pages. There are many WYSIWYG hypertext editors that are user-friendly and very powerful. They make the creation of Web pages a simple task. But there will be more on the nature of hypertext documents in the next chapter.

On the Web, every document can be linked to any other local or remote document as long as the latter's URL is known. The user's interaction with Web sites is made possible by browsers – such as the old public-domain Mosaic, or the various versions of Netscape and MS-Explorer – that rely on a basic protocol, known as HTTP (HyperText Transfer Protocol), to read Web documents, but can also access virtually any other resource available in cyberspace via several different network protocols, including the old gopher and ftp. The three basic navigation operations are:

1   browsing, i.e. reading a document;
2   interacting with a document (sending queries, using forms, operating with software online, selecting options from customisable menus and on/off switches, etc.);
3   surfing, i.e. following links from one document to another.

The Web merges the techniques of networked information and hypermedia to provide a very intuitive, visually based, global information system that is economical and extremely powerful. Since it allows negotiation of format between a smart browser and a smart server, Web technology overcomes the frustrating incompatibilities of data format between suppliers and users and has transformed cyberspace into a truly seamless information space (Internet as "the Web"), in which information in any format and accessible through any kind of protocol is (or can be) readily available to the end user in a thoroughly transparent way, via point-and-click interfaces. Clearly, the Web represents the Internet for a Windows-based culture.

The impressive growth of Web technology, with its high degree of flexibility and efficiency, has fuelled the development of a whole generation of new tools and services:

•   new programming languages such as Java;
•   new types of web computers, no longer designed as stand-alone multimedia workstations within a PC-centred environment, the so-called Wintelnet (Windows + Intel + Internet), but as powerful nodes of a network, capable of taking full advantage of online software and resources, within an Internet-centred environment, based on the old mainframe/terminal architecture. Thus we have the NC, supported by companies such as Sun, IBM, Apple and Oracle, which is no longer a Von Neumann machine but

more closely resembles a terminal provided with a powerful processor, a modem or an ISDN chip, an elementary OS, Internet-Web software and some Mb of RAM to work with networked resources, including applications; and the NetPC, supported by Microsoft and Intel, which is more like a reduced version of a standard PC, based on the coupling Windows Intel-processor. Of course, both NC and NetPC will require a high degree of semi-ubiquity. With their diffusion, functions will have definitely moved out to the periphery of the network (decentralisation);

• new formats and corresponding protocols such as the VRML (virtual reality modelling language) required to build 3D, animated, interactive, morphing, multi-user, virtual worlds accessible online;

• new business services such as Intranet and Extranet. An Intranet is a company's internal network that is managed and works by implementing the same kind of tools and services as those devised for the Internet. An Extranet is an Intranet that includes a gateway to the Internet and areas open to the anonymous user from without.

The success of the World Wide Web has been so dramatic that it has deeply affected our conception of the Internet. If the latter can be thought of as a new mass medium and a commercial tool this is only because of the Web's possibilities.

The future of the human encyclopaedia in the third age of IT: Frankenstein or Pygmalion?

The extraordinary range of possibilities offered by the Internet makes our last question – how the Internet is going to affect the nature and development of organised knowledge – almost impossible to answer. In this case, it is even hard to give an initial shape to our ignorance, since there may be much more we do not know than we can guess.

One may start by remarking that, as a synthesis of several innovative technologies, the Internet is fostering the growth of knowledge, while at the same time generating unprecedented forms of ignorance. This is a common process in the history of technology. Whenever a radical change occurs in the way we handle our knowledge, some individuals are left behind, uninstructed, and the new technology makes those who do master it suddenly aware of other domains of knowledge still to be explored. What is truly remarkable, in our case, is the impressive scale of the phenomenon in question. Not only has the Internet already enlarged our notion of illiteracy, and produced new forms of cultural isolation and discrimination, but, because it intensifies and amplifies the effects of the digital revolution, it is also transforming some of our most radical conceptions and habits. Take our conception of a text for example. The enormous importance of the new model of "spineless textuality" represented by hypertext, the virtual ubiquity of documents, the appearance of online services and electronic sources that need to be catalogued, have all changed a discipline such as librarianship in the most radical way. Even the library itself may disappear in some cases, as we move from the holding and lending library, which stores knowledge physically recorded on paper, to the consulting library, which provides access to electronic information on the network; then from an object-oriented culture, which produces multiple copies of physical entities like books and CD-ROMs for each user, to a culture which appreciates the relationship between time and information, and provides services charged per period of use; and finally from the library as a building to the library as a gate-node in the virtual space of the system of organised knowledge, which I have already called the human encyclopaedia.

The Internet has transformed the physical citizens of a modern society into the disembodied netizens of a post-modern cybercommunity, as some hackers like to say. The jargon may be a bit extravagant, but the changes are almost tangible. In the new electronic agora implemented by the Web, publicity has assumed an international scale, while privacy also means electronic privacy in our e-mail conversations. Our good manners are evaluated on the basis of a netiquette of communication. Civil rights are concerned in the way in which information about ourselves can be created and stored in databases, and then accessed and used through the network. Crimes range from electronic pornography to viruses (programs that "infect" other programs or executable applications by embedding themselves in them so that, when the latter are executed, the embedded virus is also executed, propagating the "infection" into the system in a way that is usually invisible to the user. Their effects may be just annoying messages, but some viruses may cause irreversible damage, e.g. by corrupting or deleting files); from the illegal reproduction of software to illicit intrusion into and mishandling of electronic systems; from the infringement of copyright to electronic plagiarism. Even the way we think may be affected in the long run, for relational and associative reasoning is becoming as important as linear and inferential analysis, while visual thinking is once again considered to be at least as indispensable as symbolic processing. And as the skill of remembering vast amounts of facts is gradually replaced by the capacity for retrieving information and discerning logical patterns in masses of data, the Renaissance conception of erudition and mnemotechny is merging with the modern methods of information management.

In the third age of ICT, activities like communicating, writing, publishing and editing, advertising, selling, shopping and banking, or counselling, teaching and learning are all being deeply affected. Networks easily overcome political barriers, creating "information havens" where gambling and pornography, but also civil rights and social demands may find safety. The rapidly growing phenomenon of offshore data-entry work is causing an international relocation of low-skilled data-processing activities that is increasing the gap between information societies and less-developed countries. Similar transformations are of the utmost importance, as they will determine not just our lifestyle in the coming decades, but more importantly what kind of world we shall leave to future generations. If I put the subject aside now it is only because I wish to conclude this chapter by sketching the new problems affecting the system of the human encyclopaedia and, more generally, the whole infosphere, that have already been caused, or soon will be, by such an epochal change in our culture. My impression is that there are at least eleven principal issues, concerning the growth of an information and communication network, worthy of attention. Let us have a look at them briefly, in tentative order of increasing importance.

Digital discrimination

We have already entered the stage in which digital information is sometimes preferred to non-digital simply because it is more readily available, not because of its quality (how many students now refer to MS *Encarta* as a source for their essays?). One may hope that the more high-quality resources become available, the less serious the problem will become, but it is clear that languages and cultural traditions that are not digitised run the risk of becoming marginalised and disappearing from the "literary horizon", represented by the digital space, because of the costs incurred by their documents in terms of localisation, efficient use, and availability, as well as of lack of multimedia features.

Disappearance of the great compilers

By greatly increasing the supply of data, the Internet largely satisfies the ever-growing demand for information. In this process, the use value of information has increased steadily, in parallel with the complexity of the system. Its exchange value, however, has been subject to a radical modification. Because of the great and rapid availability of data, the Internet has caused a devaluation of some intellectual enterprises, like compilations, collections of images, bibliographical volumes and so forth, whose original high value depended mainly on the inaccessibility that afflicted information in the era of the printed book. Today, some of the data that in the past had to be discovered and collected with great expense of time and energy are becoming directly available on the Internet. The result is that users will look more and more frequently for value added to works done on raw data and then on electronic sources and tools. The era of the great collectors is fading. Raw data simply will not travel through the printed medium any longer; they will be (more or less expensively) available through the digital channels of the network.

Emergence of the computerised scholar

So far, academia has been slow in acknowledging that new forms of scholarly activity have appeared, like moderating a discussion list, keeping an online bibliography constantly updated, or publishing a paper in an electronic journal. The sooner such activities are properly recognised and evaluated, the easier it will become for individuals to dedicate more time and effort to the digital encyclopaedia, and the more the latter will improve, compelling further recognition for those who have worked on its creation, and so forth, until a proper balance between work and rewards will be reached. Universities have been re-engineered all over the world, and yet too little has been done so far to accompany this with a parallel process of informatisation of academic activity. How many departments in the humanities use groupware tools and Intranet services to manage their ordinary activities?

Stored knowledge > knowledge accessible

There is more knowledge on the Internet than we can ever access. This is a truism important to remember. In the macrocosm represented by cyberspace, the fundamental imbalance between the extraordinary breadth of the system and the limited amount of information that can be accessed by an individual mind at any one time arises again because the technology responsible for the processes of management is far less efficient than the technology responsible for the accumulation of knowledge. The quantity of useful information potentially available online has increased beyond all control, whereas the technology whereby the network actually allows us to retrieve the data we are looking for has improved much more slowly. The result is that we are again very far from being capable of taking full advantage of our digital infosphere. I have already remarked that ICT developed in the 1950s partly as an answer to the explosion of the system of knowledge and information originated by the book age. After a few decades, it can be seen to have defeated itself by extending the infosphere beyond its own control. The challenge of the next few years will consist in narrowing the gap between quantity of information and speed of access, before it becomes even greater. Projects like the American Information Superhighway or SuperJANET in Great Britain are of the greatest importance, not because they will ultimately resolve all our problems of management, but because they can restore the balance between the real extent of the infosphere and potential access to it. The gap between the mind and the domain of knowledge should never be too wide, even if closing it is impossible, given that this fundamental imbalance is rooted in the very nature of the system of knowledge. We shall always lag slightly behind the growth of organised knowledge.

Knowledge accessible > knowledge manageable

This is the problem of *infoglut*, and concerns the degree to which retrievable information can actually be managed. We live in a post-scarcity information environment: compared to our present age, any other moment in the history of thought has experienced desperate shortage of data, or info-pauperism. In the past, this led to a rather voracious attitude towards information. Today, we face the opposite risk of being overwhelmed by an unrestrained, and often superfluous, profusion of data. The old heuristic rule *melius abundare quam deficere* has become self-defeating. A critical form of censorship is therefore a precondition for the individual mind to be able to survive in an intellectual environment in which exposure to the infosphere is far greater than ever before. Plato and Descartes thought that knowledge could be compared to food for our minds. If this is the case then today, for the first time in human history, we need to learn how to diet. This is not a matter of dull specialisation, of knowing more and more about less and less, as the saying goes. What we really need is a new culture of intellectual taste and selection, and tools that can help us to filter and refine what we are looking for. Otherwise, the Internet and all other cognate information systems will become a labyrinth that researchers will either refrain from entering or in which they will lose themselves. In order to avoid both extremes, one can only hope that the care now taken to avoid damaging the integrity of data or losing information during the input process – that is during the conversion of organised information into a digital macrocosm – will soon be paralleled by equally close attention to the output process, that is, efficient and economical ways in which we may select and retrieve all the information we need from the infosphere.

"404 document not found" and the forgetful memory

There are many old digital documents that are no longer readable because the corresponding technology (floppy drivers, word-processing software, etc.) is no longer available. There are millions of abandoned pages on the Internet (pages that have been created and then not updated or modified). At the beginning of 1998, the average life-span of a document that had not been abandoned was 75 days. Our digital memory seems as volatile as our oral culture but perhaps even more unstable, as it gives us the opposite impression. This paradox of a digital "prehistory" (on prehistory as human history before the invention of writing see the next chapter) will become increasingly pressing in the near future. The Internet, and more generally the infosphere, is made possible by the extraordinary progress made in storage and retrieval technologies, but memory is not just a question of storage and efficient management; it is also a matter of careful maintenance of the differences and hence of stable sedimentation of the past as an ordered series of differences, two historical processes which are now seriously at risk (Ted Nelson, for example, designed Xanadu so that it never deletes copies of old files; see Chapter 4). A site constantly upgraded is a site without memory of its own past, and the same dynamic system that allows one to rewrite a document a thousand times also makes it unlikely that any memory of past versions will survive for future inspection. Every digital document may aspire to such an ahistorical nature. The risk is that differences are erased, alternatives amalgamated, the past constantly rewritten and history reduced to the perennial *hinc et nunc*. When most of our knowledge is in the hands of this forgetful memory, we may find ourselves imprisoned in a perpetual present.

Digital parricide

The global network may cause the loss of information on paper. Some libraries have already destroyed their paper records after replacing them with a computerised OPAC (online public access catalogue), even when the original files contained information that could not be codified in the electronic database. This is unacceptable, as would have been the practice of destroying medieval manuscripts after an editio princeps was printed during the Renaissance. We need to preserve the sources of information after digitalisation in order to keep our memory alive, if only because the new global encyclopaedia is still too unstable to be trusted as a final repository. The development of a digital infosphere should not take the form of parricide (Baker 1994).

No epiphany on paper

Because increasing sectors of the infosphere will remain forever digital and online, access to the network will have to be granted to all in order to avoid the rise of a new technocratic elite.

The new language of the infosphere

ICT is the new language of organised knowledge. Its massive diffusion is creating new social outcasts, the so-called "computer-illiterate" and "electronically disadvantaged": in the future, it will be necessary to consider their problems. Elements of ICT will have to become part of the minimal education of any human being, if the freedom of information is to remain a universal right.

Intellectual space or polluted environment?

Because the Internet is free space, where anybody can post anything, it can become a dumping ground for any rubbish, and organised knowledge could easily get corrupted or lost in a sea of junk data. In the age of the book, the relation between writer and reader is clear and mediated by a number of sociological, cultural and economic filters. One may be unhappy with it, but we know how it works and, after all, such filters do provide some positive selection. On the Internet, the relation between the producer and the consumer of information (when there is any distinction at all; today we should rather speak of the new figure of "produmer") tends to be direct, so nothing protects the latter from corrupt information. Now, there is a lot to be said in favour of the free exchange of information on the network, and I do believe that any producers of data should be free to make them available online as they wish. However, I am also convinced that users should be protected from corrupt knowledge by intermediary services, if they wish to be. Unless responsible individuals, as well as academic, cultural institutions or recognised organisations, provide some forms of guides, filters, selective agents and authoritative services (e.g. rating services, quality-control services), we may no longer be able to distinguish between the intellectual space of information and knowledge and a highly polluted environment of junk mail and meaningless data. In spite of what some people are claiming, direct access to knowledge is only a temporary stage in the evolution of the network. In the future reliable intermediary services will become fundamental.

Decentralisation versus fragmentation

This is probably the most pressing issue on our agenda. By converting the human encyclopaedia into an electronic space, we run the risk of transforming the new body of knowledge into a disjointed monster rather than an efficient and flexible system. In the past, inadequate efforts were made to forecast how the infosphere would be affected by the binary revolution occurring in information management, and so to promote changes that would be appropriate to meet the rise of new intellectual demands. The consequence is that the Internet has developed in a very chaotic, if dynamic way, and today it suffers from a regrettable lack of global organisation, uniformity and strategic planning. While we entrust ever vaster regions of the human inheritance to the global network, we are leaving the Internet itself in a thoroughly anarchic state. We seem to be unaware of the consequences. Efforts at coordination are left to occasional initiatives by commendable individuals, to important volunteer organisations or academic institutions and, as usual when a need arises, new commercial enterprises are benefiting from the demand for a cheap, fast and reliable system of information retrieval, by sponsoring Web search engines and then placing them between the users and the information they wish to select.

The retrieval systems in existence are insufficient to guarantee that, in a few decades, organised knowledge will not be lost in a labyrinth of millions of virtual repositories, while efforts and funds are wasted in overlapping projects. The Internet has been described as a library where there is no catalogue, books on the shelves keep moving and an extra lorry load of books is dumped in the entrance hall every ten minutes. Unless it is properly structured and constantly monitored, the radical decentralisation of information – a positive feature – will degenerate into a neo-medieval fragmentation of the body of knowledge, a fragmentation that in turn will only result in a virtual loss of information. Already it is no longer possible to rely on the mere speed of our NIR tools to browse the whole space of knowledge, and collect our information in a reasonably short time. If global plans are disregarded or postponed, and financial commitments delayed, the risk is that information may well become as easy to find on the network as a needle in a haystack.

In the past, some people have compared the invention of the computer to the invention of printing. I have argued that the comparison can be very misleading, at least in one important sense: the appearance of the printed book belongs to the process of consolidation and enlargement of our intellectual space, whereas the revolutionary character of ICT has rested on making possible a new way of navigating through such a space. But there is another sense in which I would be inclined to accept a substantial affinity between the two phenomena; for, in the same way that the invention of printing led to the constitution of national copyright libraries that would co-ordinate and organise the production of knowledge in each country, so the Internet is in need of an info-structure of centres which, through their co-ordinated efforts, can fulfil the following five tasks:

1 guarantee the stability, reliability and integrity of the digital infosphere;
2 provide constant access to it without discrimination, thus granting a universal right to information;
3 deliver a continually updated map of selected regions of the infosphere;
4 expand the number and quality of resources available online, especially those that will not attract commercial operators;
5 support and improve the methods and tools whereby our world of paper documents is converted into a digital domain, and then networked information is stored, accessed, retrieved and manipulated.

I hope that what I am suggesting will not be misunderstood. I am not advocating the creation of some international bureau for the management of the Internet – a sort of digital Big Brother – nor do I have any wish to see national organisations take control of our electronic frontier. Such projects would be anti-historical, contrary to the fundamental rights of freedom of communication, of thought and of information and, moreover, they would be impossible to carry out anyway. On the contrary, I believe in the complete liberty and refreshing anarchy of the network. What I am suggesting is that the Internet is like a new country, with a growing population of millions of well-educated citizens, and that as such it does not need a highway patrol, but will have to provide itself with info-structures like a Virtual National Library system, which could be as dynamic as the world of information, if it wants to keep track of its own cultural achievements in real time, and hence be able to advance into the third millennium in full control of its own potential. It is to be hoped, therefore, that institutions all over the world may soon be willing to take full advantage of the new technologies available, and promote and co-ordinate such a global service, which is essential in order to make possible really efficient management of human knowledge on a global scale. Today we are giving the body of organised knowledge a new electronic life, and in so doing we are constructing the digital heritage of the next millennium. Depending on how we meet the challenge, future generations will consider us as new Pygmalions or as old Frankensteins.

Chapter 4

The digital domain
Infosphere, databases and hypertexts

The paradox of the growth of knowledge: from the chicken and the egg to the needle in a haystack

At the roots of scientific research and of the advancement of knowledge there is an old methodological dilemma: philosophers have always found it difficult to explain how knowledge can emerge and develop from a natural state of ignorance. In one of Plato's dialogues, Meno challenges Socrates by asking him (*Meno* 80d–81a):

Meno: And how will you investigate, Socrates, that of which you know nothing at all? Where can you find a starting-point in the region of the unknown? Moreover, even if you happen to come full upon what you want, how will you ever know that this is the thing that you did not know?

Socrates: I know, Meno, what you mean; but just see what a tiresome dispute you are introducing. You argue that man cannot enquire either about that which he knows, or about that which he does not know; for if he knows, he has no need to enquire; and if not, he cannot; for he does not know the very subject about which he is to enquire.

(Jowett 1953. For a more literal translation by
W. K. C. Guthrie see Hamilton and Cairns 1963)

What is the process through which knowledge grows? How can we start searching for something, if we do not know already what we are looking for? Meno's question cleverly introduces a paradox that has kept both interpreters and philosophers busy since its formulation. Plato thought that some form of innate knowledge and hence an ontological dualism had to be defended if Meno's question was to be answered successfully. As Socrates puts it, in his reply to Meno, "all enquiry and all learning is but recollection". Yet Plato's most brilliant pupil suggested a less metaphysical alternative. For Aristotle held that Meno's problem could arise only if one failed to perceive that the growth of knowledge was ensured by the cumulative efforts of a whole community of investigators. As he wrote in the *Metaphysics* (II, 993b, 1–5),

> The investigation of truth is in one way hard, in another easy. An indication of this is found in the fact that no one is able to attain the truth adequately, while, on the other hand, no one fails entirely, but everyone says something true about the nature of things, and while individually they contribute little or nothing to the truth, by the union of all a considerable amount is amassed.
>
> (Barnes 1984)

In the formulation of Meno's paradox, as well as in the acceptance of its conceptual prerequisites, there is implicit Plato's view of mental life as an utterly individualistic, *infra-subjective* and atemporal experience. No body of empirical observations fully deserves the name of science, logico-mathematical knowledge is conceived of more as a personal than a collaborative enterprise, and the practice of dialogue and teaching is meant to be a way of showing the direction in which the individual enquiry should progress, and hence have the opportunity to gain a personal acquaintance with knowledge, rather than representing a method for transmitting, improving and increasing well-tested and reliable knowledge from one generation to the following. As a result, *history* (the time after the invention of writing) represents for Plato a *degenerate* (both in the moral sense of "corrupt" and in the mathematical sense of "simpler") time, in which the essential foundation of philosophy is put at risk by dangerously allowing it to move from a personal and dialectical understanding of what is eternal and immutable to an intersubjective erudition concerning contingent and ever-changing phenomena, based on the written word (see *Phaedo* 275a and ff.). Augustine and Descartes shared very much the same view and ran into similar problems, opting for not very different solutions (Descartes's mathematisation of physics must be understood as a way of elevating the latter to the rank of science rather than as an attempt to run against the Platonist view), although with the overall important difference that the French philosopher replaced Plato's world of ideas and Augustine's Christian truths with the foundations of a new science.

In Aristotle, the notion of the unity of the mind is replaced by that of the unity of the scientific community. The Greek postulate that there can be no true knowledge of what can be otherwise is still there, but in Aristotle's philosophy there is also room for empirical research as a diachronic, *intersubjective* process of progressive construction, as long as the essential foundations, the metaphysics on which any further knowledge is based, are not affected. Interaction between individuals is not just a matter of personal education, but constitutes the only way in which ignorance can be escaped, through cumulative efforts. No matter how little knowledge each generation is capable of gaining, this accumulates and improves through time. Thus, for

Aristotle, there can be no real growth of the encyclopaedia outside *history*. It was natural that "justified-by-tradition" should become, for scholastic philosophy, a clear sign of the solidity of the building of knowledge, whereas the Augustinian–Cartesian approach relied on a subjectivist and internalist theory of justification.

The tension between the two views is inescapable and it appears in all its clarity in contemporary analytic philosophy. The attempt to reconcile Plato's anti-historical individualism and Aristotle's view of empirical knowledge as a historically based, collaborative enterprise seems to lead to a paradox. On the one hand we may adopt a "scientification" (that is, a "logico-mathematisation", "empirification" and problem-solving interpretation) of philosophical questions that justifies an engineer-like disregard for history, such as Descartes's or Wittgenstein's. On the other hand we may also try to save a neo-Aristotelian conception of philosophy as a progressively growing body of knowledge. Eventually we run the risk of being anachronistic, strategically blind and reductively superficial. We may be tempted to philosophise as if we were Platonists – living in a pre-historical time – or as Aristotelians – whose projects already have an explicit and well-grounded metaphysical justification – and only on philosophical questions that can either be reduced to, or forced to appear as, scientific problems in need of a timeless solution. It is for this reason that I suspect that Richard Rorty's position, while correctly criticising the Aristotelian part of the picture, is misguided in attempting to reconcile Plato's practice of dialogue with a *historically* based sense of a community of speakers.

Despite Descartes's understandable rebellion, it is hard to deny that there was at least a core of truth in Aristotle's suggestion. In practice, people do not suddenly find themselves in the region of the utterly unknown, nor do they seem either willing or truly able to question their past certainties and switch off even the little light there might be available, as it were. They bank on whatever humanity already knows, or thinks it knows anyway, heading towards new discoveries and improving on previous experience by trial and error. Peirce's fallibilism comes to mind, of course, with its strong Aristotelian roots and anti-Cartesian approach, and if we need another literary image to parallel Plato's myth of the cave we may perhaps turn to Edgar Alan Poe's *The Pit and the Pendulum*. In the story, the narrator suddenly finds himself in a dungeon, sentenced to death by the Spanish Inquisition and the victim of several psychological and physical tortures. He slowly recovers his memories, acquires an empirico-mathematical knowledge of his surroundings and survives twice thanks to his luck and intelligence, but he would be dead if it were not for the arrival of the French troops at the very last moment, suggesting a defeat of (an alleged) medieval obscurantism by the Enlightenment. No matter how much the Platonist hero tries, the solution comes from an Aristotelian team-working attitude.

Since the fifth century BC, western culture has been hovering between

Plato's and Aristotle's explanation, the cave and the pit, as it were. At the beginning, Aristotle's intuition came true. For centuries after the appearance of Meno's paradox, men and women did move slowly but firmly into the dark region of the unknown, no matter if it was with fluctuating fortunes. And when knowledge came to be at risk, the Middle Ages erected its *turris sapientiae*, to store and protect it carefully and patiently, in the centuries that run from Isidore of Seville's *Etymologies* (ab 570–636) to Rabanus Maurus' *De rerum naturis* (780–856). At the end of this long period, Richard de Bury (1281–1345) wrote in his *Philobiblon* that

> "the wise man will seek out the wisdom of all the ancients" [Eccl. 39]. For the disciples continually melting down the doctrines of their masters, and passing them again through the furnace, drove off the dross that had been previously overlooked, until there came out refined gold tried in a furnace of earth, purified seven times to perfection, and stained by no admixture of error or doubt.
>
> (de Bury 1970: 109, 111)

So he was convinced that Aristotle was right when

> He held that we should give thanks not only to those who teach rightly, but even to those who err, as affording the way of more easily investigating truth, as he [i.e. Aristotle] plainly declares in the second book of Metaphysics.

Nevertheless, a radical change suddenly occurred in the mid-fifteenth century, when Gutenberg and Fust had the brilliant intuition of applying some simple techniques to the mechanical reproduction of texts (the *Bibbia Mazarina* was printed in 1455). We live in a time when the loss of information is not an option, but occurs, one hopes, only as a rare and unfortunate disaster. During the Middle Ages it was simply a natural occurrence that people had to put up with. A few copies of a single work could easily disappear, and they did. Old manuscripts were re-used for new texts, so that the limited provision of physical carriers helped to determine the selection of works that future generations would inherit (what would you do if you had only one floppy disk in your entire life?). As if by magic, the invention of printing changed all this (for a cultural history of printing see Eisenstein 1993). The accumulation of knowledge became both easier and safer. The words of Ecclesiastes XII, "of making many books there is no end", became the motto of generations of humanists and Renaissance scholars. As Erasmus remarked of Manutius, one of the greatest publishers in the history of printing, "Aldus is creating a library which has no boundaries other than the world itself" (1982). Western culture stopped streaming and replacing information, saving knowledge in its castle, and began to accumulate and spread it at a rate which Meno would have never dreamed of. Printed books soon started to produce a boundless sea of knowledge and transformed information into a territory that required precise maps. It was going to be a region in which only expert people would be able to find their way.

Growing attention was paid to memory techniques, being a scholar became a full-time profession, and the equation "knowledge = power" acquired a third term, the book. Shakespeare describes the phenomenon well in *The Tempest*. Prospero loves and prizes the books of his library above his dukedom (Act I. ii) because, as Caliban reminds us,

> without them
> He's but a sot, as I am; nor hath not
> One spirit to command.
> (Act III. ii)

The closed, stable and protective *turris sapientiae* of the Middle Ages is replaced by the image of Bacon's dynamic and adventurous vessel sailing *plus ultra*, beyond the pillars of Hercules, towards the open sea, no longer condemned to eternal damnation as Dante's Odysseus was.

For about two more centuries, it looked as if Aristotle was to be praised over Plato for having forecast the future of the advancement of human knowledge with far greater accuracy – that is, until the progressive growth of information and knowledge transformed the Platonic world of ideas into a new objective reality. Human beings can flourish as persons only if deeply immersed in their cultural world, in a process of creation, transformation and transmission of the various regions of their infosphere. By the seventeenth century, part of such an intellectual space had already started to become a new universe in itself, no longer a filter for the interpretation and the understanding of reality and hence the attribution of meaning to it, but a separate and enigmatic macrocosm, with its own features and life, its physical problems and its psychological pressure. Prospero lives with his books "rapt in secret studies" (I. ii), but he is a Renaissance man still immersed in the natural world of an island, a symbol not of a Cartesian dualism between *res cogitans* and *res extensa*, but of solitude and detachment from worldly events, labours and ambitions (Prospero is inclined to neglect "all worldly ends, all dedicated/ To closeness and the bettering of mind" (I. ii)). However, it is in a high-vaulted, narrow Gothic chamber that we find Goethe's Faust, restless in his chair by his desk, asking himself:

> Alas! I'm still confined to prison.
> Accursed, musty hall of stone
> to which the sun's fair light itself
> dimly penetrates through painted glass.
> Restricted by this great mass of books

that worms consume, that dust has covered,
and that up to the ceiling-vault
are interspersed with grimy papers,
confined by glassware and wooden boxes
and crammed full of instruments,
stuffed with the household goods of generations –
such is your world, if world it can be called!

(*Faust*, Part I: 396–409)

The encyclopaedia is no longer a self-contained unity, a book looking inside itself, nor is culture a friendly environment in which to find respite from human preoccupations. Human knowledge has exploded into a whole new domain of growing sciences, technical information, know-how, intellectual forces, powerful ambitions of management, control, reproduction and forecasts. The *turris sapientiae* has been opened up and will never be closed again. People like Descartes rightly suspected that its foundations might need close checking and a new justification. Others, such as Leibniz, began to stress the importance of a new language and a new memory system (*De arte combinatoria*, 1666). Many perceived the opening of the *turris sapientiae* in the same way as that of Pandora's box. Here is a remarkable statement from the *Reflections upon Learning* by the antiquarian Thomas Baker, which I have already had the opportunity to quote in other contexts:

> learning is already become so voluminous, that it begins to sink under its own Weight; Books crowd in daily and are heaped upon Books, and by the Multitude of them both distract our Minds, and discourage our Endeavours.

> (Baker 1699: 59–60)

It was only one of the first in a long list of similar complaints that we hear uttered repeatedly in the subsequent centuries. Quoting Goethe, Nietzsche dramatically labelled this problem *das historische Wissen*:

> Wie sehr das historische Wissen tödtet, hat Goethe einmal ausgedrückt: "Hätte ich so deutlich wie jetzt gewusst, wieviel Vortreffliches seit Jahrhunderten und Jahrtausenden da ist, ich hätte keine Zeile geschrieben, sondern etwas anderes gethan."

> (Nietzsche 1903, X: 273)

(Goethe has well expressed how lethal historical knowledge can be [for any spontaneous and original thought]: "If I had actually been aware of all the [literary] efforts made in the past centuries, I would never have written a line, but would have done something else."

Auerbach, to mention a contemporary author, shows the same awareness in the Epilogue of his masterpiece:

> On the other hand it is quite possible that the book [i.e. *Mimesis*] owes its existence to just this lack of a rich and specialised library. If it had been possible for me to acquaint myself with all the work that has been done on so many subjects, I might never have reached the point of writing.
>
> (1953: 557)

Reality bites and life hurts, but it is left to the modern mind fully to realise that even knowledge and culture, which have evolved as an emancipation from reality through history, will forever transform itself into a new antagonist to the individual. When Prospero abjures his magic powers, he does so by sinking his own books "deeper than did ever plummet sound" (Act V. i), dissolving them in water and returning their secrets to nature. But Christopher Marlowe's Dr Faustus receives his books from the hands of Mephistopheles and Lucifer themselves. And when he thanks them, at two different moments, he does so in exactly the same dangerous way: "This will I keep as chary as my life". So when his life is finally close to an end and he wishes he had "never seen Wittenberg, never read book", it is no longer sufficient to get rid of his library. There is no natural way of restoring his relation with Being, no Renaissance unity of microcosm and macrocosm is now achievable. Dualism is inevitable. All his books must be completely destroyed by fire.

It is the same "modern" destiny that awaits them in Emily Brontë's *Wuthering Heights*, a story of ruthless and intoxicating passions and tragic love, which can be read as the dramatic conflict between nature and civilisation, recounted through the pages of Lockwood's diary in the years 1801 and 1802. At the beginning of *Wuthering Heights*, Lockwood saves himself from the appearance of Catherine Earnshaw's spectre on a stormy night not by force or violence, but only because "The fingers [of the spectre] relaxed, I snatched mine through the hole [in the window], hurriedly piled the books up in a pyramid against it". It is her own small library that he is using as a wall, "a few mildewed books piled up in one corner". Unknowingly, he has put between himself and death what the spectre most hated in her life ("I [Catherine] took my dingy volume by the scroop, and hurled it into the dog kennel, vowing I hated a good book. Heathcliff kicked his to the same place."). Metaphorically, Lockwood finds his safety from Catherine's aggressive force of nature in literature, exactly as Linton, Catherine's husband, had in the past (Mr Linton "is continually among his books, since he has no other society" and on her sick-bed Catherine complains: "What in the name of all that feels has he to do with *books*, when I am dying?"). Later in the story, when Lockwood confesses to the young Catherine (Catherine Earnshaw's daughter): "take my books away, and I should be desperate!", she, who has inherited her father's love of literature, replies, "I was always reading, when I had them [the books] . . . and Mr Heathcliff never reads; so he took it into his head to destroy my books. I have not had a glimpse of one for weeks." As in Marlowe's *Faust*, books have to be destroyed to be accepted again and kindle a tender love between the young Catherine and Hareton. Aware of and fascinated by the young Catherine's intellectual superiority, Hareton has stolen all her remaining books ("some Latin and Greek, and some tales and poetry: all old friends"), books so dear to her that she has, she says, "most of them written on my brain and printed in my heart". It is half a dozen volumes, which in the end Hareton, hurt and provoked by the young Catherine, "hurls on the fire". It is only once all the remaining literature in Wuthering Heights is destroyed that the two are brought together. Both "book-lessly naked" in front of nature, they can begin to understand each other. She can finally teach him how to read, and draw him from nature to civilisation, within whose boundaries we find them at the end of the novel, both absorbed in the process of reading and dialoguing together.

The flowering of a world of learning through the long period from Francis Bacon's motto *plus ultra* to Kant's illuministic reply *sapere aude*, had brought about Plato's revenge. New knowledge could obviously be found; centuries of successful accumulation prove it unequivocally. Yet the new world represented by the human encyclopaedia had become as uncontrollable and impenetrable as the natural one, and a more sophisticated version of Meno's paradox could now be formulated. How can a single scholar or scientist find the relevant information he requires for his own work? Moreover, what about ordinary people in their everyday lives? Meno could indeed ask: "how will you find, Socrates, what you know is already in the ever growing human encyclopaedia? Where can you find the path through the region of the known? And if you find what you are searching for, what will save you from the petrifying experience of *das historische Wissen*?" The original formula of Meno's paradox had relied on the interpretation of the human mind as a single entity and of knowledge as an immutable domain. The solution had been to conceive of the former as being in perfect tune with the latter innately. Aristotle had shown that the problem did not arise if such a single entity was more correctly interpreted in terms of a modular methodology, as a community of individuals, each taking advantage of the work carried out by the previous generations, and knowledge was viewed as a growing body. But now new difficulties arose precisely because the empirical universe of knowledge was not the product of a unique individual, but the result of the cognitive efforts of millions of lives, which generated a dualism more difficult to reconcile. Knowledge, as history and culture, is a strictly human business. It was left to the modern mind to discover that it can get lost, frightened and overwhelmed even in its own intellectual environment. The epoch of the individual, of the concepts of authorship and copyright is also the time when originality, as the establishment of the individuality of the self and the singularity of its production, is ever more difficult to achieve.

One of the consequences of the emergence of the infosphere as the real environment of the modern mind was that, by the end of the seventeenth century, humanity had moved from the problem of the chicken and the egg – how can one escape one's state of ignorance without already having some knowledge? – to that of the needle in the haystack, which one may suspect is there, but which one does not know how to find. It was not long before Diderot and D'Alembert thought, in 1751, that it was time for a comprehensive description of the human encyclopaedia to be collected together and made publicly available. Perhaps Voltaire would have not liked to acknowledge as much, but of course this extraordinary editorial effort had more than an Aristotelian twist.

Throughout the following century, western culture saw a countless number of similar attempts to dominate the universe of knowledge in some economic way. The new era of great catalogues, of the organisation of the national libraries, of German philology, of Hegel's new project to provide no longer an encyclopaedia of contents, but an intellectual map which could help the modern mind to find its way in the universe of thought, had begun. We saw in Chapter 1 that the wider the extension of knowledge became, the higher the hierarchy of the maps had to be. The process was often compared to the building of a pyramid. In order to keep the proportions stable, the height must increase whenever the basis is enlarged. Specific bibliographies appeared, and then bibliographies of bibliographies. Reviews had to be written in order that people could select the texts worth reading. In the seventeenth century a new form of publication had appeared, the scholarly and scientific journals. They were written in Latin and published specialised articles on any topic. After a century, they had become specialised periodicals, written in all the European languages, and were meant to deal only with a limited portion of the domain of knowledge. Lexicons of separate disciplines started to be compiled. The pyramid became a cathedral, with its secret rooms, its high peaks, nave and aisles, proving that the printed medium could cope with the extension of knowledge only vertically, by producing more and more specialised guides and then further guides of guides, in an endless hierarchy. The eighteenth century and the Romantic movement revalued and transformed the mediaeval image of the *turris sapientiae* into the ivory tower of the philosopher and the poet (Panofsky 1953). It was a symbol not only of sentimental escapism but also of increasing scientific *specialisation*, another word for the right to ignore. Gradually, even history itself became a self-reflective study, interested in human deeds but also in its own past as a discipline. The empire of knowledge eventually found that one way to survive its own growth was by breaking down into smaller kingdoms of disciplines. The Balkanisation of knowledge had begun.

"Everything must be transformed into an Encyclopaedia" (Novalis)

The growth of knowledge has followed the path of fragmentation of the infosphere and has been held in check by the new version of Meno's paradox until the second half of the twentieth century, when information technology has finally provided a new physical form for our intellectual environment and hence the medium and the tools to manage it in a thoroughly new way, more economically and efficiently and in a less piecemeal way. The managerial function of computers, rather than their immediate mathematical applications, has represented the real revolution in our culture, and it is only by relating it to the history of the infosphere that the impact of ICT on our way of living and thinking can begin to be fully appreciated. Looking at the history of thought from this perspective, the development of the information society can finally be interpreted as the latest (although certainly not the ultimate) stage in the auto-regulative process whereby western culture attempts to react to and defend itself against its own growth.

ICT is, then, the cultural answer to the terrific growth undergone by our system of knowledge since the Renaissance. This is not a new idea. In *The Postmodern Condition: A Report on Knowledge*, writing on the essential transformation brought about by ICT in the mental landscape of western civilisation, Jean-François Lyotard ventured the following forecast in 1979 (see Lyotard 1984):

> Databases are tomorrow's encyclopaedia. They exceed the capacities of any user. They represent "nature" for the postmodern humanity.

Lyotard's three observations were of differing value, and can now be used to introduce the more technologically oriented topics of this chapter.

The first forecast was correct. Lyotard's "tomorrow" is our "today", a time when we all let our computers search, at fantastic speeds, for the required needles in those huge, well-ordered, electronic haystacks that are our databases. If our time resembles the Renaissance in anything, it is in this: today we are selecting those works from the past which deserve to be put into an electronic medium – either because of their importance or because of their utility – almost in the same way that during the Renaissance humanists all over Europe selected those works from the past that would be preserved in print for future generations.

The comparison can even be extended. Just as it would have been foolish to produce new scholarly tools in the form of hand-written manuscripts in the sixteenth century, so it has become increasingly unreasonable to print them on paper in our time. CD-ROMs are our present encyclopaedias, but they won't be the last. The natural inclination of publishers to produce items instead of services (for example hundreds of CD-ROMs for hundreds of libraries instead of a networked information service) is not going to be a winning strategy in the long term. More and more, publishers will have to rethink their role in society and offer services online, thus regaining their central role in the development of human culture, just as, in the sixteenth and seventeenth centuries, families of publishers like the Manuzi, the Estiennes or the Elzevirs were not just sellers, but promoters, selectors and suppliers of intellectual services. After all, as D. F. McKenzie (McKenzie 1986: 60) has correctly reminded us, there is already an ideal continuity between the principle of buying access to a network and the functioning of an old lending library in England, thanks to which past generations of readers did not buy a book so much as the time to read it.When the network revolution is complete, the centralised control of databases online will raise new problems, ranging from the regulation of public access to information to massive censorship, from political control of the info-sources to the technical dependence of data- and access-less countries or social groups on data and access providers. Increasingly, knowledge will be synonymous with power.

The last of Lyotard's three remarks is slightly misleading because, as I have tried to explain already, it is not just the implementation and diffusion of databases, but the construction of the human encyclopaedia in modern times that has given rise to a new, mental as well as physical, environment for the individual. The force behind the emergence of such an artificial (not in the negative sense of "unnatural", but in the positive sense of "mind-originated") world of ideas is the fundamentally *constructionist* inclination of the mind, which is constantly present in the development of thought. As Cassirer put it in his *The Philosophy of Symbolic Forms*, perhaps more profoundly than Lyotard himself,

> every knowledge of the world and every action that is definable, strictly speaking, as "spiritual" and has as its own object the world, necessitates that the I draws away from the world, that in the process of contemplating as well as operating, the I reaches a certain "distance" from it.
>
> (Cassirer 1996, vol. 3: 1)

In search of its own individuality, autonomy and stability, the single mind can firmly establish itself at the crossroads of Being and Culture only by epistemically emancipating itself both from the world of things surrounding it and from the infosphere it inherits from the past, including the world of previously codified knowledge. However, in thus establishing its own individual autonomy, each single mind cannot help contributing to the growth of the infosphere, thus also generating new knowledge to which future generations will need to react. The succession of such reactions – understood as a constant activity of fixation, modification, rejection, renewal and ordering of epistemic facts by millions of individual minds – results in a continuous process of upheaval and enlargement of the domain of knowledge. Consequently, through time the mind cocoons itself in an ever-changing, intellectual space, an infosphere that constitutes the true "nature" within which it spends most of its life. Databases and cyberspace are only the latest outcomes of such a process.

I have left Lyotard's second observation to last because it was misformulated, to say the least, and correcting it finally introduces the analysis of what a database is. The difference between an encyclopaedia and a database does not lie in the fact that the latter "exceeds the capacities of any user", because this is trivially true of the former as well, but in the crucial fact that, unlike a simple book, a database can in principle provide all that the user requires and only that. A book is usually meant to be a fixed register with one-dimensional access, whereas a digital database is in principle an *interactive* and flexible memory that can be queried, re-shaped and continuously modified and updated according to the user's needs. It represents, therefore, an "artificial" revival of that culture of dialogue so praised by Plato in the *Phaedrus*. ICT is a technology that can make "history", the time of the written word, so open and light as to enable us to interact with other people and the infosphere both "anachronistically", as if we were in a prehistorical time (Plato), and historically, i.e. in Aristotle's sense of cumulative investigation. The shelter of the mind, the thing that stands as a defence against Being and Culture, is still knowledge, but knowledge is no longer brutally and quickly piled up like sandbags in a improvised dike, simply with a view to protection from the world. It now constitutes an ordered and harmonious structure, made to fit its user. It is a place where the mind finds itself at home.

What is a database system?

The time has now come to turn to less philosophical topics and take a closer look at some of the technological concepts and devices mentioned in previous pages.

According to Internet sources, among software industries, the database industry is second only in size to operating system software. In 1994, it yielded about $7 billion in revenue and in 1996 it was growing at 35 per cent per year. As might be expected, the term "database" has become part of our everyday language and is often used rather loosely, to refer to any large collection of data that can take on a variety of organisational formats and have different functions depending on requirements and applications. More precisely, however, a *database system* (DS) consists of

1   a collection of digital data, properly called a *database* (data stored in a database system may be partitioned into one or more databases), accessed by end users through

2   a friendly interface (the specific application software), and managed by

3   a dedicated suit of software, called a *database management system* (DBMS), both (1) (2) and (3) being supported by

4   some possibly specialised computing platform (i.e. hardware, operating system), which works as a storage device for data and software, accessible by possibly many concurrent users either online, e.g. via an Intranet or the Internet, or off-line, as stand-alone systems.

The physical database itself can be of any size and, in principle, it may contain any sort of large aggregations of alphanumerical, visual and acoustic digital data, such as names, logical values, pictures, sounds, video clips, animations, word-processing or spreadsheet files and so forth. Data are expected to be *persistent* (they need to have a sufficiently stable nature because volatile or transitory data would be of little use), *related* (an utterly random collection of data would also be worthless) and *auditable* (an audit is a detailed and complete record of all the computing processes which have been applied to a set of data input, that allows their reconstruction), while information standards include *accuracy, completeness, relevance* and *timeliness*. The whole database itself is then expected to be

- *integrated*: Data are organised into a functional system, minimising separation, isolation and redundancy (*normalisation* is the process of elimination of useless redundancy in a database). Note that minimal duplication of data enhances a higher degree of data integrity, but may affect the speed of data processing, so usually some *ad hoc* de-normalisation is implemented to enhance computing performance.
- *well-ordered*: Data within the system are arranged in logically structured patterns.
- *sharable*: Data are stored only once but are repeatedly usable, both in the sense of being usable many times by the same user and in the sense of being usable by different users at the same time.
- *variably accessible*: Data can be accessed in different logical orders, depending on users' requirements.
- *software independent*: Application programs only define which data are required, not their format. This *data independence* ensures that software will not need to be modified when changes are made to the data structure, thanks to the metadata managed by the DBMS (see below).
- *upgradable*: A database is usually a long-term resource, and is expected to be as open as possible to future modifications.

The DBMS is a layer of software, usually consisting of a suite of modular applications, that makes possible and regulates any interaction (including any communication) between the users (human users as well as artificial agents) and the infosphere, that is, the database with its environment (the computerised system, the OS, possibly a whole network and so forth). DBMSs have been in use for a long time and a wide variety are available, but even if commercial DBMS software packages have their own specific characteristics, they all share some essential features. Typically, a DBMS provides a user-friendly, abstract representation of data, so that users do not need to be acquainted with their exact physical representation, maintains a complete and updated catalogue and directory of database objects (the primary data in the database), ensures the constant availability and accessibility of data through user-friendly interfaces, enables the user to create/collect, insert/delete, store, access, retrieve, update, maintain (e.g. modify, organise, redefine, structure, sort, etc.), query, process (e.g. by statistical analyses) and report data to produce information in a simple and flexible way, and tends to make the technical details of data processing transparent to the user (e.g. users do not need to know the algorithms used by the DS to achieve its results). In addition, since a database is a valuable asset, a DBMS must also ensure the proper functioning of the DS, providing facilities

- to implement a description of the database, when a database is being set up;
- to maximise data *consistency* (identical data are always uniformly modified), *quality* (data should not be damaged or corrupted) and *integrity* (data should remain correct during concurrent operations);
- to allow some data *validation*, i.e. some constraints specifying which range of values are allowed; for example, validation may force an error to be reported if a letter is typed into the numeric field of a database;
- to manage transactions, specifying, authorising and checking correct logging accesses to the database by many users at once, thus controlling *concurrency* and priorities among users accessing the same data at the same time;
- to make possible regular backups and fast recovery procedures. *Resiliency* is the ability of a database to recover from system or power failures without loss of critical data;
- to enforce data monitoring and *security*, e.g. by access control, limiting access to the data by unauthorised users.

To provide all the above facilities, a DBMS is supported by specialised programming languages, called database languages, which include

- a high-level language for data description and definition (DDL): The DDL describes the database to the DBMS, provides facilities for changing the database, for defining and changing physical data structures, and enables users to access the database.
- a query language (QL), to interact with the database: Different DBMS provide different QL, but SQL (structured QL), a language for making interactive queries from, and updating relational databases, has become a *de facto* industry standard, although there are several variants.

- a data manipulation language (DML).
- other application programs.

All previous languages may be integrated into a single language, and an *application program interface* (API, a library of function calls) may provide database access to programs that use the DBMS.

Types of database systems

DS can be classified according to many different parameters, such as

- *the type of data they store*: we may distinguish between alphanumeric, iconographic, acoustic and multimedia databases. In what follows, we shall concentrate only on the former, although DBMS capable of storing and processing multimedia data will become increasingly common in the future.
- *their means of access*: e.g. via network or via stand-alone CD-ROMs, a difference that obviously affects the speed and reliability of any data processing, among many other factors. Typically, geographically distributed databases adopt a client-server design, in which a central server, running on a networked host, implements the DBMS, and clients, elsewhere on the network, login to the server and make requests to access or modify data synchronically (this is known as parallel database processing, and is not to be confused with parallel computing, an innovative architecture that will be discussed later in the book). As I have already remarked, modern publishers are still inclined to produce stand-alone databases because they naturally tend to rely on a "per user" marketing logic, rather than a "per time" approach, whereby one sells consultation time rather than objects. Predictably, in the future publishers will also move towards management of units of time, not just of physical tokens.
- *the kinds of users for whom the database is designed*: desktop DSs are essentially small, stand-alone, single-user systems, but networked and mainframe DSs are powerful, multi-user systems, which require provisions for concurrent access and update to the same data elements, for fault tolerance and for data integrity.

Finally, and more importantly, databases are characterised according to their

- *data models*: that is, the way in which they represent data in terms of sets of primitive datatypes and constructors for new types. Alphanumeric data models can initially be divided into two great families, depending on whether data are *discrete* members of consistently identifiable classes (i.e. autonomous and separable chunks of data such as proper names, places, dates, etc.) and therefore can easily be standardised and structured into tables (this is why they are also known as tabular data) to be sorted and retrieved, or *continuous* and sequential (e.g. whole texts) and require a different kind of software to be managed.

Discrete data can be variously organised according to hierarchical, network (both also known as navigational), flat file, relational and object-oriented data models. The two most common types of DBMS in the academic world are the flat file DBMS and the relational DBMS, and I shall say something more about them in a moment.

Navigational databases belong to the past. Efforts to automate bookkeeping date back to the 1960s, when record-oriented file models with a hierarchical or network structure were adopted. Files were updated in daily batches, at the end of all transactions. Until the end of the 1970s, network databases (not to be confused with a computer network) were the standard product. They used a record-at-a-time procedural language, and interconnections between the data were more easily represented, allowing for dependencies to be changed depending on the specific software or on the desired approach, but the programmer had to navigate through the database, following pointers from record to record, and if the data structure was redesigned, as often happens after a few years, then the application programs had to be rewritten.

The object-oriented data model (OODBMS) began to emerge only late in the 1990s. Object-oriented database systems allow users to model and manipulate complex data structures and objects, and hence support many new applications, such as streams of video data, graphics and animation, better than relational databases. During the second half of the 1990s OOD-BMS began to be developed as a possible alternative to the relational model, but in this context we shall not be much concerned with them. Suffice it to say that while relational databases keep units of data (structures) and instructions (functions) separate, in OO programming systems (OOPS) they are merged into software building blocks, known as objects. OODBs are so called because they can be thought of as being assembled like virtual Lego from these preassembled objects. An object (e.g. "Mary") comprises a data structure definition and its defined procedures in a single structure. Every object belongs to a class (e.g. "humanity") which defines its general properties, that is, it specifies what it is like to be an object of that class and hence what kinds of *messages* an object of a class can respond to in terms of implemented procedures (*methods*). Objects pass messages to other objects to initiate actions. Subclasses inherit the properties of their superclasses (think about the relation between the subclass "humanity" and its superclass "mammals") in a hierarchical structure. Classes, on the other hand, are collected into libraries, which provide whole catalogues of types of reusable software. We have already encountered some of the most well-known OO languages in Chapters 2 and 3.

Discrete data structures can have *n*-dimensions. When $n = 2$ we have the *flat file* DBMS: data are rigidly and hierarchically organised by datasheet *tables* (single and independent containers for raw data, looking like rectangular grids of rows and columns of cells), into records (the horizontal rows of the table, each holding data about a specific instance of the type of entity represented) and fields (the vertical columns of the table, each holding data about a specific aspect of the instance of the type of entity represented), with each cell (the smallest structural unit of a table, represented by the intersections of rows and columns) having a specific value. In this way, a table can provide sorting and formatting functions. Typical examples of flat file DBMS are: bibliographic managers, where each bibliographic item (book, article etc.) in the database may constitute a record and can be subdivided into short, standardised fields such as author, title, date of publication and so forth; and spreadsheets: applications such as Microsoft *Excel*, designed to facilitate tabular analysis and to perform automatic calculations, create graphs, sort the data, or perform statistical analyses. Note that a truth table could be considered a kind of flat file data model, namely a special type of spreadsheet used to calculate truth values.

When discrete data are more complex and voluminous, and present a high degree of interconnections and potential redundancy – let us take as an example data concerning Sextus Empiricus' manuscripts, their transmission, variants, editions and translations – they require structures with $n > 2$ dimensions, and it becomes necessary to organise them into n tables linked by the contents of specific columns, so that data from each can be combined. This is a relational database. The essential elements of the relational data model were devised in 1970 by Ted Codd, and since the 1980s relational DBMS have become the dominant standard in corporate computing. The SQL for relational databases became popular after 1982, was standardised by 1986 and, by 1990, virtually all DS (including navigational and object-oriented DS) provided an SQL interface. Today, popular commercial products include Microsoft *Access* and Borland & Corel *Paradox*. In a relational database, large amounts of different types of alphanumeric data are structured by means of explicitly interlinked tables. The common fields, used to link the data of a table T1 to the data of a table T2, are known as primary keys in T1 and foreign keys in T2, and, at least in theory, a well-designed and fully normalised relational database should store only such keys more than once, while all the other data should be entered only once. In our simple example, primary keys could be the titles of Sextus' works. Once the database is complete, each table, representing a type of datum as in the flat file model, is given a name, which may be called a relation, and the database can be queried by means of operations on tables that let the user select some of the rows or columns of interest from a table, or combine two tables to make a new one. Linked tables can be accessed, queried, combined and reorganised much more flexibly and in a number of ways that may not be immediately predictable when the database is under construction. For example, to obtain a new table listing all Sextus' manuscripts containing the first book of *Adversus mathematicos* translated into Latin by Johannes Laurentius, a possible query in SQL may have the following simplified pattern:

SELECT field name(s), in this case "title of the book" = M I

FROM database's table name(s), in this case, e.g. Sextus files

WHERE conditional clause, in this case "name of the translator" = Johannes Laurentius

We have seen that not all data are discrete or tabular. Very often we deal with machine-readable texts such as word-processed documents or whole collections of texts (*textbases*), like the *Thesaurus linguae Graecae*, the *Patrologia Latina* or the *Corpus Christianorum* (CETEDOC). In this case, special text-management tools for textbases are required. Here, it may be useful to distinguish between two kinds of software:

(1) *Retrieval software*: This is a basic utility, often part of the OS, which enables the user to locate specified alphanumeric strings (e.g. a combination of words) in any specified areas of memory (e.g. a specific set of directories on the hard disk of a PC) without pre-indexing it. Queries are performed by using keywords ("Aristotle"), wildcards ("Aristot*", or "*ristotle"), Boolean operators ("Plato" OR "Aristotle"), proximity functions (("Aristotle" within 10 words of "Plato")), context functions (("Plato" in "Aristotle")) and complex or nesting structures (((("Plato" OR "Aristotle" in "Ancient Philosophy") within 100 words after ("Commentators" in "Arabic Philosophy")))). Thus flexible retrieval software allows the user to transform her hard disk into a flexible and useful database and this, by the way, represents one of the main advantages of word-processing one's own documents;

(2) *Concordance software and parsers*: Concordancers are applications that allow the user to study a text by reorganising it independently of its sequential order, according to analytic criteria such as combinations of keywords, word-forms or concepts. As might be expected, current concordancers can easily handle only character-strings, and unless the text has been previously indexed or tagged (a tag is a meta-textual marker, which may specify a particular structure, like a paragraph or a chapter, or denote, for example, lemmas for inflected word-forms, implicit textual phenomena such as references to other parts of the texts, and so forth), the morphology and the semantics of a text cannot immediately be processed automatically. Parsers are applications that can determine the syntactical and hence grammatical structure of a written text and suggest alternatives when they encounter possible mistakes. Text retrieval programs and searchers, concordance software and parsers are of very little use for finding and understanding ideas automatically. They typically miss too much of the desired material because concepts and ideas are very often expressed by semantic relations and structures, not just by a specific lexicon. Still, computer-generated concordances remain a useful scholarly tool and are very common in literary and linguistic studies.

Unfortunately, their value is still very much underrated in the study of philosophical texts.

Data, information and knowledge: an erotetic approach

As an utterly new and revolutionary technology, databases have raised a number of philosophical issues, some of which can be briefly discussed here, but will need to be analysed in full by any future philosophy of information.

The conceptual framework provided by database technology can help us to clarify the meaning of "data", "information" and "knowledge" (DIK), by sketching a query or erotetic model (erotetic logic is the logic of questions and answers). A datum is anything that makes a difference: a light in the dark, a black dot on a white page, a 1 opposed to a 0, a sound in the silence. As such, it is a semantic atom: there can be no smaller extension of meaning, because a non-datum is a not-given nothingness, in which not even the presence of nothing is significant (recall what we said about the *Cartesian saturation* of cyberspace). From the point of view of our erotetic model, a datum can then be defined as an answer without a question: 12 is a sign that makes a difference, but it is not yet informative, for it could be the number of the astrological signs, the size of a pair of shoes or the name of a bus route in London, we do not know which. Computers certainly treat and "understand" data; it is controversial whether there is any reasonable sense in which they can be said to understand information. In Systems Methodology, information is often described as "data plus meaning" or "meaningful data" (Checkland and Scholes 1990; Mingers 1997). This is acceptable as a working definition, but can be refined, in the following way. To become informative for an intelligent being, a datum must be functionally associated with a relevant query. Thus a piece of information can be defined as a semantic molecule consisting of (datum ∧ a relevant question): 12 becomes informative once we know that it is the answer to the question "how many apostles were there?" Note that a datum does not need to be the correct answer to function as a proper compound of a semantic molecule: disinformation and propaganda are still forms of information, no matter whether wrong or incorrect. What is knowledge then? An embarrassingly old question. In our erotetic model, information becomes knowledge only if it is associated with the relevant explanation of the reasons why things are the way they are said to be. Knowledge involves understanding, not merely the contingent possession of a correct justification, and therefore insight, and can be defined as a body of (information ∧ a relevant explanation). Note that there may be more than one correct explanation, and that scepticism is possible because we can often doubt whether ((datum ∧ a relevant question) ∧ a relevant explanation) = 1. The result of the previous analysis is that there are many more data than corresponding items of information, and the greatest part of our epistemic life is based on true information, not on knowledge, since understanding is a rare and often unnecessary phenomenon. Strictly speaking, we do not know our names, our age or that "this is my hand"; we are simply informed about these facts. We may not know where we live and who our best friends are, but we are able to answer both questions correctly; most of us are only informed that water is H_2O, and that $(a + b)^2 = (a^2 + 2ab + b^2)$. Moreover, many things are just the way they are and there may be no particular explanations to give, or none that we can ever discover. "The person who will get the job owns a Ford", if true, is a piece of information that may be intrinsically unexplainable, for there may be no specific reason why that is the case, and hence no way of raising it to the status of knowledge. We need to remember that information is a common phenomenon, knowledge a rare exception.

There are times when too many data only help to hide what we are looking for, like a leaf in the forest. There are other times when we wish never to find the data we are searching for, like the name of a friend in a list of casualties. And yet, there is no sensible phrase to reassure us that no data are always good data: the wrong horse on which I bet is only one of the many reasons why. The truth is that even accurate data are nothing by themselves; information is what really matters, but the former can rise to the latter only when properly mixed with the relevant questions, no matter how implicit. That is why we always want the data, all the data, the only data which best answer our specific queries, without effort, without risk, just in time and without waiting. This is precisely what the digital system at its best can do, and the analogical has always inevitably failed to achieve, though with an important proviso. The analogical document without the digital is inflexible and risks becoming a monotonous parrot, *Plato docet*. But the digital, freed from the iron cage of the analogical, is spineless and can often deafen the understanding with its overwhelming noise, as shown by the Internet. Of course, it is also a matter of gradual education. Just as we do not eat everything in the fridge at once, and just as we do not switch on all the electric devices in our flat just because we can, likewise we need to learn to become thrifty with data, treating them like any other natural resource. Environmentalism is crucial even in a Berkeleian world in which pollution is an intellectual problem. However, training ourselves in the proper use of digital resources is only half the solution. There is also an increasing need to produce conceptual tools that combine the solidity of the analogical with the openness of the digital, mental-energy saving resources which may turn out friendly towards our intellectual habitat, green intellectual tools, as it were. Technology at the service of thought and thought at the service of the mind, this is the main goal of ICT, without ever forgetting that, in the information society, careful users now expect well-tailored information, and rightly disdain both intellectual *prêt-à-porter* and dumb DIY. I shall come back to this point when talking about the information rich and information poor.

The hyperbolic space of the infosphere and the fifth element

A database may contain four types of data:

(1) The set of *primary data*: These are what we ordinarily mean by, and perceive as, the principal data stored in the DS, e.g. a simple array of numbers, or the contents of books in a library. They are the data an information management system is generally designed to convey to the user in the first place.

(2) The set of *metadata*: These data are secondary indications about the nature of the primary data. They enable the DBMS to fulfil its tasks by describing essential properties of the primary data, e.g. location, format, updating, availability, copyright restrictions, etc. In our example, they could be library records, or the page of an Internet search engine.

(3) The set of *operational data*: The DS may also monitor and collect data regarding usage of the database, the operations of the whole system and the system's performance.

(4) The set of *derivative data*: These are data that can be extracted from (1)–(3), whenever the latter are used as sources for comparative and quantitative analyses (or what I shall call "ideometry", see below), in search of clues or inferential evidence (e.g. smoke interpreted as fire). The difference between primary and derivative data can easily be illustrated by three elementary examples. Using FRANTEXT, the electronic archive produced by INaLF (Institut National de la Langue Française), Keith Baker has studied the evolution of the idea of "public opinion" in France in the eighteenth century. In his *Inventing the French Revolution*, he has been able to show how the old meaning of "opinion", as an uncertain and unstable belief, acquired a positive value thanks to the association of the expression "public opinion" with the authority of reason, which is supposed to regulate the politician's conduct and before which the politician is expected to justify his activity. Second example. Suppose we analyse Chadwick-Healey's *English Poetry* on CD-ROM, a textbase containing the whole of English poetry. The structure of the digital collection is thoroughly flexible and we can query it at will. As a simple example, we could study the presence or absence of the two popular figures of Heraclitus, the weeping philosopher, and Democritus, the laughing philosopher, throughout the entire set of documents. A quick survey shows that the joint motif of compassion for human misfortune and derision of human ambitions was very popular between the second half of the sixteenth and the first half of the seventeenth century, as it is in this period that we find most of the occurrences of the philosophical couple. The pattern becomes even more interesting once we notice that during the seventeenth century the two Greek philosophers were portrayed in many Dutch paintings. Here is another simple example. Clusters of lexica are not the only relevant data. Derivative data may well be negative and still highly significant, as our

acquaintance with the binary system has already taught us. In his history of medieval philosophy, Etienne Gilson suggested that during the Middle Ages there were no real sceptics, i.e. no authors or thinkers who explicitly defined themselves as sceptics, contrary to what had happened in classical times and would happen again from the Renaissance onwards. Apparently, Augustine was the last Latin philosopher to take a serious interest in sceptical problems. Was Gilson right? If we consult the *Patrologia Latina* textbase we discover that the word "scepticus" never occurs, that the whole family of words related to "Pyrrhonism" and "scepticism" is absent from the lexicon of the medieval authors, and that there is only a marginal presence of terms related to "academicus" (probably because of Cicero and Augustine himself). These are all negative derivative data that are in themselves very interesting and informative if we wish to understand the development of scepticism in the Middle Ages. In all these examples, we have made the infosphere speak about itself through a quantitative and comparative analysis. Unfortunately, textbases are still published as reference tools only, and only occasionally do they make possible some elementary ideometric analyses (for example, they never include statistical applications).

Since to each type of datum corresponds a type of information and hence a type of knowledge, we now have twelve forms of contents. The infosphere consists of a countless number of DIKs. Is there any geometrical conceptualisation of this model? To begin with, we may compare each DIK to a dodecahedron (a polyhedron made of twelve regular pentagons). Each face is a possible type, and each DIK is interpretable according to the perspective from which we look at it (e.g. an instance of metaknowledge may be considered a primary datum). Now the infosphere is a closed and finite space (although it is potentially infinite in terms of expansion), that can be treated as a hyperbolic space, i.e. a space, representable like a sphere, in which, through any point not on a given line an infinite number of lines parallel to the given line may be drawn, squares do not exist and the sum of the internal angles of triangles is always less than 180 degrees. We have seen that the infosphere is a conceptual environment in which there can be no empty space, either within or without (a dataless infospace is a contradiction, as the concept of unextended empty space was for Descartes). This means that the DIKs fully tessellate the infosphere (fill the *n*-dimensional space in the same way as stones may cover a pavement). As it happens, a hyperbolic space can indeed be tessellated with right pentagonal dodecahedra. At this point, a suggestive reference to Plato seems inevitable. There are five regular polyhedrons, and in Platonist literature four of them were associated with the structure of the four natural elements (earth = cube, fire = tetrahedron, air = octahedron, water = icosahedron) while the fifth, the dodecahedron, was sometimes interpreted as the geometrical structure of the fifth element. What some Platonists taught was ether (the source is

Epinomis 981b–e, but see also *Timaeus* 55c and 58d), we now have defined as DIK contents. Metaphorically, we can define cyberspace as the ethereal zone.

The aesthetic and the ontological interpretation of databases

What has been said so far helps us now to clarify the two main views concerning the nature and hence the utility of databases.

According to one approach, a database is a computerised record-keeping system whose chief utility lies in the facility and flexibility with which we can manage *primary* DIKs and solve problems such as primary data duplication, lack of primary data integration and efficient retrievability. The database is seen as a model of a user's model or conceptualisation of a particular reality (an institution's organisation, a collection of texts, a business, etc.), implemented a posteriori and therefore third in the logical order of realities (world – conceptualisation – database). This reminds one of Plato's definition of art (see *Republic* 597a–598d): works of art consisting of copies, or imitations, of physical things, which themselves are copies of the world of ideas – the world of ideas being true reality. Following Plato, we may define this "mimetic" approach to databases as "aesthetic". The aesthetic approach can be limited by its naive realism (in which only physical entities and their perceptible properties are genuinely and authentically real) and undervalues the crucial importance of procedural and derivative DIKs. It mistakes the infosphere for a copy of a copy, instead of considering it, more correctly, the constitutive blueprint of any physical implementation, and hence what truly determines the shaping of any future reality.

This is the view shared by a second approach to databases which, still in Platonic terms, we may connote as ontological or hyperrealist. According to the ontological approach, databases are not only sources of *derivative* and *procedural* DIKs that users (scientists, managers, scholars, analysts, investors, etc.) exploit for further enquiries, analyses, or decision-making procedures, but are also strategic resources whose overall purpose is to generate new information out of old data, that is, mines of that digital gold which is at the centre of most human activities. From this perspective, the infosphere is the authentic reality that underlies the physical world, and as such it has a normative or a *constructionist* function: a clear design of the structure of a particular domain in terms of a data model or information system is either a *conditio sine qua non* for any implementation or, when the implementation is already available, an essential element that contributes to the proper modification and improvement of the conceptualised reality in question. Thus, the infosphere comes first in the logical order of realities, and it is the necessary conceptual environment that provides the foundation for any meaningful understanding of the surrounding world, one of its many possible implementations.

The epistemological difference between an "aesthetic" and a "construction-ist" approach can be further clarified by saying that in the biological and physical sciences a pre-conceptualised reality (actual entities in the external environment) comes first and its theoretical model may work as a second-level explanatory representation that can be used for predictions, whereas in mathematical and computer sciences, the relation is usually reversed. The ideal model comes first, providing the requirements that the actual implemen-tation in the real world will eventually need to satisfy. Once we adopt the latter, ontological, approach we can better understand the following issues.

Ideometry

A lot could be said about the important innovations that the development of databases and the Internet has brought about in the field of the production and management of organised knowledge. One may think, for example, of the reduction of the time-lag between the production and the utilisation of knowledge, the promotion of international co-operation and free sharing of information among researchers and scholars, or the possibility of remote teaching online. Yet most such novelties are less revolutionary than they seem, since their principal task is to make it easy and quick to do what we used to do more slowly and with greater difficulty. There are other striking innovations, however, which are more radical. One of these concerns the way in which we are able to acquire and reuse data about the infosphere itself more and more easily and efficiently. In the age of the book, primary data sets were collected and organised in structures that were necessarily rigid and unalterable. The ordering principles not only created a domain, they also established *de facto* the limited range of primary questions which could meaningfully be asked. In our previous example we saw that, if the ordering principle stated that the primary data should be all the poetry ever written in English, the final edition in several volumes of all English poems provided the means to answer properly and easily only a limited range of primary questions, such as who wrote what or when. There was a direct correspondence between ordering principles and possible questions. Computerised databases have changed all this, for it is now possible to query the digital domain and shape it according to principles that are completely different from those whereby the primary data were initially collected and organised. The structure of our particular set of digital data can be modified to fit an indefinite number of requirements, and hence provide answers to secondary questions which were not intended to be answered by the original structure.

Consider again the intellectual hyperspace of organised knowledge. Within the infosphere, data form a web of dependencies and symbiotic relations. The data output of data collection and analysis processes can be restructured to become the input of other information processes (no hierarchy is implied).

Complex relations among data-producers, data-collectors, data-processors and data-consumers constitute an ecosystem in which information may be used and recycled to acquire further information and eventually make strategic decisions or provide new explanations. The patterns that emerge from the application of quantitative and comparative queries may turn out to be meaningful and interesting for reasons that are completely extraneous to the initial ordering principle. What we may call *ideometry* is the critical study of such significant patterns resulting from a comparative and quantitative analysis of the extensional field of codified information, that is, clusters of primary data, metadata and procedural data from data-banks, textual corpora or multimedia archives used as extensional sources. Derivative data are the outcome of an ideometric analysis of whatever region of the infosphere has been subject to investigation.

Ideometry is a clear case of the ontological rather than aesthetic approach to databases. It begins by collecting, integrating, arranging and comparing data as modular and composite objects, and then re-configures (within the scope originally envisaged by the source/author) or more often re-purposes (beyond the scope originally envisaged by the author/source) the available data to construct, generate or simply reveal new information, usually subtle but very informative patterns. Two factors are crucial for the evolution of ideometric analyses:

1   the thoroughly digital nature of data and computerised tools: the signified need to be separated from their physical existence as signifiers to become the malleable, flexible, customisable digital gold processed by ideometric analyses;
2   the amplitude and scale of information phenomena, which makes a crucial difference.

Primary data need metadata in order to be manageable, so this second dimension of the infosphere can never be separate from the first. Procedural and derivative data, however, are not so directly available, and they emerge as new dimensions of our intellectual environment only when large amounts of primary data are collected in digital form, are made easily accessible to the user, and can be queried rapidly and thus re-structured via electronic tools.

Ideometry is perfectly in line with the development of the history of thought, which through time becomes progressively more and more self-reflective and metatheoretical. As a cluster of multidisciplinary methods, it has become popular in many humanistic, linguistic and social disciplines since the 1960s. Scientometric historiography, the study and edition of literary texts (Neuman 1991), the collation of manuscripts, the attribution of adespota (literary works not attributed to, or claimed by, an author), lexicography (the principles and practices of lexicon or dictionary making, Spinosa 1990), stylometry (the technique of making statistical analyses of features of a literary style, Kenny 1978 and 1982, Ledger 1989), linguistic statistics (Butler 1985 is an introduction to fundamentals of textual statistics), metrical analysis, prosopography (historical enquiry concerned with the study of political careers and family connections), citation analysis, bibliometric studies, econometrics, cliometrics (the application of economic theory and quantitative techniques to describe and explain historical economic events), and quantitative history, all use forms of ideometric analyses to deal with their data.

When simple and economical tools for studying visual and acoustic patterns also become available, ideometric analyses may be extended to the entire domain of the enlarged infosphere. Ideometry shows that digital texts, though they maintain some of the basic features of printed books and can therefore be used as surrogates, should not be understood as if they were meant to fulfil the same task, as if their physical transformation were almost irrelevant and the speed of access were the only valuable difference. We do not convert printed texts into electronic databases in order to read them better or more comfortably. For this task the book is and will remain unsurpassed. We collect and digitise large corpora of texts in order to be able to subject them to ideometric analysis and extract data they contain only on a macroscopic level. In this way, we can reach further information about the infosphere itself. What is revolutionary in an electronic bibliography, for example, is not that I can find what I need in a few seconds – for this is rather trivial – but that I can check when historical books on Analytic Philosophy started to be written, and discover how their number increased while the movement was becoming more and more scholastic. Corpora of electronic texts and multimedia sources are the laboratory for ideometric analysis. The larger the domain, the better it will be, for the ideometric value of an extensive corpora is given by the product rather than by the simple arithmetical sum of the ideometric value of each single document.

The commodification of information and the growth of the infosphere

Information, as well as the processes by which it is manufactured, can easily be commodified. Why this is so is often a matter of disagreement, owing to widespread confusion between five different phenomena: digitisation, cross-medialisation, disembodiment, reification and hence commodification of information:

(1) *Digitisation*: The codification of mono- and multimedia documents in the language of bytes not only makes possible their versatile and precisely quantifiable management, it also provides them with a common and interchangeable support, causing a

(2) *Radical cross-medialisation of the contents*, which can be manipulated, stored, imported and exported regardless of the individual carrier. The

movement from token-carrier (e.g. documents printed on paper) to type-carrier (e.g. database files recorded on any digital support) has a twofold effect:

(3) *Disembodiment*: The semantic contents, once largely carrier-independent, come to be considered fully detached from their physical bearers. It is a process of de-physicalisation of reality that begins with the mechanical reproduction of printed material (two books can contain exactly the same document, unlike two manuscripts) and is then carried on by the process of industrialisation. In a manufacturing culture, the concept of an industrial object ends up representing a mere replaceable instantiation of a universal model. This disembodiment of the things we live with has largely affected our understanding of the importance of the individual entity, now in principle always replaceable without any discernible ontological loss.

(4) *Reification*: Since digital documents are easily subject to purposeful manipulation, exact measurement and fast exchange, they also acquire a substantiality that would have been inconceivable in the past. We do things with and to digital objects, not just to their physical bearers, and thus we perceive and treat them as actual entities, appreciating their value but also their fragility and danger, their ageing and decay for example. Disembodiment and reification make possible the

(5) *Commodification of information*: Value-adding processes like collecting, sorting, analysing, packaging and exchanging information-objects lead to financial transactions between knowers and know-nots, data/information suppliers and data/information consumers, sellers and buyers. Assets become increasingly abstract, intangible and information-based. Information represents the new digital gold of a society in which people work and may commit crimes for it.

These five stages of development explain why it is a mistake to interpret the information society as a communication society, as Negroponte seems to be suggesting from a massmediological perspective (Negroponte 1995): the transformation is much more radical, because it represents an ontological evolution of the post-industrial society into a manufacturing society in which what is manufactured is no longer material *res extensa* but consists of immaterial information. From the sycophants (the word for informers in ancient Athens) to the 30 denarii, information has always been an indispensable and therefore highly valuable resource and so a potential commodity, but before its disembodiment and reification and the ICT revolution, it was very difficult to handle it and price it with sufficient accuracy. Today, the commodification of information has become an essential concept for interpreting the future both of our culture and of our society.

Rich and poor in the information economy

There is a mistaken tendency to reduce the difference between the information-rich and the information-poor to that between primary information haves and have-nots. We have inherited this perspective from the industrial society and its empiricist mentality, but in a Platonic space, the matter is somewhat more complex. DIKs can be treated as real objects but do not have an immediately perceptible nature. For example, they can be shared or sold again and again, without being lost, so simple ownership of them is an unstable form of wealth, one that is easily and quickly eroded by information inflation. On the contrary, one is truly information-rich if:

1   One has control of, access to, and can use, constantly renewed DIK-sources. Ownership is not necessarily the point here and it may even be a hindrance, as anyone who has taken advantage of fringe benefits well knows. Rather, to belong to a privileged class means to be placed in a privileged position within the infosphere.

2   One is capable of transforming primary data into primary information. This is a matter of interpretation and hence of semiotic abilities. I shall return to this point in a moment.

3   One is capable of transforming primary information into primary knowledge. The capacity for explaining and understanding information is what makes the difference between practical instrumentalism (e.g. if you wish this p then do this q) and epistemic control (e.g. p-cases and q-cases are connected because of s-relations, so if you wish to bring about this p-case it is sufficient to implement the relevant q-case and s-relation).

4   One is capable of transforming primary information into derivative information. This is a matter of intelligence, for it requires the ability to infer new information.

As in the market for raw materials, knowing how to manipulate the digital gold is at least as important as owning it. As in the financial market, derivatives are at least as valuable as the underlying assets. This explains why the information society is a little more egalitarian than the industrial one: every info-rich person is necessarily a self-made man. What really matters, in the information society, is education and the full mastering of the several languages that ontically constitute the fifth element, from one's own natural idiom to mathematics, from English to ICT, since languages are the very fabric of the infosphere. Philosophically, we are still struggling with the view that the chief goal of semiosis (the process whereby something functions as a sign) is representation and then communication. Thus we tend to endorse what is ultimately a *heteronomous* conception of language, understood as a mapping instrument which does not find its justification in itself, but constantly needs to rely on an external reference to justify its function. Yet meaningful signs (including those belonging to natural languages) do not clothe a pre-existing infosphere, they constitute it, and a long intellectual tradition, going from von Humboldt to Chomsky, has called attention to this fundamentally constructionist nature of semiotic codes, whereby languages ontologically *incorporate* reality, rather than just describing it. It seems that no philosophy of language with a narrowly aesthetic approach (i.e. representational or communication-oriented, in the technical sense just introduced) can hope to succeed in explaining the semiotic function.

ICT practical problems and computer ethics

The diffusion of ICT literacy and the accumulation (concentration in single locations) of huge quantities of fully accessible (dissemination), easily manageable (digital databases allow an increasing number of queries, thus making original collections of data usable for purposes that may be very different from those which suggested their recording) and highly valuable information naturally give rise to practical problems concerning the use of the "digital gold". These can be divided into two classes:

1   problems with the information, ranging from the lack of universal standards – a serious hindrance to the harmonisation and standardisation of the infosphere – to data security and hackers' intrusions, from the unauthorised use of databases, which may lead to data corruption or loss, to the infringement of copyright or the spread of viruses;
2   problems arising from the information, ranging from the misuse and abuse of private and confidential information to the exchange of illegal copies of software, from the publication of terrorist information to child pornography.

An increasingly large sector of the ICT industry is involved in protection of, or from, information and, on the philosophical side, computer ethics has become a whole new area of investigation, whose importance and complexity is bound to grow steadily in years to come.

Textual analysis: a constructionist approach

Computer-oriented concepts, database terminology and DBMS ideas provide a disciplined framework whose salutary precision and clarity may be of considerable benefit in approaching the analysis of literary texts from a perspective that, in line with the ontological interpretation of databases expounded above, I shall also label constructionist.

For a constructionist, a text such as Descartes's *Meditations* is not simply a structured micro-region in the infosphere, with a neighbourhood that remains well defined although constantly expanding diachronically and overlapping spatially with other texts, like the centre of a galaxy in motion. A text is, above all, a primary form of reality, that must be treated as a genuine object, a conceptual artefact that has been assembled for a purpose, often relying on and re-configuring old material, and which can really be understood only if one knows how to use it, how to disassemble it and re-assemble it, repair it and in some case improve it, exactly as if it were a conceptual tool.

Interpreting a literary text from a constructionist perspective means, therefore, to be able to normalise and categorise its DIK-elements (what they are and how they are to be re-modelled or re-conceptualised as related sets of properties), to discover their mutual relations, their internal processes, their overall structure, and to provide a textual model in which it becomes evident how far the purposes of the text-tool are fulfilled. If programs can be copyrighted because they are literary works and hence formal expressions of ideas (see for example the USA 1976 Copyright Act, amended by the Congress in 1980), then conversely literary texts can also be seen as conceptual mechanisms, complex systems that may exhibit holistic and emergent properties or have a high degree of fault tolerance (do the *Meditations* collapse because of the Cartesian circle?) and redundancy, and that may be broken after all, or in need of repair. For a constructionist, rational criticism is a way of showing how far a text can support external and internal solicitations, and reading is like working with Lego. It is from this perspective that we shall now look at the hypertext.

Hypertext as information retrieval system

A relational database can loosely be described as a hypertext, and if its records are multimedia files, we may well call it a hypermedia. We saw in the previous chapter that the Web is a gigantic hypermedia, but what is a hypertext exactly?

Although the idea of associating information with places, and hence of linking it into easily retrievable patterns to help one's memory, is as old as Greek rhetoric, hypertexts, as we know them now, are the result of the ICT revolution. (On the nature of hypertext see McKnight 1991; Nielsen 1995; Seyer 1991; on the conceptual issues concerning the technologies of writing and hypertext see Bolter 1991; Landow 1994, 1997; Ong 1982.) Our story begins in 1945, when Vannevar Bush, then director of the Office of Scientific Research and Development in the USA, published an extraordinary article, in the *Atlantic Monthly*, entitled "As we may think" (all following quotations are from Bush 1945). During the war, Bush had co-ordinated the activities of a large community of scientists. He therefore knew that "a record, if it is to be useful to science, must be continuously extended, it must be stored, and above all it must be consulted". He had also come to appreciate, however, the remarkable difficulties confronting the management of huge quantities of constantly updated information in a world in which "specialisation becomes increasingly necessary for progress, and the effort to bridge between disciplines is correspondingly superficial", whereas methods of encoding, processing, transmitting and reviewing information were still obsolete and thoroughly inadequate.

> The summation of human experience is being expanded at a prodigious rate, and the means we use for threading through the consequent maze to

the momentarily important item is the same as was used in the days of square-rigged ships.

Bush thought that a new way of managing (what we have called) the infosphere was necessary. In his article, he refers to Leibniz and Babbage among many others and then, in perfect line with the mechanical approach I already discussed in previous chapters, he sketches the project for a new *mechanism*, the memex.

Much needs to occur, however, between the collection of data and observations, the extraction of parallel material from the existing record, and the final insertion of new material into the general body of the common record. For mature thought, there is no mechanical substitute. But creative thought and essentially repetitive thought are very different things. For the latter there are, and may be, powerful mechanical aids. . . . Consider a future device for individual use, which is a sort of mechanized private file and library. It needs a name, and to coin one at random, "memex" will do. A memex is a device in which an individual stores all his books, records, and communications, and which is mechanized so that it may be consulted with exceeding speed and flexibility. It is an enlarged intimate supplement to his memory. . . . There is, of course, provision for consultation of the record by the usual scheme of indexing. If the user wishes to consult a certain book, he taps its code on the keyboard, and the title page of the book promptly appears before him, projected onto one of his viewing positions. . . . Any given book of his library can thus be called up and consulted with far greater facility than if it were taken from a shelf. As he has several projection positions, he can leave one item in position while he calls up another. He can add marginal notes and comments. . . . All this is conventional, except for the projection forward of present-day mechanisms and gadgetry. It affords an immediate step, however, to associative indexing, the basic idea of which is a provision whereby any item may be caused at will to select immediately and automatically another. This is the essential feature of the memex. The process of tying two items together is the important thing. When the user is building a trail, he names it, inserts the name in his code book, and taps it out on his keyboard. Before him are the two items to be joined, projected onto adjacent viewing positions. At the bottom of each there are a number of blank code spaces, and a pointer is set to indicate one of these on each item. The user taps a single key, and the items are permanently joined. In each code space appears the code word. Out of view, but also in the code space, is inserted a set of dots for photocell viewing; and on each item these dots by their positions designate the index number of the other item. Thereafter, at any time, when one of these items is in view, the other can be instantly recalled merely by tapping a button below the corresponding code space. Moreover, when numerous items have been thus joined together to form a trail, they can be reviewed in turn, rapidly or slowly, by deflecting a lever like that used for turning the pages of a book. It is exactly as though the physical items had been gathered together to form a new book. It is more than this, for any item can be joined into numerous trails.

The retrieval problem is a communication problem, which can be solved by devising an information system that no longer requires the user to move towards information (towards the notes at the bottom of a page or at the back of a book, towards the document referred, towards the library and so forth) but, rather, organises information so that whatever is needed can be made immediately and constantly available, coming towards the reader, as it were. It is the first seed of that semi-ubiquity of information we have seen characterising the Web.

The memex was never built, and Bush did not coin the word "hypertext", but the idea was clearly there. It was left to another pioneer, Ted Nelson, to find the right label and develop the idea of what he called a *hypertext* into a vision of a computerised system (see Nelson 1974). In the 1960s, Nelson described his *Xanadu* project (a sort of global hypermedia library, now comparable to the World Wide Web, named after Coleridge's poem precisely to suggest "the magic place of literary memory where nothing is forgotten") as a form of *nonsequential writing*, in which sets of documents are connected by links, thus allowing readers to choose alternative reading pathways. What was a visionary project turned out to be an excellent product: applications such as *HyperCard* or *Storyspace* have become common since the late 1980s and even the Help instructions in our software now come as a click-and-go hypertext.

More than half a century after Bush's visionary article, hypertexts have acquired so many features, and have developed in so many different typologies, that a comprehensive definition is now bound to be either somewhat generic or controversial. Before turning to the latter alternative, let us have a look at the former. It will help us to clarify a few misconceptions concerning the nature of hypertext, which seem to have become rather widespread in recent times.

A standard definition of hypertext

A text is a hypertext if and only if it is constituted by

1 a discrete set of semantic units (nodes) which, in the best cases, offer a low cognitive load, e.g. paragraphs or sections rather than pages or chapters. These units, defined by Roland Barthes as *lexia* (for a discussion see Landow 1997), can be

(a) alphanumeric documents (pure *hypertext*)

(b) multimedia documents (*hypermedia*)

(c) functional units (e.g. agents, services or applets; think of a logic hypertext-book in which a node is a program to calculate the truth values of a truth table), in which case we have the *multifunctional hypertext* or *hypermedia*.

2   a set of associations – links or hyperlinks embedded in nodes by means of special formatted areas, known as source and destination *anchors* – connecting the nodes. These are stable, active cross-references which allow the reader to move immediately to other parts of a hypertext.

3   an interactive and dynamic interface. This enables the user to perceive – often just visually, although acoustic and tactile hypertexts are also possible – and operate with the anchors (e.g. through a click of the mouse or the touch of a key, by placing the cursor on a highlighted element of the document or by dialling a sequence of numbers) in order to consult one node from another (e.g. in a multi-windows environment or through keypad hypertext systems in which callers select desired telephone services). The interface may also provide, though not necessarily, further navigation facilities, such as an a priori, spatial representation of the whole network structure – when the system is closed and sufficiently limited to be fully mappable (the sky-view system) – an a posteriori, chronological recording system of the "history" of the links followed (e.g. the backtrack navigation function in Web browsers), when the system is open and theoretically infinite, as is the case with Web browsers, or bookmarking facilities "on demand".

It is easier to explain which other features depend on (1), (2), (3) if we now look at some of the most common misconceptions I mentioned earlier.

(1) The *electronic fallacy*: hypertext is a uniquely computer-based concept.

Wrong. This would be like saying that a Turing machine is a computer-based concept, when exactly the opposite is the case. The conceptual and the physical levels should not be confused. As the Memex ("mem-ory ex-tender") shows, a hypertext is a conceptual structure that was originally conceived in fully mechanical terms. Bush's ideas were developed in 1932–3 and the draft of his paper was written in 1939. This may explain the wholly mechanical approach. Missing the importance of the new physics of information, Bush relied on instantly accessible microfilmed documents to describe his project. It is true that nodes and links can be implemented efficiently and on a large scale only by an information system that can, firstly, unify all documents, formats and functions using the same physical medium and, secondly, provide an interactive interface that can respond to external inputs almost in real time. And it is equally obvious that computers fit precisely such a role, but the memex or *Xanadu* are, like a Turing machine, theoretical models. Digital electronics, although practically vital for their implementation, is by and large conceptually irrelevant for their understanding. So much so that *HyperCard*, just to mention a specific example, is conceptually based on the metaphor of a stack of cards or an office "Rolodex".

(2) The *literary fallacy*: hypertext began primarily as a narrative technique and hence it is essentially a new form of literary style.

Wrong again. Hypertexts were first envisaged as, and remain above all, information retrieval systems used to collect, sort, categorise, update, browse and retrieve information more easily, quickly and efficiently (recall the origins of the Web as a scientific instrument for groupware, for collaborative and cumulative data management). This is consistent with the fact that they tend to be uncritically identified with ICT, as we have just observed in discussing the electronic fallacy. Hypertext provides a very powerful and effective means to integrate and organise documents into coherent collections with extensive, stable and readily usable cross-references between them. As a consequence, a hypertext format has become standard for interactive learning software, instructional and training tutorials, reference works, textbooks and technical documentation, or for the Web itself, whereas literary hypertext, understood as a new style of "open" narrative, remains only a marginal phenomenon. Literature, even in the broadest understanding of the term, came afterwards, almost like a curious form of experimentation in novel writing (e.g. it would be interesting to realise a "quantum" hypertext, in which, given a certain narrative on CD-ROM, the program determines the unique reading path followed by the reader once and forever, for every act of reading performed on a specific CD, like sculpting a particular statue from a block of marble that can be shaped into any statue; reading would make the hypertext collapse into a text, physically). As for the importance of hypertexts in technical documentation, the oft-quoted case of the CD-ROM containing the hyper-textual documentation for an F-18 fighter aircraft is illustrative: if printed, it would consist of about 300,000 pages, consulting it would be extremely time-consuming, updating it would be a gigantic and very expensive task, and its distribution would be a serious problem. These are the kinds of problems that have made hypertext an essential requirement.

(3) The *expressionist fallacy*: hypertext has arisen as and should be considered primarily a writing-pushed phenomenon.

If (1) and (2) are simply wrong, (3) is more controversial and somewhat hazardous. Although one may appreciate the fact that hypertexts free the writer from the overemphasised (see below) constrictions of linearity, it is much more important to stress that hypertexts are designed for the sake of the reader, chiefly to ease the tasks of searching and retrieving relevant documents, but also to allow a choice of reading-patterns, to some (usually limited) extent. This also means that texts need no longer be physically tailored to a unique readership, but may contain various levels of readability, depending on the conceptual accessibility of their contents and different types of information priorities. Overall, hypertext is therefore more correctly seen as primarily a reading-pulled phenomenon, rather than a writing-pushed one. This is what makes it a truly postmodern "technique": the empowered reader, rather than the writer, determines the format of the text, and in this case the stress is not only on the Cartesian–Kantian problem of how we should construct the future space of information (textuality as the result of a recording/writing problem), but also on how we should be moving within the now-constructed infosphere (hypertextuality as the result of a retrieving/ reading problem). Recall the information retrieval nature of the Memex. Anyone who has edited Web pages knows that documents that have to be converted from a text to a hypertext format usually need to be reconfigured, reshaped, framed and modularised to force them to reach the specific dimensions of linkable units in a hypertextual structure, which can then easily be navigated by the user. Readability and retrievability orient both the writing process and the resulting text. For not just writing but also, and more importantly, reading has become a computer-mediated process affected by the new hypertextuality. On the one hand, a new conception of writing has emerged in the last few years, thanks to the common practice of word-processing texts and writing Web pages, so that "authoring" now refers both to the process of content-generation (e.g. writing a text in English) and to the process of structure-shaping of the content (shaping the text to adapt it to the new logic of hypertext narrative, marking the text in html, constructing the network of links within which the text is embedded, organising the graphics of the text, providing a reader-orientation system, etc.). On the other hand, hypertext literacy implies (a) a high level of familiarity with computers, (b) a highly visual ability to recognise and use navigational tools and signals, such as icons, arrows, buttons, scroll bars, etc., as well as interactive sources and thus online modules, Boolean queries, etc., (c) a parallel capacity to extract information from the largely nonverbal nature of hypertextual documents (think how much the Web has contributed to undermining the culture of the word in favour of the broader culture of the sign), and (d) some experience with homogeneous and non-linear documents, lest one becomes confused and disoriented by their network structure, as if it were a labyrinth. (Consider, for example, the following three phenomena. There may be problems caused by the absence of physical peculiarities of the documents consulted: completely different types of contents tend to look exactly the same if they are in an electronic format. We may become disorientated in our navigations: the "lost in hyperspace" experience. And there is the "jumping" experience that occurs when a reader moves from one place to another: what guarantees that the next Web page to be opened up with a click of the mouse will not be deadly frightening, morally disgusting or psychologically threatening?)

Recognising hypertext as primarily a reading phenomenon means becoming aware both of the necessity of producing reader-friendly hypertexts and of the new barriers that hypertexts may represent for ICT-illiterate persons. This is not all. In its normative aspect, a writing-centred conception of hypertext also runs the risk of enhancing a certain mental laziness. From Marcus Aurelius's *Meditations* to Thomas Aquinas's *Summa theologica*, from Pascal's *Pensées* to Wittgenstein's *Tractatus*, philosophical literature includes many masterpieces in which the poetics of the commentary or of the fragment is purposefully and very successfully pursued as the least inadequate and most truthful form of expression (on philosophical writing see the essays by Landow, Aarseth, Liestøl and Kolb in Landow 1994). Hypertext editions of such works may enable one to capture more easily all the inherent interlinks in the texts. However, hypertexts, with their facilities and a writing-oriented approach, should be no excuse for the author to lapse into a fragmentary style merely for want of structuring ability or syntactical control over his narrative. It is often said that hypertext may enhance lateral thinking (that is, any way of thinking which seeks the solution to an intractable problem not "vertically", i.e. using conventional logic, but through unorthodox methods, by disrupting an apparent sequence and approaching the solution from another perspective), but even if this is the case, heuristic procedures should not be confused with expository requirements. Compare the adoption of rules in games, logic exercises or physical competitions: we discover that narrative rules are not iron-hard, but then, who said one could not touch the ball with one's hands when playing football? Intellectual self-discipline, constrained rationality and constructive control of the consequential narrative are "Aristotelian" virtues (*Poetics*, chapter 7), especially when presenting one's own ideas to a reader. The great contribution of hypertext to philosophical writing seems to be that of having made clear that now authors can choose to be linear. On the one hand, paraphrasing Beckett, I write linearly "pour m'auppauvrir", "to impoverish myself": it is the minimalist aesthetics of a Bauhaus type of geometrical linearity. On the other hand, the availability of hypertextual writing is no justification for baroque, disconnected, loose, overparatactic or disordered contents. A reader-centred interpretation of hypertext remains the best prevention against similar risks.

(4) The *"politically correct" fallacy*: with hypertext, the reader is in complete control of whatever contents or functions are available and hence is no longer subject to the writer's authority.

This is one of the most widespread mistakes. It suffers from the opposite problem encountered in (1): it still confuses the conceptual and physical levels of analysis, yet this time it does so in favour of the conceptual, disregarding what is actually the case. As far as the view is intelligible, it appears to be based on a rather odd collection of misunderstandings and confusions. On the one hand, authorship is conflated with authority and the concept of book is narrowly limited to that of a linear, closed and finite text exemplified by the novel, which is then strictly associated with the concept of hierarchy. On the other hand, hypertext is celebrated as the means through which one may finally challenge the rigid domain of the hierarchical and linear textuality of the book – and hence elements such as a definite beginning and ending, fixed sequence, and a consequent perception of narrative unity, comprehensiveness and self-sufficiency – in support of the active power of the reader. Hypertextual literature is claimed to represent a reaction against the oppressive authority of the writer, in favour of a "reader liberation movement". A whole rhetoric of multiple-centred, decentred or "eccentric" discourses, multiple authorship and multiple linearities, which would retain and extend the controlling power of the individual reader, ensues. The view that hypertext may give rise to a new style of avant-gardist literature is tinged with populist consequences. In its most extreme form, all this is plain nonsense à la Sokal and the "reader liberation movement" is a myth, but this is indeed a pity, for there is some truth in this perspective.

Let us look at the facts and compare actual hypertexts with actual books (not potential hypertexts with actual books, as it is too often done). Hypertexts are often as closed, finite, authoritative and immutable as a book, and present an equally clear path through which the reader is invited to move, an *axial narrative*. Take for example the Web pages of a site, or an electronic encyclopaedia. These hypertexts are created to provide the user with some flexibility in reading the documents, but the network of links is not meant to be alterable, and only a selection of alternatives is allowed the reader, whose degree of freedom is constrained by the author's original project and the usual costs/benefit ratio which determines the process of marking the whole set of documents. Many have theorised that the advent of the space of hypertext represents the end of "stratigraphic writing", i.e. the disappearance of a neat division between what Gérard Genette has called the *paratextual* (a whole class of structures including copyright notes, footnotes, the chapter titles, appendices, indices and all the other printed material on the logical periphery of the text) and the primary text, but the suggestion, though fascinating in theory, is utterly mistaken in practice, for it is based on two erroneous assumptions. First, the logical possibility that all hyperlinks may be equivalent relations – i.e. links which are all connected ($\forall x \, \forall y \, (x \neq y \rightarrow [Rxy \lor Ryx]))$, reflexive ($\forall x \, (Rxx)$), symmetric ($\forall x \, \forall y \, (Rxy \rightarrow Ryx)$) and transitive ($\forall x \, \forall y \, \forall z \, ((Rxy \land Ryz) \rightarrow Rxz)$ – is never actually implemented by any real hypertext. Second, the view that syntactical equivalence may be equal to, or entail, semantic equivalence is obviously unjustified. On the contrary, links in a hypertext do not usually have the same nature (e.g. some may be asymmetric, some symmetric, etc.) and hypertexts that are too large always break down into sectors, acquiring a hierarchical structure, so that all decent hypertexts inevitably end up by organising their semantic units around a backbone (think of the home page of a Web site). In practice, the hypertext author can make more than one semantic universe available for the reader, but certainly not every universe. The reader's navigation is *wilfully* constrained by the reader as well as by the writer around an axial narrative, and it is usually very clear what is text and what is paratext.

Consider now the polemic against printed texts. Books are definitely more open, connected with each other, internally structured and flexible than some of their detractors appear to think, at least seeing how skilful students are in identifying only those sections of the books they are supposed to read for their courses. Moreover, a library is full of printed texts, including books, which were not written and were never meant to be read from beginning to end: journals, magazines, newspapers, dictionaries, vocabularies, encyclopaedias, readers, conference proceedings, collections of essays and so forth. A scholar is a student who has stopped reading texts from the beginning to the end. In what sense are articles printed in a newspaper or the entries in a dictionary "linear", as opposed to the non-linearity of a hypertext? If you look at the complete printout of a hypertext, in what way is it not syntactically linear? I shall return to this point in a moment, when talking about a more positive interpretation of hypertext. The fact that electronic hypertexts may provide marking and annotation facilities at a meta-level only shows, all the more clearly, that the hypertext in itself, at the object-level, is often locked, as a collection of "read only" files. The degree of *creative* interaction that hypertexts offer to the reader remains practically limited. Likewise, on the Web we should not be misled by the opportunities offered by the limitless possibilities for linkage. There is a huge difference between a fully marked hypertext, that is a whole network of nodes and links, and the single connection with another hypertext which is not directly under the author's control: it is the same as the difference between the network of internal roads on a number of different state-islands and the single boat that connects the whole archipelago. If it is of the single boat that we are talking, then in what sense are books not equally interconnected, e.g. by their Dewey decimal classification, or their internal system of references, indexes, contents pages, tabs, footnotes, bibliographies, etc.? Anyone who speaks of hypertexts as potentially infinite is usually voicing a platitude that applies to books as well (recall the quotation from Ecclesiastes). Finally, cases of open and collaborative hypertexts, as opposed to single-authored books, are somewhat misleading: of course, if a group of people decides to collaborate to write a number of Web pages, they may all have the right to modify what they read, but then they will do so as co-authors and, conceptually, they could do so even if they were using pencil and paper. Again, there seems to be a very narrow conception of printed text at work here. To mention a final example, humanists may tend to forget that virtually all scientific texts are co-authored, and were so well before the appearance of hypertexts (but see Landow 1997).

(5) The *obsession with the rhetoric of syntax*: hypertext is non-linear writing

and challenges the bookish assumption that contents have to be presented in a linear fashion.

In this case, the confusion arises because of the misleading way in which hypertexts are negatively defined as mere *non-linear* texts. It is a poor definition because hardly informative, since linearity may stand for at least four different phenomena, and it is unclear which one we are negating. An information system can already be connoted as linear if it satisfies at least one of the following conditions:

(a) It is *syntactically sequential*: its constitutive *signifiers* (i.e. its physical letters, numbers, symbols, words, etc.) are ordered one after the other, in a physical structure that is reducible to a one-dimensional, unique and non-branching sequence of occurrences.
(b) It is *semantically sequential*: its *signifieds* (i.e. the meanings conveyed by the signifiers) constitute a one-dimensional, linear and progressive narrative, as in the case of a train timetable.
(c) It is *t/c-serial*: its *signifiers* can be transmitted/communicated only one at a time, one after another.
(d) It is *a/r-serial* its *signifiers* can be accessed/retrieved only by retrieving all the previous signifiers.

Now most books are linear only in the sense of (a) and perhaps of (c). The physical layout of printed words consists necessarily of a continuous thread of consecutive words or symbols, whose order, in western cultures, proceeds from left to right and top to bottom, so books can also be seen as "interfaces" which transmit one symbol after the other. However, books are not a/r-serial documents: their contents can be accessed in a number of different ways, so they are instances of RAM. But most importantly, books are hardly ever semantically sequential in the sense of (b), for the flux of meanings – the time of the signifieds, that is the multi-dimensional order in which events happen, as opposed to the time of the signifiers, the order in which events are narrated – is virtually free from physical constraints (compare the narrative order of a timetable with the narrative order of the *Odyssey*) and can be variously shaped in any non-linear form. The point may be further clarified if we consider a film, a form of document even more linear than a book. A film is syntactically sequential (a set of frames, one after the other), t/c-serial (frames are transmitted only one per time) and, unlike a book, a/r-serial (if you wish to see a frame you need to go through all the previous frames). Nevertheless, it is a document whose semantics are intrinsically non-sequential: the story told may contain many simultaneous events, or events narrated in inverted order from the end to the beginning, with gaps, anticipations, flashbacks, postponements, iterations, there may be internal references to previous or later episodes, citations from other documents, including other films, etc. No crime story would be of any interest if it had to be narrated in a semantically sequential order. Likewise, the syntactical sequentiality and t-seriality of a book may constrain, shape and guide the process of writing/reading but this does not mean that a book needs to be any more semantically linear than a film, for language, like any other semiotic medium, is free to construct any arrangement of meanings.

At this point, it should be clear that documents could be ordered according to their degree of linearity. A timetable may have linearity 4/4; a film has linearity 3/4 (it transcends linearity of type (b)); a novel's linearity is equal to 2/4 (it transcends linearity of type (b) and (d)); and a hypertext has linearity 1/4, for it transcends linearity of type (a), (b) and (d) but it is still linear in the sense of (c): although the information space has acquired a three-dimensional syntactical nature, the non-linear nature of a hypertext means that the text is fragmented and multi-linear but that any individual path through hypertext is still linear. The reader still perceives (or tries to perceive) items serially, with a beginning, and end, a linear development and a sense of unity. Strictly speaking, then, no medium can truly transcend all forms of linearity without seriously affecting its intelligibility. There is a sense, however, in which hypermedia may be considered as documents with linearity 0/4. Not even hypermedia can transmit more than one token of a specific type of signifier per time without creating confusion in the receiver, but they can transmit tokens of more than one type of signifier simultaneously, a text with images and music, for example, and this kind of multi-level linearity may well be taken to be a way of transcending linearity also in the sense of (c). We shall see the importance of this point in a moment.

(6) The *mimetic fallacy*: hypertext mimics the associative nature of the human mind and therefore is better suited to its activities.

This cognitive view, already held by Bush, as the title of his paper makes clear, is partly questionable and partly the source of an interpretative confusion. On the one hand, we know that there is no reason to confine the ways in which the mind works just to predominantly associative processes, as opposed to, say, linear, computational, inferential, constructionist processes (such as various forms of psychological self-narrative) or even the development of innate intellectual abilities and cognitive modules. On the other hand, even if the mind worked exclusively as a big associative engine, this would still be very far from proving that therefore an information system, implementing the same logic, would necessarily be any better than a linear system. It is the usual naturalistic fallacy of inferring the normative from the descriptive: even accepting the general premiss, one could still argue that, despite the associationist nature of the mind, we really ought to make an effort to reason linearly (straight, as philosophers like to say), and not indulge in hypertextual thinking, for a hypertext may run the risk of becoming a mere 1:1 map of the mapped object and thus fail to be informative.

(7) The *methodological fallacy*: hypertexts will replace printed books.

Although what I have said so far suffices to make it clear that this view too is mistaken, a further point may deserve to be emphasised. People who support the replacement thesis often do so on the following basis: in the same way that nobody nowadays reads illuminated manuscripts, in the future nobody but scholars will read old printed books. They are committing a rather common mistake. Suppose P is a technological problem and A and B are two technological products, developed at different times, both solving P, in such a way that B is both later and better than A. It seems reasonable to conclude that, once B appears, it will soon replace A. But this simplistic evolutionary model of technological development is far from adequate, for two reasons. Firstly, because not all technological products are solutions to exactly the same immutable problem – think for example about the compact disc, which has fully replaced the vinyl disc but not the audio tape – and secondly, because not all technological problems are simple. It is often the case that technological problems have an aggregate nature, and new technologies contribute to reshaping them by splitting what were single exigencies into new sub-problems. In this case, the appearance of B creates new necessities as well as answering old ones, and therefore may well coexist with A. It is sufficient to refer to the evolution of analogue and digital watches, of bicycles and motorbikes, of disposable razors and electric razors, of fountain pens and ball pens: in each case the B products have not displaced the A products, but increased the range of choices. The same applies to printed and electronic texts. If this is sometimes forgotten it is only because infomaniac technophiles are as extremist as technoanxious Luddites in that they equally lack a historical perspective.

Hypertext: the structure of the infosphere

We can now move on to a more controversial interpretation of hypertext. We have seen that books and printed documents in general can be conceived of as "calcified hypertexts". Because they lack a digital nature and a properly formatted structure that would make them easily consultable, their accumulation may result in a hindrance to the further development of knowledge. Hypertext, as the innovative organisational principle or topological structure of our intellectual space, fluidifies what would otherwise be petrified, thus opening the infosphere to a boundless growth. Hypermedia have linearity 0/4 and, technically speaking this makes them hyper-real because reality itself and live events still present a linearity of at least 1/4, for they are semantically sequential and asymmetric. (This is the arrow of time problem that troubles philosophers so much; nothing can really happen twice, and we cannot invert the order in which things happen.) It thus seems reasonable to describe hypertext as the logically *constitutive* principle of organisation of the hyperspace represented by the infosphere. On the other hand, hypertextuality is also a matter of perspective, that is how closely one is analysing a document, and what one takes to be a semantic atom. Consider the node of a hypertext: is it not by itself linear? But then consider a whole collection of books organised by topics and analogies, such as the Warburg Institute library, for example, or the library of a philosopher: is it not the case that their hypertextual structure is so macroscopic, with each volume representing a particular node, that their network structure merely escapes our immediate perception to become somehow invisible? Rather than trying to impose a sharp line of division between different types of documents, it seems more useful to recognise that hypertext, as a relational organisation of digital documents, has helped to unify, make more finely grained and eventually fully accessible the inter-textual and infra-textual structure of the infosphere.

The characterisation of hypertext as the conceptual structure of the infosphere brings with it a number of consequences of philosophical significance, which unfortunately can only be sketched in this context.

First, we can now abandon the common view that hypertext (the conceptual structure, not the actual products) is simply an epistemological concept, variously understood as a mere interface technology – a way to negotiate the user's access to what would otherwise be an overwhelming domain of DIKs – or an external, and perhaps even arbitrary, ordering principle, in itself extraneous and impartial with respect to the domain to be ordered, namely the infosphere, allegedly existing independently of it. As the system of relations connecting the DIKs, hypertext is the very backbone of the infosphere and significantly contributes to its meaningfulness in an *ontical sense*, i.e. by helping to constitute it. Syntax is not semantics, but it is an essential prerequisite of it. Think of a truth table in which the organisational structure and all spatial relations are erased: whatever remains, a heap of capital letters and connectives, is virtually useless by itself. Likewise, in the infosphere aspects such as location, neighbourhood and relations become crucial, and the hypertextual structure is a vital component, without which the infosphere loses much of its present intelligibility and future potential, since, as the grammar of our intellectual space, hypertext enables us not only to understand it, but also to construct it.

Second, the space of reason and meaning – including the narrative and symbolic space of human memory – is now externalised in the hypertextual infosphere, and this brings about four more consequences concerning the rhetoric of spatiality. (1) A linear narrative, which is necessarily associated with time, makes room for a multi-linear narrative that is naturally associated with space. In the past, writers constructed their narrative space virtually within the mind of the reader. Now writer and reader live within a common infosphere and the former no longer needs to weave the narrative, diachronically, within the mind of the latter, as an ongoing textual Web, since all signifieds can co-exist synchronically outside, in the public and intersubjective environment represented by the hypertextual infosphere. (2) In this public domain, writing and reading become spatial gestures, and if time still plays a role, this is only as far as the fictional time of narrative is replaced by the real time of information transmission and retrieval. (3) Consequently, a whole new vocabulary develops, one based on extensional concepts borrowed from the various sciences of space: cartography, geography, topology, architecture, set theory, geology and so forth. (4) It follows that logic, broadly understood as the science of timelessness, hence as intrinsically a *topo-logy*, tends to displace history, broadly understood as the science of the timed, i.e. a *chrono-logy*, and we have seen in the previous chapter how this radical topologisation of the infosphere may unfortunately lead to the paradox of a forgetful memory.

Finally, it is important to realise that a philosophy of mind may investigate the nature of the self, and the consequent problems of identity and dualism, from the information perspective just introduced, by developing a Humean theory of personality in terms of narrative development of a region of the infosphere. The new topological vocabulary would then replace the chronological one we constantly use to analyse the mind (for example, there is a clear sense in which the "I" evolves chronologically, growing and ageing, but does not have a temporal nature, for the "I" either is or is not). The individual person – with her mind and body understood as the two poles of a continuum, ultimately constituted by packets of information such as her DNA, her past memories, her sexual tastes, her biological structure and so forth – becomes a unique element in the infosphere, a steadily evolving hypertext, which is kept together and remains identifiable through its evolution thanks to the special access and awareness it enjoys with respect to its own states, the uniformity of its own reflexive narrative (the person never stops reconstructing herself, like a hypertext capable of updating itself in real time, continuously, recognising herself as herself also on the basis of an ever-changing environment) and the presence of links or lack thereof. The narrative nature of the self, as the axial line of development of the person–hypertext, would then explain its potential instability and fragility, its necessary reliance on memory and on all mental and bodily information that constitutes it as a subject and an agent, as well as its social dependence and constructability (the self as a collaborative enterprise).

Conclusion: a Renaissance mind?

It is to be hoped that one of the direct effects of the transformation both in the ontology and in the organising logic of the infosphere may be an inversion of a secular tendency towards the diffusion and reinforcement of specialisation. The explosion of the world of knowledge in the modern age has prompted a constant compartmentalising of scientific interests. Researchers and scholars gave up the ambition of being able to dominate even a small galaxy in the universe of human knowledge a long time ago, forcing themselves to concentrate their efforts on necessarily limited sectors, which more often than not acquire the status of small niches in too vast a system. Now if the phenomenon seems a sad and yet inescapable necessity in other scientific areas, in philosophy it has been even more frustrating and dangerous. Frustrating, because philosophical knowledge constitutes the epistemic field which more than any other needs to keep its own investigations unified within a single framework of reference, no matter how articulated and rich in contrasts, in firm opposition to an endogenous tendency towards fragmentation and dissolution of its own specific nature. Also frustrating because a philosophy divided into rigid areas of specialisation, done by "experts", seems to be in flat contradiction to the universal and unifying ambitions of a rational reflection which, by its very nature, aims to be the ultimate threshold of theoretical understanding. Thus, the necessity of stressing the importance of the epistemic managerial functions implemented by ICT rests also on the crucial role that the latter may have in weakening the concept of compartmentalisation. We have seen that the age of the book, providing a rigidly structured context, invited vertical specialisation, not only in science but also in the humanities. On the other hand, the computer as *ordinateur* – a word that in the eighteenth century signified the Supreme Being, recalling the *Dieu horloger* of Voltaire – may now promote forms of horizontal interdisciplinarity and multi-disciplinarity which could soon start bearing fruit. The more open and flexible the whole space of knowledge becomes to the individual mind, the more "diatopic" its approach to it can be. It is difficult to limit oneself always to the same confined, epistemic space, if one can navigate so easily across the disciplinary boundaries. This is one of the reasons why the computer age has also been described as a return of the Renaissance mind.

Chapter 5

Artificial intelligence: a light approach

GOFAI

Artificial intelligence is an old dream but a fairly young discipline, which has developed since the late 1950s as an interdisciplinary branch of computer and cognitive sciences aiming at computational models of human cognition. In its strongest version, the one which was predominant for at least the first two decades of its history, between the mid-1960s and the mid-1980s, and is now often labelled Strong AI or GOFAI (good old-fashioned artificial intelligence), AI worked on the theoretical basis of the construction of software and hardware, and hence computers and robots, whose behaviour would eventually be at least comparable, if not superior, to the behaviour characterising intelligent human beings in similar circumstances, e.g. recognising one's car among many others in the street, driving it to the supermarket safely but at a reasonable speed, parking it successfully, remembering to lock it carefully and then inferring that one will not be able to drive it home because one has locked the keys inside, and so one had better get someone to help.

To achieve its goal, GOFAI attempted to steer a middle course between two approaches:

(1) *rationalist dualism* (Cartesianism), according to which

    (a) intelligence is completely independent of the presence of a biological body – and therefore would in principle be implementable by other "bio-bodiless" and a-social (stand-alone) forms of cognitive systems, which may not have a biological brain or any interaction with other intelligent beings, for example God, angels, ghosts and computers – but

    (b) intelligence is also wholly mind-dependent, thus requiring a personal, psychological inner life (the individual "I") so evolved that a vegetable, a machine or even an animal can never achieve it; and

(2) *materialist monism*, according to which

(a) intelligence is nothing but a complex property of a physical body (epiphenomenalism = mental processes are secondary effects accompanying, and being caused by, physical brain processes in such a way that asymmetric causal relations can link brain states with other brain states and brain states with mental states, but not vice versa) – and therefore would in principle be implementable by other forms of equally embodied cognitive systems, including animals, extraterrestrial beings and computers – but as such

(b) intelligence is also a direct manifestation of life and cannot be disjoined from the whole physical behaviour, bodily experience and natural interaction of a *living organism* both with other living organisms and with its concrete environment within the world, something an engineered machine can never achieve.

The first half of each position is favourable to GOFAI, while the second half makes it unfeasible. As a solution, GOFAI accepted a controversial form of

(3) *computational materialism*, not unlike Hobbes's computational and mechanistic account of the mind, according to which intelligence is *biologically* body-independent and stand-alone, as in (1a), but also completely mind-independent, as in (2a), and therefore is in principle implementable by a (brainless, mindless and lifeless) general-purpose, logico-symbolic system enjoying no psychological or bodily experience nor any emotional or social involvement with other similar systems. (For a defence of the view that programs are models of mental processes see Simon and Newell 1964; see also Newell and Simon 1976.)

The only way GOFAI could make (3) a consistent position and support its "computational materialism" was to endorse the following reduction:

(4) intelligence = ratiocination = symbolic processing = computation
and adopt, as a criterion of normative assessment, some form of

(5) *functional behaviourism*, whose most well-known version is represented by Turing's Test.

Programs are formal representations of states and state-transitions. In principle, they are executable by any kind of computational "engine". Thus effective computation is indeed mind-independent and can be implemented by any non-biological stand-alone hardware whose performances can then be evaluated by a purely behaviouristic method. The trouble is that for over twenty years GOFAI insisted that (4) was not a *reduction* but an *equation*, thus forgetting that intelligence is an utterly individual property, that no two intelligent minds are identical, that intelligence also evolves as an eminently social phenomenon within a cultural milieu to which we contribute but that is and remains largely independent of ourselves, that a fully developed intelligence requires some powerful semiotic medium which is also socially based, and that not even mathematical thinking can ever be reduced to algorithmic operations, let alone less formalisable processes. It thus committed what Peirce described as a "malignant heresy":

> first, nothing of importance can be deduced from a single premise, and secondly, from two premises one sole complete conclusion can be drawn. . . . This couple of heresies, being married together, legitimately generates a third more malignant than either; namely, that necessary reasoning takes a course from which it can no more deviate than a good machine can deviate from its proper way of action, and that its future work might conceivably be left to a machine – some Babbage's analytical engine or some logical machine (of which several have actually been constructed).
>
> (Peirce 1931–58, IV: 610–11)

Research in AI developed as if thinking and behaving intelligently were just synonymous with algorithmic computing, while background conditions, experiences (inspirations, passions, intuitions, insights, education, know-how, imagination, sensibility, common sense, taste, aspirations, bodily sensations, consciousness, communication, fears, desires, etc.) and social interactions were not essential components of an individual's unique intelligent life. The human ability to deal with the world intelligently was seen to be fully and exclusively dependent on human ability to think rationally about the world, and rational thought was seen to be identical with stand-alone, symbolic processing and hence with effective computation. Since GOFAI's regulative ideal was *Star Trek*'s Lt Comdr Data, it achieved little but crude caricatures of intelligent human behaviour, and one may wonder what would have happened to the GOFAI research programme without the huge military funding – we are talking about hundreds of millions of dollars – that for decades has been made available for strong AI projects. Some of these were either aimed at the construction of weapons or were directly weapons-related (this is the sense in which some AI projects can raise substantial moral questions in computer ethics, in terms of improper, wasteful or even dangerous applications, see Forester and Morrison 1994: ch. 7).

Turing's Test

The birth of GOFAI can be dated to the opening of the Dartmouth Summer Research Project on Artificial Intelligence, organised by John McCarthy (the developer of LISP, one of AI's most popular programming languages) in 1956, but it was Alan Turing who had set up the whole agenda for

GOFAI several years before (all following quotations are from Turing 1950). Turing reduced the question "can machines think?" – which he rightly believed (but too many have since then forgotten) "to be too meaningless to deserve discussion" – to a famous "imitation game", now known as Turing's Test:

(TT): Take a human interrogator IN, a digital computer C and a woman W, place the latter two in separate rooms and make sure they can both communicate with IN only via email (Turing's teleprinter). IN can now ask both C and W all sorts of questions. If IN fails to discover the correct identity of the two interlocutors on the basis of their answers, then C and W are obviously incapable of showing sufficiently different behaviour.

IN's questions are the input of the system, W's and C's answers its output and the test aims to show the possibility of intelligent machines by applying a weaker version of Leibniz's law of the identity of indiscernibles: if, *ceteris paribus*, significant differences between W's and C's outputs are indiscernible then W and C are interchangeable, that is, given the same input, the outputs a human and a digital processor can generate are such that the differences between the two are insufficient for the purposes of unmistakable recognition.

Turing's mental experiment is a test in so far as it provides a specification, not an implementation, for an intelligent machine, that is, it specifies an operational criterion for establishing the intelligence of a machine. Turing himself thought that

> in about fifty years it will be possible to program computers . . . to make them play the imitation game so well that an average interrogator will not have more than 70% chance of making the right identification after five minutes questioning.

In a superficial way, he was over-pessimistic; in a more significant sense, he was definitely wrong. As early as 1964–7, Joseph Weizenbaum had written and tested a program, called ELIZA, consisting of a language analyser and a list of instructions enabling the machine to "improvise" around a certain topic, mocking, for example, the behaviour of a psychotherapist. A person, let us say IN, could "converse" in English with ELIZA through a typewriter. The reference to Eliza Doolittle, the character in G. B. Shaw's *Pygmalion*, was not accidental: feedback functions assured that the program could also "learn" to speak increasingly well. ELIZA was a masterpiece in deception. Here is an example of a typical conversation with a young woman, as reported by Weizenbaum himself (Weizenbaum 1976):

YW: Men are all alike.
ELIZA: IN WHAT WAY?
They are always bugging us about something or other.
CAN YOU THINK OF A SPECIFIC EXAMPLE?

Well, my boyfriend made me come here.
YOUR BOYFRIEND MADE YOU COME HERE?
He says I'm depressed much of the time.
I'M SORRY TO HEAR YOU ARE DEPRESSED.
It's true. I am unhappy.
DO YOU THINK COMING HERE WILL HELP YOU NOT TO BE UNHAPPY?
I need some help, that much seems certain.
WHAT WOULD IT MEAN TO YOU IF YOU GOT SOME HELP?
Perhaps I could learn to get along with my mother.
TELL ME MORE ABOUT YOUR FAMILY.
etc.

ELIZA could carry on similar conversations for ever, and indeed, it played this special imitation game so well that people "dialoguing" with the program soon became emotionally involved and tended to anthropomorphise it. After a short time, some practising psychiatrists even thought it might develop into a nearly completely automatic form of psychotherapy. To Weizenbaum's greatest surprise, a large number of people seemed to believe that ELIZA was somehow intelligent. Yet the software only implemented a limited number of instructions that allowed it to fake a conversation by associating simple questions, predetermined responses, standard platitudes or just slightly modified repetitions to particular patterns of input. It was cruising on automatic pilot, as it were, using standard phrases and clichés to maintain a state of apparently true interaction – anyone who has attended at a formal dinner or college high table knows very well what this means – but it did not even count as an expert system, for it embodied no knowledge database, and could not be described as being intelligent in any significant sense of the word. Nevertheless, it seems it could pass a decent version of Turing's Test. Something had gone wrong.

Four limits of Turing's Test

Although this brief section cannot undertake to provide a full assessment of the philosophical and technical implications of Turing's Test, it is useful to analyse four of its shortcomings because the history of GOFAI can then be conveniently summarised as the failure to overcome them.

(1) The mimetic ambiguity
Turing's Test is deceptively simple, but a moment of reflection suffices to make one wonder what it really purports to establish. Does TT show that C's and W's answers can become indistinguishable from each other because the former's resemble the latter's, or rather because the latter's cannot really differ from the former's anymore? The second claim is virtually uncontroversial but also much less interesting than the first: a TT would simply be any

irreversible process through which a sufficient loss of information makes the sources of the outputs no longer distinguishable or re-identifiable, in the same way that we cannot reconstruct the complex and different inputs of two logic gates from their identical, simple outputs. Turing himself wrote that

> the idea behind digital machines may be explained by saying that these machines are intended to carry out any operations which could be done by a human computer. The human computer is supposed to be following fixed rules . . . we may suppose that these rules are supplied in a book, which is altered whenever he is put on to a new job. He has also an unlimited supply of paper on which he does his calculations.

Ideally, a meticulous and patient scribe, a kind of tireless idiot savant, provided with an unlimited amount of time and stationery, could do everything any Turing machine or classical computer can do. That in most cases he would arrive too late or not understand what he is doing – as this is the case with Searle's Chinese room example, in which the scribe successfully operates on Chinese symbols he does not understand (Searle 1980 and 1990; Van Gulick 1998) – is explicitly not the point addressed by TT. Nobody can justifiably disagree about the possibility of a computing scribe. Arguments based on Gödel's theorem (Lucas 1961, 1996; Penrose 1989, 1990, 1994; see Detlefsen 1998 for a brief introduction), for example, purport to show that there is an ineliminable difference between a human mind and a Turing machine in the sense that anything our computing scribe can do can also be done by an intelligent scribe, but not vice versa (a TM cannot prove the true Gödelian well-formed formula concerning its own consistency). But then, isn't this enough to explain why IN is unable to establish whether C and W are (a) two computers, (b) two persons acting like computers, or (c) a mixed couple, one a computer and the other a person with no option but to act as if she were one? Turing set up his test with certain conditions:

- only written communication;
- only yes/no questions possible ("We are of course supposing for the present that the questions are of the kind to which an answer 'Yes' or 'No' is appropriate");
- no critical questions requiring C's or W's personal approach, such as "What do you think of Picasso?" (this is Turing's example);
- no context-sensitive questions and hence the irrelevance of the environment;
- no symmetrically interactive dialogue, since W and C can answer questions but cannot ask them, cannot exchange their roles, and cannot be asked to pretend to be other "people" (it may be argued that a computer can mimic some human behaviour, but a human being can mimic any behaviour, no matter how badly);

- no linguistic–pragmatic context (can a computer master the rules of Grice's conversational implicature, whereby a sentence that literally means p is actually used to communicate a message other than p?).

Because of these conditions, the lack of significant differences between W's and C's answers may well be caused by the downgrading of the human agent to the level of the computer, rather than vice versa. TT would be a "blurring machine", aiming to show the possibility of W's human stupidity rather than C's artificial intelligence, especially if we also endorse the reductionist assumption.

(2) The reductionist assumption

TT-conditions are so constraining that all intelligent behaviour of both C and W is strictly reduced to symbolic processing tasks. No pattern or sound recognition skills are taken into account, for example, since C would not be able to appreciate the difference between *Guernica* and *The School of Athens* (Picasso once said: "When I was their age, I could draw like Raphael, but it took me a lifetime to learn to draw like them."). Is this restriction truly irrelevant when Turing's general conclusion that "We may hope that machines will eventually compete with men in all purely intellectual fields" is formulated on its grounds? Prima facie, it would seem obvious that "purely intellectual fields" encompass much more than just the capacity to handle well-formed strings of symbols according to finite sequences of instructions. Indeed, one may even argue that the latter capacity is not central to many intellectual skills. In either case, the test is not sufficiently cogent to support the much more substantial conclusion drawn by Turing. Things get even worse once we bring to light the linguistic fallacy.

(3) The linguistic fallacy

TT presupposes that IN, W and C all speak and understand the same language, otherwise they would not be able to play a convincing part in the test. This is clear if one recalls that, to introduce TT, Turing first presents another version of the test, in which the actors are a man and a woman, and IN is shown to be unable to discover the sex of his interlocutors. Of course, the language in question must be so powerful, rich and hence "natural" as to allow a satisfactory if constrained level of conversation between IN and W and provide no clues about the artificial nature of C. Let us call such a language TT-adequate. To be TT-adequate, the linguistic–semiotic skills of C already presuppose an intelligent agent, whose behaviour is superior not only to that of a brainless coelenterate such as a jellyfish, but also to that of mammals such as dolphins and chimpanzees, which are known to be able to learn only an extremely limited range of linguistic skills, insufficient to pass the test. It follows that the very mastering of such skills by C counts as a significant instance of fully-grown human intelligence. After all, ever since

Plato the process of thinking has been described dialectically, as inner discourse, rather than mathematically, while Descartes, as a good Platonist, embraced intuition (the light of reason, with its strong stress on mental visualisation) as a fundamental stage of any epistemic process. It was only Hobbes who later suggested a strict comparison with computing, under the influence of the Cartesian revolution:

> For seeing life is but a motion of limbs, the beginning whereof is in some principal part within, why may we not say that all automata (engines that move themselves by springs and wheels as doth a watch) have an artificial life? For what is the heart, but a spring; and the nerves, but so many strings; and the joints, but so many wheels, giving motion to the whole body, such as was intended by the Artificer?
>
> .   .   .
>
> When man reasoneth, he does nothing else but conceive a sum total, from addition of parcels; or conceive a remainder, from subtraction of one sum from another: which, if it be done by words, is conceiving of the consequence of the names of all the parts, to the name of the whole; or from the names of the whole and one part, to the name of the other part. And though in some things, as in numbers, besides adding and subtracting, men name other operations, as multiplying and dividing; yet they are the same: for multiplication is but adding together of things equal; and division, but subtracting of one thing, as often as we can. These operations are not incident to numbers only, but to all manner of things that can be added together, and taken one out of another. . . . In sum, in what matter soever there is place for addition and subtraction, there also is place for reason; and where these have no place, there reason has nothing at all to do. . . . For reason, in this sense, is nothing but reckoning (that is, adding and subtracting) of the consequences of general names agreed upon for the marking and signifying of our thoughts; I say marking them, when we reckon by ourselves; and signifying, when we demonstrate or approve our reckonings to other men.
>
> (*Leviathan*, Introduction and ch. 5)

Consider now the following example. One day, some fascists went to see Picasso. Referring to *Guernica,* they asked him, "Did you do it?"; he replied, "No, you did". Apparently, the reply was good enough to save Picasso any further trouble. Would a computer be able to understand a similar dialogue? It would have to, if its language is to be TT-adequate, but if C is granted such a degree of linguistic competence surely the test loses all its probatory value, as it is simply begging the question: technically speaking, full linguistic competence is recognised to be an AI-complete problem, i.e. a problem whose solution *presupposes* a solution to the "strong AI problem", namely the synthesis of a human-level intelligence. Therefore, it would be equally valid to argue that, since C cannot have behaviour as intelligent as W's, it cannot be granted fluency in any TT-adequate language. In each case, a processor capable of mastering a natural language well enough to play TT will also show sufficiently intelligent behaviour. The problem then becomes whether we can justifiably assume that C is already fluent in a TT-adequate language. The answer must be in the negative, of course, unless one wishes to maintain only that it is *logically possible* that C may come to master a TT-adequate language. In which case, the whole test comes to be based on the fallacy of modal indeterminacy.

(4) The fallacy of modal indeterminacy

Turing's Test shows that "carbon chauvinism" is unjustified: thinking machines are *logically possible* – there is nothing contradictory in the hypothesis that a brain may not have a neuro-physiological nature but an electro-mechanical one, or that a machine may be able to speak a natural language properly – hence GOFAI cannot be ruled out as being impossible in principle, yet this is very far from establishing that silicon intelligence is also even vaguely plausible, likely to evolve, or *empirically feasible*. The distinction is crucial, but it is often overlooked. It is one thing to prove that doing *p* involves no contradiction and hence is logically possible, and an utterly different thing to infer that doing *p* is therefore possible, without further qualifications (for example, think of the possibility of guessing exactly how many people have used the London Underground each day since it was opened). Miracles, such as living forever, though extremely improbable, can still count as logically possible; it is just that nobody these days is inclined to develop scientific theories on their likelihood.

Turing presented TT only as the basis for a conjecture. He honestly recognised that he had no positive arguments in favour of the actual possibility of GOFAI, only negative ones against its critics. Consequently, he was able to show that it was a mistake to consider non-biological intelligence logically impossible. In computer science, however, indirect proofs of purely logical possibilities bear no weight, for only constructive methods are truly effective, and after so many failures there seems to be some clear evidence that true AI may not be empirically feasible. The reply may be that GOFAI projects just need more time to develop.

Here is an argument against GOFAI's empirical feasibility that relies on the complexity of the programs required by any real AI application and the standards of reliability that we have come to expect in all other areas of engineering. Given the incidence of faulty software (ironically, we are used to paying for updated versions, which are not necessarily better, often simply because we were sold software whose bugs had still to be discovered; this is so true that software is one of the few common goods that is not usually provided with a warranty, thus showing its potential unreliability) and given that computers are increasingly failure-prone, the more sophisticated they become (how many times has your computer crashed in the last six months?), it is unlikely that any AI system will ever become sufficiently reliable. Testing and debugging – attempting to detect, specify and eliminate the possible causes of programs' malfunctions – is not a science, it is a Sisyphist art, for bug-free software is almost a contradiction in terms (see Fetzer 1998 for an overview of the epistemological debate about verification). The more complex a piece of software has to become, to cope with a larger variety of evolving tasks, the more common the occurrence of serious programming errors (a serious bug does not just cause misbehaviour, but puts an end to any behaviour at all, like a stroke). Unfortunately, the scale of combinational complexity of any non-trivial software (programs with more than 100,000 lines of code; consider that automatic bank tellers are often run by software containing more than 700,000 lines, and common software for Windows can easily contain more than 500,000 lines) is so high, that errors cannot be exhaustively detected (let alone fully fixed) by means of empirical tests. This is because the software can exist in literally billions of discrete states, and each state could be the source of an error and hence a *catastrophic* failure in the Greek sense of the word, i.e. a sudden collapse – so that we soon run out of time (the process would require longer than the life of the universe to be feasible).

Of course, a completely foolproof universal debugging program D would be able to determine whether any application A terminates successfully, for all initial situations. However, trying to prove that D is possible would be equivalent to trying to prove that there is a program that solves the halting problem, and we have seen in Chapter 2 that this is impossible. The empirical fallibility of software is here to stay. Error detection is a matter of dedicated testing programs, which are not in themselves error-proof and may or may not discover all the main faults of the software in question. Even when some bugs are discovered (and this often happens only thanks to extended use by millions of users, a posteriori and inductively), the probability of introducing new severe errors when debugging such complex software is known to be so high that it has become common practice to correct only the smallest possible fraction of the original errors, and then, rather than tampering further, users are warned of any other known circumstances in which the software may not work properly, in the same way that every drug indicates its potential contraindications, i.e. the potential negative results that may be caused by the complexity of its interactions with the body of the patient and other secondary effects.

A GOFAI application requires software so complex (billions of lines of code) that it would be "undebuggable" in principle, and therefore never absolutely reliable in practice. Mad computers behaving erratically could become a reality. To get some idea of the scale of the problem, consider that the computerised system for the space shuttle contains about 25,500,000 lines of code, whose development required some 22,100 man-years, but that the whole computer system does not even come vaguely close to being a fully artificial brain like Hal in *2001*. Currently, there are no existing techniques that deliver software of fully warranted quality and reliability. The solution may lie in the development of better error-proof programming languages and programming techniques, and much more powerful tools for software verification and derivation (derivation is verification on-the-fly, a method of showing that the software works properly while it is being written), but much as both areas may bring fruitful results in the future, verification and derivation programs can currently handle software of only very modest size, and neither of these approaches is likely to eliminate the substantial problem. For verification, if applied consistently, would limit the programmer's freedom to the point of becoming a serious hindrance to any high-quality GOFAI application, while derivation can succeed in limiting the damage but can never eliminate the possibility of some catastrophic dormant bug.

To return to the fallacy of modal indeterminacy: if anyone argues that a computer roughly as intelligent as an ordinary human being is a logical possibility, or that a robot that behaves, feels and has qualitative experiences roughly like an ordinary human being is logically possible, then there is not much to object to, beyond remarking that there is very little gain in showing that a thinking machine is not a contradictory concept. However, it may just be interesting to ask the "logical-possibilist" whether an omniscient and omnipotent creator, who is equally logically possible, may still be able to spot the difference between his artefact and ours. If the answer is in the positive, we may rest content that the computer and the robot are not exactly like a human being. If the answer is in the negative, as I suspect it ought to be, then we would have no reason to complain: there are worse idle speculations than those concerning science fiction scenarios.

The application-areas of AI

GOFAI developed as the empirical research project that aimed to make Turing's claims come true. It was based on questionable assumptions – the logical possibility of non-biological intelligence – and unrealistic expectations, so it could not succeed in its most ambitious plans, despite the huge amount of human and financial resources to which it helped itself. This does not mean that AI has not achieved remarkable results. In the course of its attempts to construct a TT-adequate computer that could perform tasks usually supposed to require some form of human intelligence, research in artificial intelligence has come to be organised around the following main areas:

(1) *Theorem proving*: Historically, this is the first and most successful application of AI and yet, in so far as decision procedures are known for the theorems in question, as in the case of propositional logic theorems, most scientists and philosophers would not consider it real AI, since such theorems could also be proved by a well-constructed windmill or our dull ("brainless") scribe. On the other hand, theorems for which no mechanical procedures are known are much more intractable, and non-computable solutions are based

on *ad hoc* algorithms designed by human experts and intelligent programmers. So much so that when the latter are no longer available, as is often the case after some time, if there is no documentation and the software needs to be updated it is easier to start again from scratch than try to interpret what the experts had in mind and actually did.

(2) *Game playing*: In this case too, games for which a decision procedure is known, such as noughts and crosses (tic-tac-toe) are easily implementable, but can hardly be considered instances of full artificial intelligence. Other board games, such as checkers, chess or monopoly, require databases and the discovery and application of heuristic procedures, i.e. rules of thumb and general problem-solving techniques. The issue then becomes an empirical one and needs to be further analysed, as we shall see in a moment.

(3) *Information processing*: This is perfectly achievable in terms of the processing of strings of symbols, as in word-processing, mathematical programs, parsing software or statistical applications, as we saw in Chapter 4. When understanding is in question then see (6).

(4) *Planning for robot behaviour via means–ends analysis*: Means–ends analysis is a computing technique used in AI to achieve goals by formulating plans. The system implements a plan, constituted by a sequence of actions, and the sequence is constructed by comparing the goals that each action achieves (means) with the goals and predicted actions that must be achieved (ends). This is perfectly achievable as long as the environment and the tasks are limited and can be fully formalised. We shall discuss this point more fully later in the chapter.

(5) *Expert analysis and advice in applied fields, such as medical diagnosis*: This is feasible as long as the expectations are moderate. For example, in medicine, expert systems have been developed that analyse the disease symptoms, medical history, and laboratory test results of a patient, and then suggest a variety of possible diagnoses to the doctor.

(6) *Fluency in a natural language* (building a system that can understand and speak a written and spoken natural language as well as a human being): Some restricted sectors of a natural language or specific formal languages, i.e. languages with identified meaning in fixed contexts, can be understood and processed by machines. There are programs that enable a computer to generate grammatically correct sentences, to establish links between data inputs/ outputs and concepts, to recognise written or spoken information and to produce summaries, answer specific questions, or redistribute information to users interested in specific areas of this information. However, interpretation and fluency in a natural language is a human activity *par excellence* that our present computers will never achieve. The use of a natural language is a constantly evolving ability, which is made possible by, and is intrinsically rooted in, our complex experience of a physical and psychological life and on our being human agents interacting with the world from inside a human body, within a specific human society and a determined culture. Above all,

being able to use a language means being able to shape the world of experience. TT takes the possibility of a computer's linguistic proficiency for granted, but while phonetic and graphical features (the physical aspect) as well as lexical and syntactic aspects (the logical structure) of natural languages have been subjected to formalisation rather successfully and there are hopes that they may be fully controlled by a computerised system, semantics, pragmatics and hermeneutics, i.e. the problems of meaning, contextual understanding and interpretation, have remained largely intractable and appear to be beyond any translation in terms of functions effectively computable by a Turing machine. Here it is important to recall a promising programme of research in applied computational linguistics, namely statistical semantics: loosely speaking, the computer suggests the most reasonable meaning of a word W by analysing the most consistent system of N words forming a cluster around W, which is useful for projects concerning automatic information retrieval and extraction from digital documents. This shows the limits of GOFAI (in this case the full simulation of human language competence) and the value of a more pragmatic approach to AI in the area of automatic translation of unrestricted texts, and in the area of computer understanding and generation of natural language, and hence human–computer communication. Computers cannot master a language like a human being, but software systems can greatly simplify the work of human translators and improve our present interfaces. One can easily think of a number of successful applications, such as voice recognition programs, automatic grammar checkers for word-processing software, intelligent email filters and routers, text classification systems, systems for information extraction from semi-standardised texts and so forth.

(7) *Informal, non-deductive reasoning and universal problem-solving*: This would require computers to be able to argue or reason, to hold and defend views. It is a largely intractable problem without resort to human intelligence and *ad hoc* programming.

(8) *Visual and acoustic perception and pattern recognition*: Pattern recognition systems are currently able to classify data (patterns) thanks to either statistical information, extracted from the patterns themselves, or a priori labelling information provided as previous input. They consist of three basic components:

- a sensor, which collects the data to be described/classified;
- a feature-extraction mechanism, which computes symbolic or numeric information from the collected data, usually using one or more of the following approaches: statistical (or decision theoretic), syntactic (or structural), or neural. The statistical approach is based on statistical characterisations of patterns, assuming that the patterns are generated by a probabilistic system. The syntactic approach is based on the structural interrelationships of features. Neural pattern recognition employs the

neural computing paradigm that has emerged with neural networks (we shall discuss pattern recognition in more detail in the section headed "Artificial neural networks" later in the chapter;

- a classification or description scheme, which describes or classifies the pattern, relying on the extracted features. The classification or description scheme is usually based on the availability of a set of patterns that have already been classified/described (groups of measurements or observations, defining points in an appropriate multi-dimensional space). A learning strategy based on training sets of a priori labelling patterns is characterised as supervised, but learning can also be unsupervised when the system itself extracts the patterns from the statistical regularities of the observed data.

Perceptual tasks (the acquisition, classification or description of observations) are, in different ways, performed by all forms of life, but have proved to be very difficult for digital machines, except in fully formalisable instances. In particular, computer vision (building a system that can see as well as a human) remains a recalcitrant problem, despite its military importance (note that for a missile "pattern recognition" really means "target individuation").

(9) *Experience, common sense, self-consciousness, introspection, awareness of and detachment from time–space situations, knowledge, understanding, sense of pertinence, insight, judgement, evaluation, imagination, feelings, taste, intentionality, interpretation*: these are all largely intractable phenomena, since it is still unclear whether and how knowledge – as opposed to data – and other cognitive or mental states may be analysed in such a way that a computer could be said to "understand" or "feel" something and hence apply its "understanding" or "insight" to relevant cases with at least some good common sense. We shall see that this is an extreme case of the kinds of problems addressed by knowledge engineers when designing knowledge representation and automatisation systems, and devising general rules and algorithms for the automatic recognition of meaningful and relevant information, in connection with large databases.

(10) *Self-reproducing and self-learning*: Both seemingly intractable. Intelligence appears to have its own entropy: below a certain threshold, a system is able to construct only a range of more simplified systems, whereas a brilliant child can have very dumb parents. As for self-learning, when understood as a general capacity, comparable to that of a child, AI systems as we know them have proved to be incapable of achieving it. A Universal Turing machine is an "innate" and "orthodox" machine: unable to grow and develop by dialoguing with the environment, it can nevertheless deal with situations that sufficiently approximate its internal microworlds, as long as this does not require it to behave in a heterodox fashion, i.e. in a way that is neither random nor in accordance with pre-established patterns of rules or instructions, but adequate to the novelty of the situation.

The conditions of possibility of AI and the paradox of GOFAI

On the basis of the previous analysis, the crucial conditions that make AI projects more or less successful can be conveniently summarised under five headings:

1 *Effective-computability* (see Chapter 2);
2 *Epistemic-independence*, i.e. whether no knowledge/understanding is relevant, or alternatively whether all relevant knowledge/understanding that is presupposed and required by the successful performance of the intelligent task, can be discovered, circumscribed, analysed, formally structured and hence made fully manageable through computable processes;
3 *Experience-independence*, i.e. whether the task is based on universal and "timeless" instructions carried out by the system, or alternatively whether all practical experience, both relevant as a background condition and necessary for the successful performance of the intelligent task, can be discovered, circumscribed, analysed, formally structured and hence made fully manageable through computable processes.
4 *Body-independence*, i.e. whether the intelligent task can be performed by a disembodied, stand-alone intelligence, or alternatively whether all "perceptual intelligence", both relevant as a background condition and necessary for the successful performance of the intelligent task can be discovered, circumscribed, analysed, formally structured and hence made fully manageable through computable processes.
5 *Context-freedom*, i.e. whether the context is irrelevant, or alternatively whether all relevant information concerning the context within which an intelligent task is performed, and which indeed make the task intelligent, can be discovered, circumscribed, analysed, formally structured and hence made fully manageable through computable processes.

Points (2)–(5) state that a classical computer can cope with intelligent tasks, which necessarily require knowledge, experience, linguistic capacities, bodily involvement and social interaction with the context when performed by a human being, only by internalising all relevant data, i.e. by transforming the strongly constrained domain of application into a microworld subject to Leibniz's law of pre-established harmony. The specific construction of a microworld "within" a computerised system represents a combination of ontological commitments that programmers are both implicitly ready to assume when designing the system and willing to allow the system to adopt. This tight coupling with the environment (immanency) is a feature of animal and artificial intelligence, its strength and its dramatic limit. On the contrary, what makes sophisticated forms of human intelligence peculiarly human is the equilibrium they show between creative responsiveness to the environment and reflective detachment from it (transcendency). This is why animals and computers cannot laugh, cry, recount stories, lie or deceive, as Wittgenstein reminds us, whereas human beings also have the ability to behave appropriately in the face of an open-ended range of contingencies and make the relevant adjustments in their interactions. A computer is always immanently trapped within a microworld. The broader its ontological environment, the less obvious the spectrum of ontological preclusions engendered by the system, and the easier it is for the user to be caught within its limits of scope and domain, and the more difficult it becomes to realise the inflexibility of the machine's real ontological commitments and apparent interactions.

There are many cases, however, such as when we try to implement common sense notions, linguistic skills or learning abilities, in which intelligence proves to be an ontologically diatopic property. That is, it is a general way of behaving and thinking flexibly, constructively and in dynamical interconnection with the surrounding reality, which is not bound to a specific and constrained area of application. In these "transcendent" cases the divergence rule applies: the more a computer interacts with the environment the more its microworld tends to differentiate itself from its reference, until there is no longer a correspondence between the two and it becomes obvious that the computer is behaving according to an internal representation that can only cope with a limited number of external variables. To satisfy conditions (2)–(5), the internalisation would require the computer to predict, potentially, every contingent novelty that may occur in the physical or conceptual environment within which it operates and hence to be nothing less than potentially omniscient. This is known as the "frame problem". The computerised system must have a formal representation explicitly containing at least all the rules for generating, and taking into account, all possible microworlds within which it is operating and foresee all the intended consequences and unintended effects of its actions. This sort of Leibnizian pre-established harmony is not an impossible achievement in a simplified and limited environment, but anything as complex as a Lego-like game already poses substantial difficulties. In the best cases, the computational pre-established harmony becomes a sort of occasionalism: the proper interaction between the system and its physical or conceptual environment needs to be constantly regulated and mediated by human agents, *dei ex machina*, as it were.

The paradox behind GOFAI thus appears obvious: the better a task fulfils conditions (1)–(5) – as is often the case in domains of application which are the result of construction out of explicit rules (board games, well-known fields of mathematics, specific databases, etc.) – the more easily it can be "stupefied" and hence the more feasible the relevant AI project becomes, but then the less we are inclined to connote as *necessarily intelligent* the agent (not the task) capable of performing it. A good example is provided by a machine capable of demonstrating theorems in propositional logic. On the other hand, a task fulfils conditions (1)–(5) less and less the more it is sensitive and "open" to completely occasional novelties, requiring non-formalised, non-procedural creative thinking, grasping of the appropriate context, mastering of the relevant information, possession of the right experience, enjoyment of a bodily involvement, social interactions, inventiveness, sensibility, intuition, understanding, linguistic skills and so on. And the less a task fulfils conditions (1)–(5) the more the agent capable of performing it is expected to be truly intelligent, but the less feasible the relevant AI project becomes. Clearly, as the nature of intelligent tasks ranges from the total "stupefiability" of regimentable and routinisable games such as noughts and crosses or draughts, to the complete openness of abilities such as mastering a natural language and laughing at a good joke, the development of successful AI projects becomes a matter of degree and of empirical trial and error. What a computer can do empirically, not just in principle, is a practical question, whose answer depends on the nature of the specific task under examination and on whether there are efficient methods to analyse it in such a way as to make factors (1)–(5) sufficiently liable to an AI treatment. GOFAI committed the mistake of considering, a priori, the whole spectrum of intelligent tasks as its own domain, because it started from the wrong end of that spectrum, namely Turing's assumption that C is already capable of managing a TT-adequate language. Unlike Strong AI, Light AI (LAI) places itself more pragmatically at the other, "stupid" extreme of the spectrum, and tries to advance as far as it is empirically feasible towards its "open" end. The perspective is radically different and so is the approach to what an "intelligent system" could be like.

From GOFAI to LAI

GOFAI endorsed Turing's suggestion that, since a single machine should be able to cover the whole spectrum of intelligent tasks, the best thing for it was to simulate the only other "engine" capable of a similar undertaking, namely the brain/mind. However, GOFAI was not only mimetic, it also set things upside-down. To see why, it is useful to draw an analogy with the history of flying machines. It was wrong, if natural, to think that, if human beings could fly one day, they would do so like Icarus, using some sort of flapping wings. As long as aeronautics tried to construct bird-like vehicles, however, it did not score a single success. To become truly achievable, the task, flying from one place to another, had to be detached from the particular manner in which birds performed it and pursued in ways more amenable to engineering solutions, thus adopting a *functionalist* approach:

- identification of a set F of relevant functions performed by the system S_1;
- abstraction of F from the specific nature of the system S_1;
- identification of the necessary and sufficient conditions C for the implementation of F;

- implementation of C by means of a new system S_2, capable of performing the relevant functions listed in F.

Since GOFAI could start from an ideal prototype, i.e. a Universal Turing machine, the mimetic approach was also sustained by a reinterpretation of what human intelligence could be. Thus, in Turing's paper we read not only that

1   digital computers must simulate human agents,

but also that

2   they can do so because the latter are, after all, only complex processors (in Turing's sense of being UTMs).

The suggestion was that all (at least seemingly) cognitive entities (AI applications, people and other living organisms) are computational systems in the "effective" sense of computation discussed in Chapter 2, which carry out their operations by manipulating symbols and transforming, through sequences of internal steps, static input representations (patterns of activity) into other static output representations. It is as if, having constructed a Montgolfier balloon while trying to enable man to fly like a bird, one had decided to fill all birds with hot air or hydrogen to make sure any flying system behaved uniformly like a balloon. A neat solution, yet completely wrong. As I have argued in Chapter 2, even if the brain is a "computing machine" this does not mean that it is necessarily comparable to a classical computer (i.e. a Universal Turing machine), so (2) above is at least controversial. Although we need to remember that GOFAI developed in a context in which crude IQ tests were very popular, it is still surprising to see how an empirically minded culture could be led so astray by its materialist project of a thinking machine as to forget that the physical nature of the brain does not prove that it functions, technically speaking, like a binary data-processor with a program, following finite lists of predetermined instructions establishing how strings of symbols need to be processed sequentially by logic gates, and that there are no ultimate reasons to believe that intelligence is a brain rather than a mental feature and "mind" just another word for "brain", and finally, that human knowledge and understanding do not resemble information-processing phenomena very closely. Attempts to shift the paradigm in favour of parallel, interactive, complex, digital, analogue, networked or quantum systems show how unsatisfactory the GOFAI picture is. The generic possibility of modelling the brain as an input–process–output device, often useful for explanatory purposes, was confused with its actual nature and the failure of GOFAI was therefore the failure of a rather primitive epistemological model of human intelligence.

The Cartesian nature of LAI

LAI has slowly risen like a phoenix from the ashes of GOFAI. While the latter attempted to "stupefy" the mind, assuming an elementary computational model of the brain itself, and hence was bound to fail, the former aims to remodel the specific tasks in question according to the logic and functions of the machine ("stupefication" of the process), and so has been far more successful. The point is that LAI is performance-oriented or *constructionist*, not *mimetic*. It recognises that the same tasks can be accomplished equally well in completely different ways and that the difficulty lies in discovering whether, given a specific task, there is a "computer-way" to accomplish it satisfactorily. Therefore, it attempts to engineer problem-oriented applications that do not necessarily simulate but rather emulate (often do better, although differently) what a human being could do in the same situation. We do not want a program that can mechanically prove a logic theorem exactly as a human being would, because we do not need either the latter's mistakes and distractions, or his or her insights and intuitions. The problem of image recognition provides a useful example. Infrared radiation is electromagnetic radiation of wavelengths between about 0.75 micrometers and 1 millimetre. All bodies with a temperature above absolute zero absorb and radiate infrared radiation, which is invisible to the human eye. Above a certain threshold, we perceive infrared radiation as heat, but a computer can easily process infrared wavelengths well below that threshold and show them on a screen as additional colours. So infrared radiation is used in many fields such as medical photography and treatment, chemical analysis, military applications and astronomy. It is a "smart" LAI computing solution that solves a problem GOFAI found intractable.

Both GOFAI and LAI endorse a Cartesian problem-solving procedure but only the latter can correctly be defined as Cartesian in spirit. Like Descartes, but unlike GOFAI, LAI rejects the feasibility of a thinking machine capable of cloning human intelligence. Nothing could be more illuminating and contrary to Turing's project than the following statement from Descartes's *Discourse on Method*:

> I made special efforts to show that if any such machines [these are what we would call AI robots] had the organs and outward shape of a monkey or of some other animal that lacks reason, we should have no means of knowing that they did not possess entirely the same nature as these animals; whereas if any such machines bore a resemblance to our bodies and imitated our actions as closely as possible for all practical purposes [this may be called strong behaviourism], we should still have two very certain means of recognising that they were not real men. The first is that they could never use words, or put together other signs, as we do in order to declare out thoughts to others. For we can certainly conceive of a

machine so constructed that it utters words, and even utters words which correspond to bodily actions causing a change in its organs (e.g. if you touch it in one spot it asks what you want of it, if you touch it in another it cries out that you are hurting it, and so on). But it is not conceivable that such a machine should produce different arrangements of words so as to give an appropriately meaningful answer to whatever is said in its presence, as the dullest man can do. Secondly, even though such machines might do some things as well as we do them, or perhaps even better, they would inevitably fail in others, which would reveal that they were acting not through understanding but only from the disposition of their organs. For whereas reason is a universal instrument which can be used in all kinds of situations, these organs need some particular disposition for each particular action; hence it is for all practical purposes impossible for a machine to have enough different organs to make it act in all the contingencies of life in the way in which our reason makes us act.

(Descartes 1984, I: 139–40)

The possibility of increasing the number of "stupefiable" tasks, together with the radically constructionist (non-mimetic), non-materialist and Cartesian nature of LAI, explain some of the specific successes and orientations of LAI and clarify an important mistake often made in the anti-AI literature. We shall first concentrate on the latter in order to introduce the former.

Deep Blue: a Cartesian computer

"Computers cannot play chess better than a Grand Master": even critics of GOFAI as acute as Dreyfus and Dreyfus seem to have made the mistake of arguing for this view (Dreyfus and Dreyfus 1986: 109ff.). Today it is easy to point out that, by defeating Kasparov, IBM's Deep Blue has dispelled any remaining doubt. The problem with Dreyfus and Dreyfus's or similar approaches did not lie in the inadequate understanding of the game or its phenomenological analysis, but in

- treating all AI approaches as necessarily mimetic,
- considering conditions (1)–(5) analysed above as inevitably "binary", i.e. either fulfillable or not, while they are "analogue", i.e. subject to degrees of and therefore to cumulative satisfaction, and hence
- undervaluing the fact that, in each chess game, the whole context, elements, facts, rules, memory of past moves, problems, heuristic strategies and evaluations, etc., make up a logical model which, though extremely vast, is very well-defined (entities, their properties and mutual relations, legal and illegal moves are all fully determined and nothing is left to chance), can be analysed in discrete terms (board games are digital and

not analogue like ball games) and hence subject to progressive data processing.

It is true that a Grand Master may well have a holistic and visual approach to the game, based on intuition, insights and inexpressible experience, but this is irrelevant to non-mimetic LAI, since a computer may play chess better than any human being without even approximately simulating any human thinking process, very much in the same sense in which we can fly faster than any bird. Likewise, it is true that there are tasks, such as understanding a natural language or translating from one to another, which remain beyond the capacity of a machine, for they are too "open". But chess, being a limited game, is not one of them, and can have its (1)–(5) features subjected to gradual and increasing fulfilment. In order to play chess decently, a computer cannot compute all possible combinations, since there are billions of alternative branches to be explored (nobody seems to know how many alternative chess games there really are, and depending on the author, estimates range from 10^{40} to 10^{120}. This is known as combinatorial escalation; to get some idea of the size of the number, you may recall that the number of protons and neutrons taken together in the whole universe is often estimated to be 10^{80}). However the computer does not need to go to this length, for it is usually sufficient to combine three essential operations:

- generate static lists of legal moves, i.e. board positions, restricting the number of moves to a relatively small number that enables it to produce a reply within a reasonable time (the depth of the search, technically known as the size of the search space, is usually five moves, i.e. ten ply, which already generates half a quadrillion moves on average). There are other ways to limit the scope of the search and hence improve its depth;
- assess the value of a particular series of moves by means of evaluation functions, that is, assign numeric values to each given board position on the basis of a set of features, such as material or positional advantage, strong attack, control of the board, development, etc., and/or a minimax strategy that attempts to maximise one's gain and minimise the opponent's; and finally
- choose the move that yields the highest value.

The first operation is a function of mere computable power; the second contains heuristic strategies based on what can be learnt from great players and implemented in terms of rule of thumb, such as ways of evaluating gambits. There are four basic chess values that a computer must consider before deciding on a move: material, position, king safety and tempo. The performance of such operations is obviously subject to improvement through time, not least because they can be supported by a steadily enriched knowledge database of millions of opening games, which has fully codified the 15 to 20 most strategic opening moves for each game, endgames and played games. On the whole, a better "stupefication" of the game is progressively achieved. This is combined with a dramatic improvement in the hardware – Deep Blue is a RISC System/6000 Scalable Power parallel system (SP) high-performance computer – and an obvious increase in the machine's capacities to calculate variations – the system contains 256 chess-specific processors working in parallel to partition and solve a chess-board problem, each one capable of searching 2 to 3 million positions per second, so that Deep Blue can calculate 50 to 100 billion moves within three minutes. And since it is realistic to assume that all the previous variables will be subject to further improvement, it becomes perfectly reasonable to expect that computers will soon be undefeatable by any human player. Of course, this does not mean that we shall stop playing chess, for after all we still enjoy other computable games such as draughts, nor does it make Deep Blue any more intelligent than ELIZA. Here is a nice quotation from the people who constructed it:

> Does Deep Blue use artificial intelligence? The short answer is No. Earlier computer designs that tried to mimic human thinking haven't been very good at it. No formula exists for intuition. So Deep Blue's designers have gone 'back to the future'. Deep Blue relies more on computational power and a simpler search and evaluation function. The long answer is No. "Artificial Intelligence" is more successful in science fiction than it is here on earth, and you don't have to be Isaac Asimov to know why it's hard to design a machine to mimic a process we don't understand very well to begin with. How we think is a question without an answer. Deep Blue could never be a HAL-2000 (the prescient, renegade computer in Stanley Kubrick's *2001*) if it tried. Nor would it occur to Deep Blue to "try". Its strengths are the strengths of a machine. It has more chess information to work with than any other computer, and all but a few chess masters. It never forgets or gets distracted. And it's orders of magnitude [are] better at processing the information at hand than anything yet devised for the purpose. "There is no psychology at work" in Deep Blue, says IBM research scientist Murray Campbell. Nor does Deep Blue "learn" its opponent as it plays. Instead, it operates much like a turbocharged "expert system", drawing on vast resources of stored information (for example, a database of opening games played by grandmasters over the last 100 years) and then calculating the most appropriate response to an opponent's move. Deep Blue is stunningly effective at solving chess problems, but it is less "intelligent" than the stupidest person. It doesn't think, it reacts. And that's where Garry Kasparov sees his advantage. Deep Blue applies brute force aplenty, but the "intelligence" is the old-fashioned kind. Think about the 100 years of grandmaster games. Kasparov isn't playing a computer, he's playing the ghosts of grandmasters past. That Deep Blue can organise such a storehouse of knowledge – and apply it on the fly to the ever-changing complexities

on the chessboard – is what makes this particular heap of silicon an arrow pointing to the future.

(from: http://www.chess.ibm.park.org/deep/blue/faqs.html#ai)

If a comparison is in order then, we may borrow a term from the military context and say that Deep Blue is only "smarter" than ELIZA is because it can stupefy more. As a test of the value of our interpretation it is reassuring to find John McCarthy, one of the fathers of AI, complaining that Deep Blue has very little to do with Strong AI. I would add that it is precisely in this difference that lies the condition of possibility of its success.

The success of LAI

Defenders of GOFAI sometimes protest that the threshold of intelligence is constantly and unfairly raised whenever a machine is shown to be able to reach it, yet it should be clear now that their complaint is unjustified. It is not that some intelligent tasks, like playing chess, no longer enjoy their intellectual status, but rather that they are discovered to be *also* amenable to successful computational treatment. As a human being, one will always need some intelligence to play chess well, but as a machine, one can do without it completely. The possibility of a LAI treatment does not diminish the value of a task; it enriches it with a new dimension. The success with game playing shows that better philosophy also means better results. A program is found to have more chance of succeeding if the problem it deals with is carefully defined, the tasks it performs are reduced to sequences of special-purpose heuristic procedures and repetitive instructions, and the context of application is severely restricted to a sufficiently small possible-world, consisting of stereotypical situations and standard cases, that is, to a microworld in which relevance, significance and total novelties are either absent, successfully constrained or fully predetermined by the programmer. Thus, in each of the ten fields listed in the section 'The application-areas of AI', LAI approaches the problem of devising smart machines by attempting to improve one or more of the five (a)–(e) conditions of possibility of AI. LAI projects aim to extend the scope and sophistication of tasks amenable to computation by means of fuzzy logic systems, artificial neural networks, parallel computing and quantum computing; to extend the number of knowledge and practical-experience sensitive tasks performable by a computer by means of knowledge engineering and expert systems; and to extend the number of body-sensitive tasks performable by a computer by means of robotics. Such solutions may combine with each other and with the development and improvement of new algorithms and the elaboration of increasingly large databases, which provide a computer with enough information about the task-environment so that the performance of the task itself becomes as context-free as possible (i.e. the computer is able to construct a model of everything that is relevant). They may thus help to devise *ad hoc* machines or programs that can cope successfully with an increasing variety of well-specified context-sensitive tasks. In this chapter we shall have a brief look at each field, focusing on some of the features that are conceptually most interesting.

Fuzzy logic systems

Fuzzy logic (FL) can be interpreted as a superset of Boolean logic (BL) (two introductory texts are Klir and Folger 1988 and Kosko 1992; for a full presentation of fuzzy logic see Zimmermann 1991). It is common to explain this relation by saying that BL associates only two truth-values to any wff (well-formed formula) P(x), i.e. $\{0,1\}$, so that in BL any wff has a discrete or crisp (yes-or-no) alethic form, i.e. it is either completely false or completely true, depending on whether or not x satisfies P. On the other hand FL employs the concept of "partial truths" to establish how far x satisfies P, that is, continuous or fuzzy (more-or-less) truth values between the Boolean 0 and 1. (Note that such values should not be taken for probabilities, since they do not need to sum to one, have no forecasting significance and do not refer to the statistical strength of evidence supporting the assertion that x satisfies the property P.) Although such terminology is slightly misleading, the distinction is intuitive. We can now make it a little more precise by referring to a few basic notions of set theory.

Suppose Σ is a non-empty set ($\Sigma \neq \{\}$) whose members $\{x_1, \ldots, x_n\}$ need to be assessed according to whether or not they satisfy a property P. In BL, we can construct a new set in terms of a mapping $\Delta_{BL}: \Sigma \mapsto \{0,1\}$ from members of Σ to members of the set $\{0,1\}$. The mapping is formally defined as a function $\mu_{BL}(x): \Sigma \mapsto \{0,1\}$, which is called the membership function of Δ_{BL}, and this clarifies why one often speaks of the function or of the resulting set interchangeably. The function $\mu_{BL}(x)$ generates a set Δ_{BL} of ordered pairs $<x, y>$, such that

1   Δ_{BL} is a subset of the Cartesian product $\Sigma \times \{0,1\}$, which satisfies the property of being equipotent with respect to Σ (there is one and only one ordered pair in Δ_{BL} for each element of Σ and vice versa)
2   $\forall x \forall <x, y>(x \in <x, y> \rightarrow x \in \Sigma)$, the formula means that every x in any $<x, y>$ is a member of Σ
3   $\forall y \forall <x, y>(y \in <x, y> \rightarrow y \in \{0,1\})$
4   0 = non-membership
5   1 = membership
6   $y = 0 \leftrightarrow \neg P(x)$, that is, $y = 0$ if and only if x does not satisfy the property P
7   $y = 1 \leftrightarrow \Pi(x)$.

The set $\Delta_{BL} = \{(x, \mu_{BL}(x)), x \in \Sigma\}$ is a Boolean set, out of which we can construct the set consisting of all interpretations of x in any $<x, y> \in \Delta_{BL}$ which are not associated with y = 0 or, which is equivalent (and this shows the binary nature of BL), that are associated with y = 1. Γ_{BL} is a "crisp" subset of Σ ($\Gamma_{BL} \subseteq \Sigma$) consisting of all members of Σ which satisfy the property P. Obviously, the truth-value of the statement x $\in$ Γ_{BL} is equivalent to the truth-value of P(x) and can be established by checking each member of Δ_{BL}. The statement is true if the second element of the ordered pair is 1, and the statement is false if it is 0. A similar analysis can now be extended to FL.

Suppose now that $\Sigma \neq \{\}$, $\Sigma = \{x_1, \ldots, x_n\}$ and that each x in $\{x_1, \ldots, x_n\}$ needs to be assessed according to the *degree* in which it satisfies the property P. In FL, we can construct a new "fuzzy" set in terms of a mapping Δ_{FL}: $\Sigma \mapsto [0,1]$ from members of Σ to members of the set of some numeric values in the range of real numbers [0.0, 1.0]. On the basis of the membership function $\mu_{FL}(x)$: $\Sigma \mapsto [0,1]$, $\mu_{FL}(x)$ generates a set Δ_{FL} of ordered pairs <x, y> that is similar to Δ_{BL} as far as properties 2,4,5,6 above are concerned, but now every y in <x,y> can be a real value from the closed interval [0,1], so that:

1   Δ_{FL} is a subset of the Cartesian product $\Sigma \times [0,1]$ which may or (more often) may not be equipotent with respect to Σ (Σ is referred to as the universe of discourse for the fuzzy subset Δ).

Note that, although y in <x, y> can take any value in the range of real numbers [0.0, 1.0], this does not mean that, given a specific model for FL, there is actually an infinite number of interpretations of y available, since each system always sets up a finite range of values for y approximate to n decimals. Formula (3) for BL becomes now

3    $\forall y \forall <x, y>(y \in <x, y> \rightarrow y \in [0,1])$

and formula (7) for BL becomes now

7    $(y = 1 \rightarrow P(x)) \wedge (P(x) \rightarrow 1 \geq y > 0)$ or, more simply, $1 \geq y > 0 \leftrightarrow P(x)$.

This means that, in FL, the two values 0/1 are only the low and upper bound of the set, so while they are still used to represent "complete" non-membership/membership, a selection of values in between is used to represent what are in fact degrees of possession of a certain property, but may be called, for the sake of simplicity, "intermediate degrees of membership" or "degrees of truth". No actual "fuzzification" of truth is in question, however, and this becomes clear once we realise that:

•   Contrary to what is sometimes stated in the literature, neither D_{BL} nor Δ_{FL} is a proper subset of Σ; only $\Gamma_{BL} \subseteq \Sigma$ and $\Gamma_{FL} \subseteq \Sigma$.
•   While in BL both Γ_{BL} and Δ_{BL} are "crisp", and hence we can use them interchangeably, in FL only Δ_{FL} may be considered fuzzy and only in the sense of having been constructed by means of a mapping from members of Σ to a selection of real values from 0 to 1 whenever the cardinality of the selection >2.

- Strictly speaking, and hence more correctly, even in FL Γ_{FL} remains crisp, since it is still the case that x is or is not a member of Γ, no matter to what degree x does satisfy the property P. Γ_{FL}consists of all interpretations of every x in any <x, y> that are not associated with y = 0, and the non-binary but multi-valued nature of FL is shown by the fact that, contrary to what happens in BL, this is not equivalent to saying that Γ_{FL} consists of all interpretations of every x in any <x, y> that are associated with y = 1. It is still the case, however, that Γ_{BL} consists of all members of Σ that satisfy, to some degree greater than 0, the property P. Obviously, the truth-value of the statement x $\in$ Γ_{BL} is still equivalent to the truth-value of P(x) and can be established by checking each member of Δ_{BL}. The statement is true whenever $0 < y \leq 1$, and false if y = 0.

To define FL as the logic underlying modes of reasoning that are approximate rather than exact, to assume that the importance of fuzzy logic derives from the fact that most modes of human reasoning, and especially common-sense reasoning, are intrinsically approximate, and to declare that BL cannot satisfactorily describe "humanistic" problems, means to have misunderstood both logics. It is natural to translate "it is true that the flower is fairly red" into "it is fairly true that the flower is red" because, working with a natural language in an informal context, it is often unclear to what degree a flower satisfies the property of being red, but in a formal language and a mathematical domain capable of sharp precision, the former equivalence is a syntactic fallacy, which simply misunderstands the scope of the adverb. Hence, in a fuzzy set an object can have numerous different membership values or "grades", but it is only for the sake of simplicity that we speak of degrees of truth or membership when referring to the alethic values of P(x). What is fuzzy is not the alethic value of P(x), but the property P, which is satisfied by x to a y degree that can be made as precise as one needs. To have a less mathematical analysis, you may try to think of degrees of falsehood. You will soon perceive the absurdity of the whole idea of a Negative FL.

Since in FL the truth-functional values of P(x) give the precise degree up to which P is satisfied by x, for any wff ϕ it is possible to generate a formal calculus by adopting, for example, the following definitions of the set theoretic operations and logic operators (henceforth I simplify the notation by leaving the specification FL implicit):

- $(\Delta = \{\}) \leftrightarrow \forall x \, (x \in \Sigma \to \mu(x) = <x, 0>)$
- $(\Delta_A = \Delta_B) \leftrightarrow \forall x \, (x \in \Sigma \to \mu_A(x) = \mu_B(x))$
- $\Delta_A' = 1 - \mu(x)$, which is equivalent to
- $(\neg \, \phi) = 1.0 - (\phi)$
- $\Delta_A \subseteq \Delta_B \leftrightarrow \mu_A(x) \leq \mu_B(x)$
- $(\Delta_C = \Delta_A \cup \Delta_B) \to (\mu_C(x) = \text{Max} \, (\mu_A(x), \mu_B(x)))$, which is equivalent to
- $(\phi \vee \psi) = \text{Max} \, ((\phi), (\psi))$
- $(\Delta_C = \Delta_A \cap \Delta_B) \to (\mu_C(x) = \text{Min} \, (\mu_A(x), \mu_B(x)))$, which is equivalent to

- $(\varphi \wedge \psi) = \text{Min}\,((\varphi), (\psi))$
- $(\varphi \rightarrow \psi) = 1.0 - \text{Min}\,(\varphi, 1.0 - \psi)$

If the truth-values are restricted to $\{0,1\}$ then clearly the truth tables of the special FL in question are exactly the same as BL's. This is known as the extension principle: any result in BL can be obtained in FL by restricting all fuzzy membership values to $\{0,1\}$ and FL, as described above, i.e. as a multi-valued logic, is interpretable as a generalisation of classical set theory and standard two-valued logic. If more than two values are admitted, then in FL some properties of BL, most notably the law of excluded middle, idempotency and distributivity, acquire different interpretations, depending on the specific axiomatisation adopted. To give a trivial example, to keep BL and FL as close as possible one would have to define a tautology not as any wff which is always true, but rather as any wff which is never false, so that $(\varphi \vee \neg\varphi)$ is a tautology both in BL, where its value is always 1, and in FL, where the value of $\text{Max}(\varphi, \neg\varphi) = $ the value of $\text{Max}(\varphi, 1.0 - \varphi)$ and the latter is always necessarily greater than 0. This set of "tautologies" in FL is called the support of a fuzzy set.

For a less formal approach, consider now the following case. Suppose we take the universe of discourse Σ to be 10 people in a classroom. The property B = "being born in Oxford" is "crisp" or digital: the set Δ will consist of ten ordered pairs $<x, y>$, where x is the name of a person in the class and y is either 0 or 1, and Γ will contain only people who are B, i.e. names associated with 1. If we consider now the property C = "living close enough to Oxford", we see immediately that C is necessarily "fuzzy" or analogue: the "fuzzy" set Δ will still consist of ten ordered pairs $<x, y>$, but while x is the name of a person in the class as before, y takes now different real values from 0 or 1, depending on our way of assessing the distance of each person's accommodation from the city centre. The resulting set Γ, however, still consists of names of people who simply satisfy the property C, the difference being that they can now be ordered according to the value of the associated y, i.e. according to the degree in which they satisfy the property C. Oxford University Regulations, for example, state that undergraduates must live within six miles of the city centre, hence our values will range from "distance from the centre > 6 miles" = 0 (if John lives more than 6 miles from the centre he does not satisfy C) to "distance from the centre = 0" = 1 (if Mary lives in the centre she satisfies C completely), with other students living x miles from Oxford for x < 6 all counting as members of Γ, although ordered according to the degree in which they satisfy C.

Fuzzy logic was first introduced by Lotfi Zadeh to treat fuzzy concepts in natural languages (Zadeh 1965 is the classic paper that marks the beginning of FL). It began as a typical project in GOFAI, based on the classic mimetic assumptions, and as such it remained for a long time little more than a promising theory. Only once it underwent the usual transformation common to many other GOFAI ideas did it become a successful component of advanced technology. FL applications are becoming increasingly popular especially, but not only, in control systems that deal with inherently analogue processes – processes that move through a continuous range of values, generate fuzzy data and cannot be easily modelled by linear analysis – and are usually implemented by means of digital processors capable of dealing only with well-defined numeric values, though "fuzzy" processors are also available. Very schematically, a typical fuzzy system consists of three components or logical stages:

(1) Input stage

A set of membership functions $\{\mu_1(x), \ldots ,\mu_n(x)\}$ makes possible the fuzzification of the source data, i.e. the conversion of a crisp value into a fuzzy value by associating the inputs x with values of y. We have seen that the logical form of each membership function is $\mu_m(x)$: $\Sigma \overset{m}{\mapsto} [0,1]$, where Σ consists now of a collection of source data $\{x_1, \ldots ,x_n\}$ provided by input devices such as sensors, switches, thumbwheels, etc., while both the range of values $\{y_{[0,1]1}, \ldots ,y_{[0,1]n}\}$ between [0,1] to be associated with each member of Σ, and the number of functions (the value of m in $\mu_m(x)$ and $\overset{m}{\mapsto}$) and hence of the resulting fuzzy sets, are specified by the system according to previously established requirements. Note that membership functions are often n-dimensional (e.g. a 3-dimensional membership function may map data from sex, age and qualification to profession). The result of the input stage is a "fuzzified" set Δ of ordered pairs $\{<x_1,y_{[0,1]}>, \ldots ,<x_n, y_{[0,1]}>\}$. Example: a car antilock braking system (ABS) directed by a fuzzy logic controller (FLC). To achieve smooth slowing down of the car, the controller needs to provide precise operational instructions to the ABS based on information concerning the nature of the surface (wet, dry, greasy, etc.), the speed of the car (mph), the brake temperature and many other variables in the system. All variables change gradually from one state to the next and in each case the continuous transition cannot easily be governed by means of rather arbitrary thresholds, which would result in a discontinuous and abrupt change whenever the input value exceeded that threshold. So a FLC may be adopted, which defines the input of each variable using some membership function $\mu(x)$ in such a way that the input variable's state, i.e. the y in <x, y>, loses value in one membership function while gaining value in the next. For example, at any one time, the y of the brake temperature will usually be in some degree part of two membership functions: 0.7 nominal and 0.3 warm, or 0.6 nominal and 0.4 cool, and so on.

(2) Processing stage

A set (usually dozens) of inferential rules $\{R_1, \ldots , R_n\}$ of the form "IF a certain specified pattern of data occurs THEN perform the specified action", generates another fuzzified set Ω from the fuzzified set Δ. The entire set of rules is usually known as a *rulebase* or *knowledge base*, and the program that determines the rule fireability, selects rules for firing and executes the consequent instructions is called an *inference engine*. In each rule, whose logical form is $\Delta^n \to \Omega_n$, Δ is the antecedent provided by the fuzzified input reached in the input stage (1), and Ω is the consequent, an equally fuzzified output established on the basis of a computation of the values $y_{[0,1]}$ in $\{<x_1,y_{[0,1]}>, \ldots, <x_n, y_{[0,1]}>\}$. Usually, rules have complex antecedents, constructed by connecting several values using the FL operators as defined above. For each n in $\Delta^n \to \Omega_n$ the inference engine invokes the N relevant rule and generates a specific fuzzified result usually involving some *linguistic variables*, such as "negative high, negative low, zero, positive low, positive high", for assessment. Hence, the antecedent describes to what degree the rule applies, while the conclusion assigns a membership function to each of one or more output variables. Rules can be solved in parallel in hardware or serially in software. There are several different ways to define the result of a rule, i.e. to determine the value of the output as a function of the rule premiss's computed degree of truth, such as the MIN inference method we have seen above when discussing the AND operator, and the PRODUCT inference method. A second stage involves the COMPOSITION of all the fuzzy subsets assigned to each output variable, which are finally combined together to form a single fuzzy set Ω. Rules for COMPOSITION are usually MAX or SUM. We have seen the MAX composition when discussing the OR operator; the SUM composition constructs the combined output by taking the pointwise sum over all of the fuzzy subsets assigned to the output variable by the inference rule. Again, at each passage the appropriate N rules are specified according to previously established requirements. Example: having fuzzified its input, the FLC now elaborates the operative instructions for the ABS on the basis of a set of rules such as: if the brake temperature is WARM and the speed is NOT VERY FAST then the degree in which brake pressure increases is MODERATE.

(3) Output stage

In the output stage, the system may need to convert the combined fuzzified results provided by (2) back into a crisp variable which is now the representative value corresponding to the specific control value to be implemented. This is known as defuzzification, and it is not always necessary, since there are systems that can cope with fuzzy sets. There are many techniques of defuzzification, but two of the most common are the CENTROID method, which is based on the selection of the centre of gravity of the fuzzy set, and the MAXIMUM method, whereby one of the variable values, at which the fuzzy set has its maximum y, is chosen as the crisp value for the new output variable. Example: the FLC defuzzifies the output of the set of rules to provide a specific "crisp" instruction to the ABS, such as the actual brake pressure expressed by a single numeric value.

Fuzzy control systems are designed empirically, following the usual trial and error methods and adopting precisely that "stupefication" strategy that we have seen to characterise LAI. A detailed analysis and precise documentation of the system's operational specifications, inputs, outputs, rulebase and defuzzification methods (if required) is essential, and is followed by tests. Given its empirical adaptability, fuzzy logic can be fruitfully employed whenever a system is difficult to model, e.g. because it is the result of the experience of a human being, or where data and processes with continuous values are common. Since FL simplifies the design complexity, while often improving control performance, it also shortens the design development cycle and simplifies the implementation of the system (FL controllers can be based on cheap sensors and low-resolution analogue-to-digital converters), thus making the latter process less expensive. Moreover, FL systems are intrinsically easily upgradable by adding new rules. All this explains the success of FL controllers. Unfortunately, this also seems to have spread three erroneous conceptions.

As regarding the philosophy of fuzzy logic, we have already discussed the misleading idea of "degrees of truth" and "degrees of membership": a logic of fuzzy values is not, strictly speaking, a theory that is itself intrinsically fuzzy. As Schroedinger once wrote, "there is a difference between a shaky or out-of-focus photograph and a snapshot of clouds and fog banks" (Haack 1979 is a well supported criticism of FL interpreted as a logic of fuzzified truth-values; Fox 1981 is a critical discussion of Haack's article). Nor is FL a logic that deals with ambiguity, vagueness or confusion, unless the latter words are superficially used to refer to continuous, degree or analogue values as opposed to discrete binary values. Truly ambiguous, vague or confused information remains so unless it is further regimented. Examples are sentences such as "perhaps I do not like it as much as I should, or maybe I do, after all", which immediately appear to lack a definite context-free meaning, or sentences that are semantically or syntactically ambiguous like "when she met us she thought we were going to the pub", which a computer could interpret in thirteen different ways. In any case, a fuzzified logic, wrongly understood as a theory of degrees of truth, could only make them *irremediably* ambiguous, vague or confused by isomorphically adapting itself to it. In database jargon this is sometimes called the GIGO rule: Garbage In, Garbage Out.

As regarding the philosophy of fuzzy technology, some people seem to believe that FL is the first method that allows the precise and reliable computation of continuous quantities, as if infinitesimal calculus had not been devised. It is true that FL controllers can efficiently replace traditional PID (proportional-integral-derivative) control systems in areas such as consumer electronics, industrial robotics, automation, information systems, diagnosis and other expert systems (DBMS, information retrieval), in pattern recognition, in connection with neural networks (image processing, machine vision) and in decision support systems, but the reason is not that FL controllers allow us to do something utterly new, but rather that PID controllers, though highly reliable and effective, require sets of differential equations to define the system response to its inputs, which are much more difficult to formulate.

Consequentially, PID systems are very demanding in terms of processing power and memory, may not be as effective as systems based on empirical rules such as FL controllers, and are certainly more expensive and much less flexible and adaptable. It is an obvious case of technological evolution, rather than revolution, and perhaps it would be useful to adopt the logic of fuzziness even when interpreting the development of fuzzy technology.

Finally, in the philosophy of artificial intelligence there seems to be a tendency to attribute FL's success to the alleged fact that somehow it resembles/captures, much better than BL does, the way in which human beings reason, take decisions and solve problems on the basis of certain but "approximate" data. It is the old mimetic postulate of GOFAI that often permeates the less technical and more "philosopherish" interpretations of FL. Thus supporters of FL systems may misinterpret the latter in terms of brain/mind-mimetic functions or reality-isomorphic properties, and hence expect FL to be able to solve problems whose intractability does not depend on the kind of mathematical logic employed. Surfing the Internet one may come across views according to which FL will make possible the construction of

> Vast expert decision makers, theoretically able to distil the wisdom of every document ever written. Sex robots with a humanlike repertoire of behaviour. Computers that understand and respond to normal human language. Machines that write interesting novels and screenplays in a selected style, such as Hemingway's. Molecule-sized soldiers of health that will roam the blood-stream, killing cancer cells and slowing the ageing process
> (http: //www-dse.doc.ic.ac.uk/~nd/surprise_96/journal/vol4/sbaa/
> report.future.html.bak)

or that "the first fuzzy logician was the Buddha". This is nonsense, or rather science fiction of the worst kind combined with a pinch of deeply misunderstood spiritualism. It is evidently true that in our minds we rationally conceptualise our experience of the world according to a logic which may often be described as fuzzy – so much so that it is worth formalising such logic into a more precise calculus – but the resulting calculus should not be mistaken for a reliable description of the ways in which we actually perceive the world, think and perform intelligent tasks. To the objection that no human being seems to be conscious of any process of fuzzification, rule-based analysis and defuzzification of the information in her or his possession, the reply can only be that all this must then take place at a subconscious level, but the subconscious is a land where only psychoanalysts and metaphysicians dare to tread. It is off-limit to computer scientists, and as epistemologists we should probably be content to acknowledge that, although the logic may change, the hope that it will one day describe the Laws of Thought (as Boole dreamed) is as tenacious as mankind's useless efforts to make it come true.

Artificial neural networks

Fuzzy set theory maps elements of an object space into a space of n > 2 membership values. Now, such non-linear mapping can be variously parameterised and can also be fruitfully combined with *artificial neural networks* (ANN).

Although there are a lot of different approaches to ANN technology, and hence many specific implemented systems that can be very unlike each other, at the core of neural computation we find the concept of distributed, adaptive and non-linear computing so, as a general introduction, it may be sufficient to present an ANN (also called *artificial neural system, connectionist architecture*, PDP, i.e. *parallel distributed processing* and *neuromorphic system*) as a multiprocessor computing system. (Aleksander and Morton 1995 provides a good technical introduction which also contains informal sections useful for philosophy students with little mathematical background, their methodological approach is highly "mimetic". On the theoretical side see Churchland and Sejnowski 1992; Grossberg 1988; Horgan and Tienson 1991. On connectionism in philosophy see Ramsey *et al.* 1991; Fodor and Pylyshyn 1988, and Dawson and Shamanski 1994, criticise connectionism in the philosophy of mind.)

An ANN understood as a multiprocessor computing system can be logically described as a matrix of

- a finite set of individual nodes $\{PE_1, \ldots, PE_n\}$, working as processing elements (also known as *units, processors* or *neurons*), whose function is to map patterns of inputs into patterns of outputs, and
- a finite set of asymmetric (unidirectional) relations $\{C_1, \ldots, C_n\}$, working as communication channels connecting members of $\{PE_1, \ldots, PE_n\}$, whose function is to enhance or inhibit the transmission of patterns of signals by increasing or decreasing their numeric weight (also called strength). The greater the weight, the greater the effect a connection has in determining whether or not the relevant PE will fire (be activated).

The processing power of an ANN consists in its capacity to adapt to, or learn from, a set of training patterns by dynamically adjusting the weight of its inter-PE connections on the basis of a non-linear, parallel processing of specified inputs, and according to a pre-established proportional difference between the desired output and the actual output. Depending on how $\{C_1, \ldots, C_n\}$ is implemented, the topology of an ANN may vary from fully connected (see below the Hopfield and Boltzmann networks) to sparsely or just locally connected, but typical feed-forward (see below) ANNs are usually not even weakly connected, i.e. they satisfy the formal property $\neg(\forall x \forall y$ $((x \in \{PE_1, \ldots, PE_n\} \wedge y \in \{PE_1, \ldots, PE_n\}) \rightarrow (Cxy \vee Cyx)))$. Hence, ANNs have fixed hierarchical structures: disjoint subsets of $\{PE_1, \ldots, PE_n\}$ are rigidly ordered into multiple layers from ground-input to top-output level, with inter-layer and infra-layer connections. Since layers are numerable, and their order always includes an input layer IL, n ≥ 0 hidden layers HL and an output layer OL, and both IL and OL are inevitable, a common way to classify ANNs is by referring to the number of their HLs (usually, an ANN has several HLs).

PEs may have a small amount of local memory, and they operate only on local data, each working in parallel with other PEs, usually asynchronously. They may act just as a simple threshold discriminator but, more often, a PE employs a threshold function – typically a sigmoid or logistic function – which makes it possible to regulate the PE activation for output, in the following way. Each PE can take many inputs having different weightings but provides only one output, which depends on the inputs. When a pattern of signals is received by its input connections with a sufficient weight, a PE "fires", i.e. maps the input modified by the interconnection weight into another pattern of signals, generating a further output and interconnection weight. In order to do so, the PE processes the input and interconnection weight by a summation function (typically a weighted summation) to yield a sum that is passed to a non-linearity called a transfer function (typically a sigmoid). The output of the non-linearity is the output of the PE, which is sent, through output connections, to another PE. Hence the operations of each PE are fully determined by the network structure (cardinality and organisation), the connection weights, the inputs received from other PEs belonging to no higher layers via the connections, and finally its own threshold function. The mathematical functions determining the processing behaviour of $\{PE_1, \ldots, PE_n\}$ are embedded in the network and, although they can vary depending on the specific tasks and needs in question, they are not subject to constant adaptation while the network is working. What makes an ANN flexible are the different degrees (which may be fuzzified) of weight that its internal connections are capable of acquiring in the course of the mapping process. Thus, ANNs are not programmed to perform a specific task "top down" but "learn by example" (bottom-up organisation) how to process a particular input satisfactorily, before they are employed in an application. To cope with another task, they need to be retrained.

The process of training a neural network involves the following stages:

1   The untrained network is presented with carefully selected patterns of typical input data.
2   The network maps the data into an initial global pattern of output data.
3   The network adjusts the weights of its connections using a variety of functions and according to how much the resulting output patterns differ from what they are expected to be. A training file is developed, consisting of data for each input node and the desired response for each of the network's output nodes. The adjustment of the weights is a matter of

trial and error, does not follow rigidly programmed instructions and involves no software programming.

4   Step (3) is repeated for many typical input patterns, so that the actual output of the network converges with the output desired (by the trainer).

5   When the gap between actual output and desired output falls below a pre-established threshold of accuracy (set by the trainer), the training process is complete; the network operates satisfactorily and is ready to be used as a predictive or diagnostic tool, to process new selections of the kind of input patterns for which it has been trained.

Depending on their methods of data processing and training, ANNs can be classified as

- *feedforward*, when they have no feedback and simply *associate* inputs with outputs. This type of ANN is normally used for simple pattern recognition;
- *recurrent*, when they implement feedback relations (closed loops) needed to create a self-regulating, dynamic system that will produce the appropriate pattern. This type of ANN is normally used for pattern reconstruction;
- *supervised*, when they require a human trainer to tune the ANN to the desired output. The most widely used *supervised* ANNs are known as Back Propagation ANNs. They are multi-layered, feed-forward networks which are trained using an error criterion. The network's output is compared with the desired output to produce an error measure; then an algorithm "back-propagates" the error from the output PE to the input PE iteratively in order to adjust the weights increasingly well so as to reduce the error. The network is trained by repeating this process many times. Once the error parameter has decreased below a specified optimal threshold, the network is said to have converged and its training is complete. Back-propagation ANNs are used for classification and prediction tasks. Hopfield and Boltzmann networks are special types of multi-layer ANNs characterised by improved features that make more likely the irreversible (Hopfield) and optimal (Boltzmann) self-stabilisation of the system;
- *self-organising*, when they can learn to identify structures in the data by adapting automatically in response to particular types of inputs, according to pre-established requirements. The most widely used *self-organising* ANNs are known as Kohonen and they are networks in which the PEs compete with each other for the "right" to respond to an input pattern. They are trained with unsupervised algorithms that can cluster patterns of data into families on the basis of measured attributes or features (as philosophers, we would say "family resemblance"), serving as inputs to the algorithms. Self-organising ANNs can be used for pattern discovery tasks.

Since ANNs are multiprocessor computer systems, in principle they can process any function computable by a Turing machine or Von Neumann machine (VNM). Furthermore, we have seen in Chapter 2 that there are mathematical models of ANN that are much more powerful than TMs, the so-called Super Turing machines, and it has been shown that neural networks can be classified into an infinite hierarchy, depending on their different computing capabilities. However, *in practice*, implemented networks face enormous difficulties when dealing with problems involving symbolic processing and memory resources (e.g. number crunching), while they are much more successfully employed to simplify many computational processes involving patterns of data that would be virtually intractable by ordinary computers. In particular, networks can be extremely useful whenever large amounts of structured data form patterns – not necessarily sensory patterns, such as a picture or a spoken word, but also logical structures, as is the case with statistics or sampling models – which are then available as training input, and when there are classification or mapping needs (clustering and synthesising data, forecasting) that cannot easily be satisfied by the elaboration of computable algorithms or efficient heuristic rules. Since networks "learn" from their examples, they are tolerant of some imprecision and can generate models effectively even from noisy data, without having to discover possible constructive algorithms.

To summarise, the functions and advantages of ANNs are:

1 They can map patterns of data by adapting their structures to input examples.
2 They can generalise patterns of data thanks to (1).
3 They can deal with multi-variable, non-linear clusters of data.
4 They can deal with noisy, distorted, imprecise and incomplete input data when doing (1)–(3) (but recall the GIGO rule: unclear, uncertain, vague data are not subject to fruitful mapping).
5 They can do (1)–(4) according to specified problem-solving requirements, either by training or automatically (self-organisation).
6 They can require advanced mathematical solutions – at least to determine the state function (e.g. the summation function), the transfer functions (e.g. sigmoid function) and the training algorithm (e.g. back-propagation) – but no software programming to do (1)–(5). It is common to formulate such a property by saying that ANNs do not require algorithms, but we have just seen that this is slightly misleading. ANNs approach problem-solving tasks in a different way from rule-based computers, which follow lists of instructions and hence require programs in order to perform their computations, but ANNs still require increasingly sophisticated mathematical functions to perform their tasks successfully.
7 They have a relatively short development time because of (6).
8 They can operate at high speed.

9 They can be implemented on parallel hardware for even greater speed of operation.

10 They can be employed in real time operations because of (8)–(9).

11 They have some fault tolerance and are subject to graceful degradation (since no individual PE is either necessary or sufficient, a partially damaged network may still perform some of its essential tasks satisfactorily) because of their architecture and the redundancy in their information coding.

It follows that their conditions of applicability are that:

- the problem to be dealt with can be expressed as a mapping problem (necessary);
- sufficient samples of typical sources of data to be mapped are available (necessary);
- tolerance for errors and context sensitivity is required;
- the problem allows no computable algorithmic solution or only algorithmic solutions that are too complex or difficult to formulate.

And their areas of application are:

- pattern recognition, detection and reconstruction;
- data classification and generalisation;
- functional prediction/projection (conclusions are generalised for new patterns from past patterns);
- system modelling of physical processes for which there are no algorithmic interpretations or for which algorithmic interpretations are too complex and difficult to find;
- control problems, where the input variables are measurements used to control an output actuator, and the network learns the control function.

More practically, some real-world, typical applications of ANN technology include: voice and visual recognition, spectra identification, chemical structures, biomedical instrumentation, medical diagnosis, credit rating (loan risk evaluation), forecasting of future sales, investment analysis, where predictions can be attempted on the basis of patterns provided by past data, market performance, economic indicators, writing recognition (especially signature verification, when new signatures need to be compared with those stored), signal processing and compression, automatic control and monitoring, production requirements, quality control, oil and gas exploration.

ANN is an expanding technology, especially in the area of artificial perception, but it has not always been so successful. Its "prehistory" can be identified with cognitive associationism, whose first roots Hobbes thought could be traced back as far as Aristotle. This is one of the chief unifying traits of empiricism's conception of the mind. To simplify, the mind is conceived of as devoid of any innate knowledge but endowed with the capacity of forming ideas by manipulating basic sensory experiences (sensations). At the end of the nineteenth century, the development of what is now called neuropsychology led to a plausible, very general account of how some mental processes might be underpinned by the interactions of neurons in the brain. The brain began to be mapped and functions to be localised. In this context, it became increasingly clear that the behaviour of nerve cells is also as much determined by their chemico-electrical excitation, and that an excited cell can "fire" and thus cause the neurons to which it is connected to become excited as well. It was then further suggested, more controversially, that associations might be formed between two cells when they tend to become excited simultaneously.

In 1943 the neurophysiologist Warren McCulloch and the logician Walter Pitts – inspired by Ramon y Cajal's theory of the neurone structure, by Charles Scott Sherrington's theory about the excitatory/inhibitory synapses and by Alan Turing's work on computing machines – proposed an abstract mathematical model of the first artificial PE (processing element). Their aim was to discover how a brain might engage in logical reasoning and how this psychological functioning might be explained on a neurophysiological basis. Different configurations of McCulloch–Pitts artificial neurons were found to be able to perform the same logical operations that are carried on by a Turing machine. Later, Frank Rosenblatt developed a model of a network of McCulloch–Pitts artificial neurons capable of responding to different patterns, which he called "perceptrons". ANN applications began to be envisaged in the late 1950s, but in 1969 Marvin Minsky and Seymour Papert (Minsky and Papert 1969, rev. 1988) showed that there were a number of specific patterns that Rosenblatt's networks, having no hidden units, could not model (these patterns constitute what is often labelled the hard learning problem). They further claimed that this limitation probably made connectionist networks inappropriate as models of human cognition.

There followed more than a decade of stagnation of research in the field. Perceptrons were limited in scope and too demanding in terms of resources even to solve simple pattern recognition problems such as horizontal/vertical line discrimination. Interest in ANN grew again only in the 1980s (Hopfield 1982), once parallel architectures and mathematical algorithms became sophisticated enough for general applications. In particular, the recovery of the whole program of research, the so-called neo-connectionism, was possible thanks to developments in the study of multi-layered networks, an extension of Rosenblatt's original design that can overcome the limitations of the former by means of back-propagation algorithms, formulated in 1986 by David E. Rumelhart and Jay L. McClelland. Their *Parallel Distributed Processing: Explorations in the Microstructure of Cognition* is unanimously recognised as the starting point of today's renewed fortunes of ANN technology and applications (for philosophical approaches to connectionism see Churchland 1990; Clark 1989 and 1993; Smolensky 1988).

Even this sketchy summary is sufficient to show that ANN technology has achieved its successes only because it has abandoned its initial mimetic ambitions and has endorsed a purely engineering approach. ANNs are collections of mathematical structures with the ability to modify their format. They can be designed as computer models, but when they are implemented they are often software simulations rather than hardware systems, so that while a BNN is always "a piece of hardware" an ANN could be nothing more than a sub-routine written in C, which will typically have been automatically generated by a neural net development kit. Their design and modelling is driven by and tested against technological aims, and the construction of powerful analytical tools to solve a variety of practical problems is pursued by developing more efficient mathematical algorithms and architectures that can easily be transferred to silicon chips. Interestingly, the more they evolve, the less biologically plausible ANNs seem to become. This is not a problem, since neo-connectionism in computer science is a successful technology that is not concerned with physiological or psychological phenomena in BNNs and should not be confused with either neurophysiological, cognitive or philosophical theories. Of course, connectionism is also a neurobiological theory and a standard model of the brain and its functioning, but the fact that neurobiological connectionism is a successful programme of research does not mean that ANNs must have significant relevance for neurobiology, or that LAI could really benefit from a good understanding of information-processing in BNNs. As we shall see in a moment, the more we understand them the more we realise that biological networks have little to do with artificial ones, and if we exclude the handy use of some common terminology – which may also be rather misleading sometimes – it is often remarked that all ANNs have in common with BNNs is a couple on "Ns" in their name. Understandably, however, successes in computing and neurobiological connectionism have given rise to new hopes for an equally successful, yet old-fashioned "mimetic connectionism" in cognitive science and in the philosophy of mind. This is despite the anti-mimetic orientation of technological neo-connectionism, the non-technological nature of neurobiological connectionism, and the fact that actual ANNs work increasingly well precisely because they do not try to mimic biological nets anymore. The contradiction is obvious, and attempts to overcome it often lead to a number of popular mistakes. What follows is a small "gallery of errors".

(1) What ANNs can do.
In the "pro-mimetic" literature, artificial networks are often claimed to be "biologically plausible" because they show at least the following major "biological features":

- They can derive meaning from complicated or imprecise data.
- They are capable of abstraction.

- They can formulate predictions about possible future events.
- They are highly adaptive, and can mimic the human brain's most powerful ability, namely that of pattern recognition.

However, none of these anthropomorphic claims is actually supported by the technology in question:

(a) ANNs are useful complex tools for mapping patterns of data, but whether the latter are *meaningful* or not, and what their plausible meaning may be, remains up to the human user to establish. This also applies to the *post hoc* discovery of how a network has managed to generate the "meaningful" data it has achieved.

(b) ANNs' capacity to discover structural generalisations and similarities between different patterns is sometimes overemphasised in a way which reminds one of Locke's simplistic yet erroneous theory of how universal ideas are "constructed" from an elementary process of abstraction. Not only is a network not a magic hat out of which one may get new information not already present in the training examples – ANNs are not epistemically creative, and whatever information they can obtain from the data must already be encoded in the data – but the process of artificial as well as biological abstraction of similar features shared by a set of individual examples, while certainly capable of leading to the construction of a *more general* model (cf. Locke's universal idea), is always based on the assumption that all members of the set in question do share such similar features, since we need a well-defined membership rule to construct the initial set. In other words: a network may reconstruct the face of a burglar out of a limited number of snapshots, only if (i) the relevant features of the person are actually captured by the pictures and (ii) the latter are all of the same person – two silly requirements that are easily forgotten.

(c) ANNs can only provide projections from previous data, they do not "interpret" the future.

(d) ANNs are highly adaptive only as a *type* of technology but not as *tokens*. Each individual ANN stores "experiential knowledge" of the right way of mapping its patterns isomorphically, i.e. as a particular matrix of PEs and connection weights which represents the "solution" to a problem. Hence, each individual ANN is always a dedicated system, which is capable of mapping different kinds of patterns of data only if it is completely retrained, but retraining means the loss of the old format. To have more flexible solutions the best thing is to have hybrid systems of symbolic and connectionist computation, combining ANN technology with programming algorithms that can store and retrieve the specific formats of ANN-matrices (Minsky 1990 is in favour of the hybrid approach suggested here). One may think of the famous piece of wax in Descartes's hands. As a kind of substance the wax is highly malleable, meaning that a piece of wax can take any shape we may fancy, yet the same piece of wax can take only one shape at a time. Finally, it is plainly wrong to say that pattern recognition is the human brain's most powerful ability, but even if it were, ANNs do not mimic it. To understand why, we need to consider the next two popular errors.

(2) ANNs learn as human beings do.

The mistake here should already be clear from what has been said above, but let us consider a couple of examples from the standard literature. First case: a 4-input PE is trained to fire when the input is 1111, and not to fire when the input is 0000. After applying the generalisation rule the PE will also fire when the input is 0111, 1011, 1101, 1110 or 1111, it will not fire when the input is 0000, 0001, 0010, 0100 or 1000, and when any other input is present, such as 1001, it will produce a random output. Second case: we digitally input a photographic image for a neural network to identify, "guessing" which circuits to fire to recognise the photograph and output the correct answer. In both cases, we train the ANN by strengthening the connections between individual PEs (resistance turned down) when the task is performed correctly and weakening them (resistance turned up) if the task is performed incorrectly. In both cases, the neural network can "learn from its mistakes" and give more accurate output with each repetition of the process. Now, if a person behaved in the way just described we would be very worried indeed, for more than one good reason. First, neither a human brain nor a human being necessarily needs to be trained in an *iterative* way to learn to recognise a pattern, e.g. the shape of a new, strange-looking, revolving door in order to be able to evaluate whether one can pass through it. Second, not even Augustine – despite what Wittgenstein writes – held a naive theory of merely ostensive learning. Most of our cognitive organisation of the world surrounding us seems to require much more than mere exposure to spatial patterns, since it is usually associated at least with experiential memory, expectations, interaction, education and language, and is the result of a constructionist conceptualisation. Besides, human experience has the intrinsic propensity to become atomic. Two human beings do not recognise a particular pattern in the same way: one will immediately (non-inferentially) perceive a television screen, the other will immediately perceive a computer screen; one will immediately perceive a Triumph Spitfire 1300, the other only a car. The same individual, trained to recognise different types of cars, will have lost the capacity to see only vehicles. Third, it is odd to be forced to remind ANNs' supporters that a human brain can learn an infinite variety of tasks, including recognising an extraordinary range of patterns, but none of them "erase" the previous ones, yet we have just seen that this is the case with ANNs' matrices. ANNs are often praised for the massive parallelism of their computations, yet lacking short-term memories they are practically unable to do more than one thing at a time. Finally, there is the problem of levels of analysis. It is extremely unclear whether people defending the similarities between artificial and biological learning processes are limiting themselves to comparisons between an ANN and a brain, i.e. with the way in which neurons and synapses behave, or wish to extend the comparison to how people actually learn to recognise patterns. The frequent reference to a child learning to recognise the shape of a dog inclines one to suspect that the latter may be an unfortunate case, but then the absurdity is manifest, since one may learn to recognise the pattern of a graph, for example, by associating it with one's favourite shape of cake, a round pie, and neurological, psychological and mental levels, if they are levels and not just independent phenomena, should not be confused. The point is not worth pursuing any further, but if a comparison cannot be avoided altogether, then it is a bit less misleading to compare ANNs' training to the way in which photographic film is impressed by light.

(3) ANNs closely mimic the internal structure of the brain and closely simulate its behaviour.
A reply to the previous criticisms usually takes the form of a quick retreat and a counter-attack. Artificial networks are indeed different from biological brains because they implement a much simplified model. Nevertheless, the architecture and the processes are still very much the same, even if on a smaller scale, and by studying the former, we may learn a lot about the latter. There seems to be an odd mixture of mistakes here. To begin with, the contrast between ANNs and BNNs is not a mere matter of scale or magnitude but is essential, and current ANNs are not just incredibly simpler than BNNs, they are substantially different. What lies behind the opposite view is a combination of

- some form of functional associationism about how mental contents come to be shaped;
- a structural atomism, according to which the whole has at most only amplified properties inherited from its components, and grasping the nature of the most elementary components will lead to a reconstruction of the properties of the whole; and
- a methodological modularity, according to which the whole can be reconstructed piecemeal by a progressive combination of elementary components, and therefore functions that can be implemented correctly in a restricted domain can also be gradually enhanced until the domain eventually approaches the real world in complexity and other features.

But the first tenet is too naive, and the latter two are exceedingly simplistic. A complex ANN may consist of hundreds, perhaps even thousands, of PE and connections, but compared to a brain it has the complexity of a grain of sand, and it is hard to see how such an impoverished knowledge representation system can give rise to higher-order concepts or intellectual activities. The brain consists of about one trillion ($10^{12} = 1$ thousand billion) cells (neurons) with output fibres (axons) and a network of a thousand trillion (10^{15}) button-like terminals representing the endparts of the fibres (excitatory or inhibitory synapses), where each neuron receives an average of 5,000 inputs from the axons of other neurons. Now numbers here are not mere factors which allow us to grasp the nature of a BNN simply by multiplying by billions the features we find in an ANN. "Numerical advantage" is only another way of stressing the fact that systems have emergent as well as "submergent" properties: the former are not present in their parts but appear more and more distinctly only in whole combinations of them, the latter are present only in the parts and gradually disappear when the size of their bearers is scaled up, so "bigger" is usually equivalent to "different". These emergent/submergent properties often represent what is really interesting in the system. The rich texture of a pencil stroke, the sponginess and taste of a cake or the strength of an army are just a few simple cases of emergent properties; the lightness of a pebble, the brittleness of a sheet of paper and the actual computability of a problem are examples of submergent properties. Now, nobody would suggest that we may assess the strength of an army, for example, simply by observing the strength of a single platoon, even if the platoon was exemplary, nor would anybody think of attributing the mobility of a platoon to the whole army. Yet, in the case of the present comparison, to view ANNs as just smaller models of BNNs is like trying to reconstruct and understand the whole military history of World War II by looking at the behaviour of a platoon on a Pacific island (note that even then the relation is not correct, as there were only a few tens of millions of soldiers fighting). Not only is this not a merely quantitative problem, it is above all a matter of completely different properties. An atomist and modular approach in the philosophy of mind may, then, lead to a few initial successes concerning some elementary functions, typically in the area of conscious perceptual experience, but is bound to fail when more general explanations are required. As Dreyfus has written, climbing a tree is not a first successful step towards reaching the moon, it is the end of the story.

Although the life of the brain's electrochemical universe is still largely unexplored, we do know not only that neurons can promote, amplify, block, inhibit, and attenuate the micro-chemico-electric signals which are passed on to them and through them, somehow like PE, but also that, unlike PE, neurons are self-repairing and self-wiring; that there are many neurotransmitters of several different types (chemical agents that can transmit the activity of peripheral nerves on to their target organs) whose chemical properties, not just electrical intensity, deeply affect the behaviour of neurons; that the threshold membrane potentials in real neural networks are not completely plastic; and that they are probably not homogeneous processors. It turns out that even the platoon we are talking about belongs to a completely different army. The objection is often made that, no matter how macroscopic the differences may be, we are after all still dealing with the same logical models, and it is at this abstract level of description that similarities between ANNs and BNNs can and should be appreciated. The best that can be said in reply is that nobody denies that, historically, neural computing was loosely inspired by investigations into modelling nervous system learning, nor indeed that a simplistic and rather superficial analogy concerning the very general structure of both ANNs and BNNs can be drawn. Like the brain, we have seen that ANNs can be thought of as consisting of interconnected neurons linked together by synapses and capable of firing electro-chemical signals. What needs to be recognised is the crucial fact that this is as far as the analogy is worth pursuing, especially once we realise that, with a bit of effort, a logical model of London's traffic lights system could be provided on the same basis. Some people seem to forget that there is a very wide variety of different types of ANN, and that if a model, and not just one particular type of ANN, must be chosen as the proper interpretation of the brain (is the brain a Kohonen net, a simple back-propagation network, a Hopfield network, a Boltzmann network or what else?), then its logical description needs to be so generic as to become, in the end, uninformative.

(4) Symbolic *versus* connectionist approach is an ultimate alternative.
The success of ANNs is often explained on the basis of a philosophical assumption: if ordinary VNMs are unable to perform some intelligent tasks, most notably pattern recognition, this is because they lack the kind of structure and functioning we find in biological neural networks. By reproducing more closely the physical architecture of the brain – it is further argued – it will become possible to simulate brain functions increasingly well. From what has been said so far, it should be clear that such a view is mistaken because ANNs are not sufficiently similar to BNNs and because pattern recognition can be done successfully on conventional computers too, although writing the software is more difficult and time consuming, and the system will generally have a slower response. The symbolic approach – sometimes also called "classic", according to which the brain is just a physical symbol system, i.e. a mechanism for interpreting and manipulating formal representations – and the connectionist approach to GOFAI competed with each other for some time only because they were both mimetic, i.e. they both tried to devise the ultimate, unified theory of the brain, a goal that allowed only one winner. One may recall, for example, that the aim of McCulloch and Pitts was to show that an ANN could implement a Turing machine. But we know that neither a VNM nor an artificial neural network is necessarily meant to be a model of the brain or that it simulates its functioning closely enough, and that symbolic, software-based computers and connectionist, artificial neural networks only offer different approaches to computing that, contrary to popular belief, are not in competition but are complementary. So much so that ANNs are normally implemented on conventional computers and the latter are often used to supervise the neural network in order to perform at maximum efficiency. It turns out that a statement such as "artificial networks are better models of the brain than conventional algorithmic computers" is

not very helpful, for these are not alternatives. Both approaches can share the questionable mimetic view that the brain is a special instantiation of a computing machine.

Much more could be said on the topic, but I hope that the previous discussion has sufficiently clarified the main issues. There is no good reason to believe that ANNs and BNNs necessarily share anything more than a general conceptualisation of their models. The construction of ANNs was *inspired* by the discovery of the densely interconnected, parallel structure of the brain, and the construction of *neuromorphic systems* was an actual programme of research when GOFAI was still thought to be possible. It failed. Today, actual ANNs do not work successfully *because* they mimic the brain's structure and functioning, and the context of discovery should not be confused with the context of justification, nor taken together with the technological success of ANNs as a good reason to defend "mimetic connectionism" in philosophy or in cognitive science. The construction of ANNs does not need and can perfectly well afford to ignore any further "neural inspiration". As for "cognitive connectionism", in so far as it supports the general view that cognitive functions depend, as emerging properties, on neuro-chemical events distributed throughout the brain in processing elements linked by neural connections, its position is perfectly safe, if perhaps philosophically uninteresting. But when cognitive connectionism moves further, and attempts to reduce higher-order mental states, including consciousness and feelings, to such neural distribution, modelling the "sub-conceptual" level of description of cognitive processes using methods offered by technological ANNs, then it loses all neurological realism and much of its scientific value, opening the path to all kinds of speculation. ANNs do not resemble BNNs closely enough to attribute their successful performance to such an isomorphism, and technologically interesting applications will more easily escape our attention as long as we waste our resources trying to clone an electronic model of the brain in order to simulate its intelligent behaviour.

Parallel computing

ANN technology can be interpreted as a branch of parallel computing. As such, it is hardly the most successful, for the alternative, represented by CPU-based applications, is the most promising development for computing in the near future.

Suppose you are in a magic castle. All the rooms have one-way doors that allow you to move only in one direction. There is a treasure in the castle, and your task is to discover it. It is a search problem (where is the treasure?) which can easily be transformed into a decision-making one (is the treasure in room 1? Is it in room 2? etc.). The solution can be achieved by going through each room (the problem space) systematically. You would be acting as a *vector*. You may be lucky, and find the treasure in one of the first few rooms you visit, or the magic castle may be so big that you never enter the right room. How can you improve your chances of discovering what you are looking for? The options are few:

1   Run as fast as possible from one room to the other.
2   Improve the organisation of your searches, e.g. walk through the corridors looking inside the rooms without entering to them.
3   Ask Merlin to scale down the castle and make it as well-structured as possible. The number of rooms remains the same, but they are now small and placed in neat rows, so options 1 and 2 become even more efficient.

Of course, the castle/treasure/hunter system is just a very simplified analogy of a classic computer. We have seen that VNMs have remained conceptually the same since they were first invented. The real difference has been made by our ability to exploit their computational powers more and more successfully. Present computers have a faster clock, use better algorithms and have increasingly efficient architectures, while nanotechnology has greatly reduced the size of their circuits. Is this an endless process, that will allow us to find any treasure more and more quickly, or is there something that will escape our search for ever? Some reasons for pessimism are evident. There are physical boundaries to how many logic elements can be packed into smaller and smaller volumes and clocked at higher and higher frequencies. Below the threshold of 0.1 micrometre (and present technology has almost reached that threshold) circuit patterns begin to blur and the ultraviolet light currently used to etch them is absorbed before it reaches the surface. Correspondingly, at the atomic level very thin wires begin to interact, while they may not be able to withstand the current density required by the functioning of the chip. Then there is heat generation. The level of power dissipation of a transistor is incredibly high. Unfortunately, the smaller the device the more difficult it is to keep it cool and at a microlevel a transistor runs the risk of fusing itself. Finally, strategies (1) and (3) face the physical constraints represented by the speed of light and atomic scale (the value of research into optical computers – standard VNMs capable of processing very fast pulses of light instead of slower pulses of electricity – can better be appreciated from this perspective). Indeed, one may reckon that our technology is not very far from running up against these constraints. Strategy (2), however, offers a different perspective. Software development is largely a matter of human ingenuity and there is no theoretical boundary to the number of new algorithms that can be devised, or to the extent they can be further improved. This explains why (2) can also lead to a fourth solution of our treasure problem:

4   You may plan your search by organising a team of treasure hunters, e.g. by assigning a floor to each one of them.

This is known as parallel computing, and it is made possible by algorithms and procedures that can efficiently network and orchestrate multiple processors to execute parts of the same program simultaneously. The conceptual strategy is "Fordist" in nature, hence simple and powerful: the physical constraints, to which the computational power and maximum execution speed of a machine are subject, can partly be overcome if long and difficult instructions, constituting a single computing task (vectorial analysis) are broken down into smaller and easier instructions, which can then be more quickly executed independently of each other by a series of collaborating PEs, working simultaneously as components of a single *parallel processing computer* (PPC).

A common way to introduce a simple model of a PPC is by considering it a multicomputer, based on the Von Neumann model of computation – a number of CPUs, connected together into a network, access instructions and data from their own memories and execute different sub-tasks serially – or an abstract model of a parallel multiprocessor, called PRAM (Parallel Random Access Machine), in which identical processing units can access any element of a commonly shared memory in the same amount of time. More generally, we may say that a PPC consists of

- a set (from hundreds to thousands) of central processing units (often termed, in this case too, PE, processing elements) with a high computational rate, using a large and fast memory (either local or shared);
- high-speed interconnection network and/or bus connections linking the PEs. Traffic among the PEs may be more or less intense, since, depending on the architecture, the PEs may run independently of each other, possibly under the control of another processor, or may need to co-ordinate themselves constantly; and
- special algorithms (often written in Fortran77, C and C++) required to carry on the organisation and synchronisation of "parallel tasks", i.e. the temporal co-ordination and execution of the logically discrete sections constituting the computational work.

If future computers are able to perform any more "intelligent" tasks, this is very likely to be because of our improved capacity to make them work in teams. What cannot be sufficiently stupefied to become manageable by a single Von Neumann machine may be a pushover for an army of them. And yet a word of warning is in order. For it would be a mistake to assume that nothing can resist the "parallel force" of a PPC. We shall return to this problem in the next section. Here, we need to recall that, when evaluating the advantages of parallel computing, four essential factors must be taken into account, and these are sufficient to show the limits of any PPC.

(1) The appropriate nature of the problem to be solved
Not all computational problems are "parallelisable", i.e. suitable to logical partition of tasks, or such that they can really benefit from it. Problems that either lack a structured solution or have only a vectorial solution (a

concatenated solution with a serial structure in which there is a rigid, linear dependence between tasks, whose order of execution affects the results of the overall computation) present no logical features that a parallel system can fruitfully exploit. They can still be processed by a PPC, but their relative speed-up (the ratio between real time of serial execution and real time of parallel execution) is equal to 1. Compare two typical examples: the computation of the potential energy for each of several thousand independent conformations of a molecule and then of the minimum energy conformation is a parallelisable problem; the computation of the Fibonacci series (1, 1, 2, 3, 5, 8, 13, 21, ...) by use of the formulae $F_0 = 0$; $F_1 = 1$; $F_{n+2} = F_{n+1} + F_n$, for $n \geq 0$ allows only a linear approach. In this case, a PPC would be no more useful than a standard computer.

(2) The appropriate nature of the parallel architecture used to treat (1)
Suppose we are dealing with a fruitfully parallelisable problem, such as our treasure-hunting problem. What kind of parallel architecture is best suited to treat it? Parallel computing functions can be implemented in several ways. Flynn's classical taxonomy – based on the combination of the number of instructions which can be executed at a time, and the number of data (data streams) on which a computer can operate at a time – distinguishes between four classes:

(a) SISD (*single instruction and single data stream*): This is the traditional model of a sequential computer (VNM), such as the simple PC discussed in Chapter 2, in which instructions are executed one by one, on a unique series of data retrieved from memory. Note that if a SISD machine needs to perform the same instruction on many different data, then it must fetch the same instruction many times, once for each datum. Things get even worse when there are loops that force the machine to execute many instructions for each piece of data. Because of this architecture, an ordinary VNM can perform much more slowly than the arithmetic unit is capable of doing.

(b) SIMD (*single instruction and multiple data streams*): This multiprocessor machine is one of the typical models of a PPC: all PEs execute the same instruction (search for the treasure) synchronously, but on their own data (in different series of rooms) retrieved from their own local memory, under the control of a supervising CPU.

(c) MIMD (*multiple instruction and multiple data stream*): This is the typical multiprocessor model of a PPC, in which synchronisation is no longer a necessary requirement, and each PE can execute different instructions on its own data, and communicate asynchronously whenever needed.

(d) MISD (*multiple instruction and single data stream*): This is not an implemented model of computation.

Another standard classification of parallel systems, based on memory and communication models, turns out to be orthogonal to Flynn's:

(i) SM (shared memory) system, in which multiple PEs access and use the same global memory, communicating very rapidly via common memory locations, so that a PE writes to a location, and another reads from it;

(ii) DM (distributed memory) system, in which each PE has its own local memory, and communicates (more slowly than in (i)) with other PEs by creating and sending data packets (messages) which are received and used by other PEs. DM systems are therefore also known as "distributed memory, message passing systems".

Combinations of (b)–(c) and (i)–(ii) give rise to hybrid models and, more significantly, to shared memory MIMD systems and distributed memory MIMD systems. Now, different parallel architectures may be more or less appropriate to solve different parallel problems, depending on the "granularity" of the latter, i.e. the amount of computation that can be done in parallel tasks. Granularity of parallelism ranges from fine to coarse. If the granularity is fine, then the task has a high degree of modularity (its solution can be reduced to a large but still finite series of sub-tasks, each of them rather small in terms of number of instructions and execution time) and requires a low degree of distributed computational power (only a limited amount of computational power is needed to carry on each sub-task). If the granularity is coarse, then the degree of modularity of the problem is low and the required degree of distributed computational power is high (the solution can be reduced to a rather small series of sub-tasks, and each of them can be solved concurrently but using a large amount of computing power). Clearly, the more finely grained a problem is the greater the potential for parallelism and hence speed-up are and the better it can be computed by means of a SIMD system, whereas the more coarsely grained it is, the more suitable a MIMD system will be. However, the finer the granularity, the greater will be the parallel overheads (time wasted in running parallel tasks as opposed to executing computational instructions) of I/O tasks, synchronisation and communication latency (time wasted by a PE waiting for messages to be sent/received; this is not to be confused with bandwidth communication overhead, which refers to the rate at which data are exchanged between PEs). In addition, there will be an increased risk of other serial bottlenecks (lists of instructions that must necessarily be executed one after the other), negative load imbalance (an uneven distribution of work among parallel tasks resulting in some PEs being idle while waiting to begin the next computational instructions) and even deadlocks (all tasks waiting to receive data, but no one sending them).

(3) The specific elaboration of appropriate algorithms to match (1) and (2)
Even if a problem can be successfully parallelised by exploiting the right architecture, parallel methods still require the elaboration of specifically designed algorithms. Everyone is acquainted with the difficulties inherent in

co-operative problem solving, which usually need a clear assignation of tasks and a rather firm division, if not a hierarchy, of responsibilities. Likewise, detailed and precise instructions for partitioning the overall problem into separate tasks and allocating tasks to processors are vital. Methodologically, parallel software should then satisfy four conditions:

- modularity (the partition of complex tasks into more simple sub-task components);
- high concurrency (capacity of parallel multi-tasking);
- high scalability (capacity to maintain a satisfactory performance when the number of processors involved increases); and
- (possibly) high locality (maximum reduction of time spent in send/ receive processes in favour of read/write processes), since access to data stored in local (same PE) memory is less time-consuming than access to data stored in remote (different PE) memory.

(4) Efficiency of the parallelisation (low degree of overhead) and the upper limit of parallelisation

There are limits to how far a problem can fruitfully be treated by a multi-processor system and the boundary of efficient parallelisation is well formu-lated by Amdahl's Law (named after Gene Amdahl): if 1.0 denotes the whole computational task, and S is the fraction of the computation task that is intrinsically sequential (at least the unparallelisable I/O stage), then $1.0 - S$ is the fraction of the computation that can be parallelised, and the ideal max-imum degree of speed-up achievable using N processors is given by the ratio $1.0/(S + (1.0 - S)/N)$. Of course, Amdahl's Law ignores all other real-life fac-tors, but it is useful to clarify two facts. First, the speed-up tends towards but can never be equal to 10, the more processors we employ in our system, since every computational problem has a sequential component that will eventually limit the speed-up of its parallelised version. Second, and more interestingly, there is an optimum threshold of costs/benefits beyond which adding more processors is no longer worthwhile. For example, assuming that the problem is 90 per cent parallelisable, that $S = 0.1$, and that a system has

- 5 processors, we will have an ideal speed-up $= 1.0/(0.1 + (1.0 - S)/5) = c.$ 3.57
- 50 processors, we will have an ideal speed-up $= 1.0/(0.1 + (1.0 - S)/$ $50) = c.$ 8.47
- 500 processors, we will have an ideal speed-up $= 1.0/(0.1 + (1.0 - S)/$ $500) = c.$ 9.82.

Clearly, the effective jump is from 5 to 50 processors, while adding another 450 processors is exceedingly expensive and does not speed up the perform-ance of the system significantly. More technically, the slope of the function can be directly related to the degree of scalability of a parallel system, to which the addition of more processors (additional CPUs are added to absorb the increased transaction volume or more complex processes) yields a proportionate increase in parallel speed-up. More trivially, two people working on the same task are much better than one, but three may not make a big difference, while four may be a hindrance.

In the short history of computing, parallel technology is a relatively new phenomenon. In 1982 two Cray-1 supercomputers linked in parallel (the Cray X-MP) proved to be three times faster than a single Cray-1, and the following year Thinking Machines Corp. and Ncube began to promote parallel processing as a commercially viable solution. Because of their power, PPCs are also sometimes known as *supercomputers*, while they have also been denoted by the expression *high performance computers* because of the HPCC programme (High Performance Computing and Communications) launched by the US Government in 1991, although in both cases the expressions included other systems not necessarily based on parallel architectures. In 1997, only one of the twenty fastest supercomputers relied on a vectorial approach; all the others were parallel processors. This advancement in parallel computing caused the USA to become the leading country once again in a sector which had been dominated by the Japanese industry since 1990: sixteen of the supercomputers in question were built by American companies, only four in Japan.

This short history does not mean that the advantages of a PPC are either marginal or unclear. On the contrary, given the same computational power, it is already becoming more cost-effective to produce a PPC using a number of fairly fast but inexpensive processors, whose cumulative memory can also be very large, than a PC based on the last Intel model. Interestingly, dual-processor capability was already a required feature for entry-level workstations during the first quarter of 1998. A dual-processor PC has a motherboard that contains two CPUs and is designed to run an OS such as Windows NT, which supports symmetric multiprocessing (SMP). SMP is a multiprocessing, scalable architecture in which two or more CPUs, connected via a high-bandwidth, share the same memory and hence the same programs, and are managed by the same OS in a roughly non-hierarchical way ("roughly" because one of the CPUs is still responsible for the booting procedures). The presence of more than one CPU may improve fault resilience – the system may still be able to work with only one processor available – and obviously boosts the performance of the system, since applications can be run by the several processors interchangeably, and all multi-threaded applications, multi-tasking or concurrent operations are parallelisable and can be executed simultaneously. This is not yet full parallelism, for software is not specially written for multiprocessor computers, but it certainly represents an interesting step towards it.

In a world more and more pervaded by digital networks, it is to be hoped that PPCs will be able to take advantage of the growing distributed computational power that is increasingly becoming available. It is already possible to devise a networked computer as a PPC, rather than just a dumb terminal. Distributed computing and the possibility of concentrating computational resources on important computational problems is one of the next crucial challenges for ICT. PPCs address the possibility of scaling up some computational problems (solving bigger problems in the same time) rather than just speeding them up (solving the same problems in less time). This means widening the possibilities for computational applications. I remarked in Chapter 1 that numerical models and simulations are a fundamental complement to theory and experimentation in engineering and scientific research and have also become crucial for the development of entertainment products. Computational enquiry is more and more often employed in the study or reproduction of all sorts of phenomena that are either too complex (e.g. because of the time scale), expensive or dangerous to be dealt with directly, through realistic physical experiments. The number of fields of application is constantly increasing, and include what have been identified, within the HPCC project, as the "Grand Challenges": fundamental problems in science and engineering, with potentially broad social, political, and scientific impact, that can be advanced by applying high performance (including massively parallel) computing resources. The following list is an extract from http: //www.ccic.gov/pubs/imp97/48.html:

1   Computational chemistry (CC): parallelise key chemistry codes that permit researchers to study environment problems, using techniques such as self-consistent field (SCF), second-order many-body perturbation theory (MP2), and Configuration Interaction (CI) codes.
2   Computational structural biology: develop methods for modelling components of genomes and a parallel programming environment for structural biology.
3   Mathematical combustion modelling (MCM): develop adaptive parallel algorithms for computational fluid dynamics and apply these methods to key problems in commercial burner design.
4   Quantum chromodynamics calculations: develop lattice gauge algorithms on massively parallel machines for high energy and particle physics applications.
5   Oil reservoir modelling: construct efficient algorithms for parallel systems to model fluid flow through permeable media for better oil recovery methods from wells.
6   The numerical Tokamak project: develop and integrate particle and fluid plasma models on MPPs as part of a study of Tokamak fusion reactors.
7   Global climate modelling (GCM): develop and implement versions of large-scale atmosphere and ocean general circulation models for MPPs.

8   Groundwater transport and remediation (GTR): design and implement a multiphase groundwater transport code with interface tracking, fracture flow, microtransport.

9   First principles simulation of materials properties: develop scalable parallel algorithms for performing local density approximation simulations of materials to novel properties for the Materials Properties Grand Challenge (MPGC).

At the end of FY 1996, Phase I of the GC program was terminated. An RFP was published for Phase II of the program with project starts early in FY 1997. The intent and grant procedures of Phase II are similar to Phase I but the projects now incorporate [an] infrastructural component to insure that the projects have the computational resources to complete their proposed goals.

This is a list that standard literature on the topic easily extends to include the improvement of services such as airline scheduling, mutual fund management, or video-on-demand; environmental modelling of past and potential air and ground pollution; car crash simulation; integrated design and manufacturing systems; design of new drugs for the pharmaceutical industry by modelling new compounds; simulation of electromagnetic and network properties of electronic systems, and so forth. These numerical models, simulations and applications require a tremendous amount of computing power which goes well beyond the resources of traditional sequential computing systems and can be provided only by massively parallel computing systems (MPPS), capable of performing more than three teraflops (three trillion floating-point operations per second). As a result, it is easy to predict that the next era of computing is going to be dominated by parallel technology. There remains a major, methodological problem, however, which is widely acknowledged but which only time will solve. For decades, the whole world of computer science and technology has focused on monoprocessor architectures. All that work now needs to be reconsidered. There is a great need for scientific and technological research on software, operating systems, programming languages, algorithms, applications, hardware implementations, programming tools and methods and other standards for parallel computing. This is probably the greatest of all challenges faced by PPC technology.

It may not be long before PPCs are as common as PCs, and one may wonder whether by then the philosophy of mind will have been influenced by the new computational model of not-ANN parallel processing as much as it has been by Turing machines, neural networks, and the now-fashionable quantum computer models.

Computational complexity

When searching our magic castle, in the previous sections, we have noticed that strategies (1)–(4) are still insufficient to solve all theoretically computable problems. To understand why, we need to introduce a few more technical explanations (Garey and Johnson 1991; Jones 1997; Lewis and Papadimitriou 1998; Moret 1998; Sipser 1997).

A computational problem P has a *descriptive* and a *computational* complexity. The descriptive complexity of P is a precise indication of the "semiotic" costs incurred in the description of P in some logical formalism, in terms of the amount of symbolic resources required by the codification of P. The computational complexity of P connotes its degree of difficulty, and is a precise indication of the costs incurred in the computation of the solution of P. It is calculated in terms of the relative amount of resources employed by an algorithm A – or, equivalently, by a Turing machine TM implementing it – to complete its task and solve the problem, independently of the programming language in which the algorithm is written (hence computational complexity does not refer to the size of the algorithm or the nature of the hardware). The two forms of complexity are mathematically related, but in this context we need to concentrate only on computational complexity.

We already know from Chapter 2 that the main resources used by a computer are time and memory space, so when we talk about the computational complexity of P we may refer to either

- its space complexity (SC) = the amount of storage memory required by TM to run A and solve P, or
- its time-complexity (TC) = the amount of time required by TM to run A and solve P.

Given SC and TC, the overall complexity of a problem can be classified according to the rate of growth of the memory space and the time required to solve it. Now, time complexity is usually taken to be more important because space is re-usable, so let us further limit our attention to TC.

TC is calculated in terms of number of time steps that the algorithm takes, as a function of the problem size, and for the worst case input. In Chapter 2, we saw that the size of the data to be manipulated by an algorithm to solve a problem can be quantified in terms of the number of symbols and length of tape used by TM as input. Assuming that n gives the measure of the length of the data input x to be computed by TM to solve P, we can organise computable problems into classes depending on their n. The standard way of describing complexity classes is by classifying formal languages Ls that can represent decision problems and can be recognised (i.e. solved) by a TM, but in this context we may adopt a more informal approach. Let us suppose that A is a specific algorithm for solving a particular class of problems C and that TM_A is a Turing machine implementing A. We know that TM_A must perform a certain number of operations O on its x data to solve $P \in C$ before it halts (if TM_A does not halt then O remains undefined, see the halting problem in Chapter 2) or, more briefly, that $O(TM_A, x)$. The complexity function $f_A(n)$, for all non-negative integers n, now gives an upper limit to the maximum number of elementary operations that TM_A needs to perform on x of size n to solve P. This gives us

the complexity function: $f_A(n) = \max (O(TM_A, x)$ for $|x| = n)$.

The complexity function indicates the *running time* of the algorithm A, but does it also indicate the time-complexity of the corresponding class of problems C? Not yet, because there can be several known algorithms $\{A_1, \ldots, A_m\}$ and therefore TMs for solving the same class of problems. Since they may have different degrees of efficiency, the time-complexity of C or (for the sake of simplicity) C complexity must be defined as being equivalent to the *lowest* degree of complexity of the best algorithm, among all known algorithms devised to solve C, based on the data input set x that results in the *longest* possible time, that is

$$TC(P) = \min (f_1(n), \ldots, f_m(n)).$$

The formula indicates how the number of operations required for the solution of P may vary depending on n according to the most efficient algorithm. For example, if the best algorithm to solve P has complexity $TC = n^2$ this means that, when the size of the data input of P doubles, the solution requires at most four times as many operations. We say *at most* because, as in the magic castle, the computer could find the solution before that, hence the function sets only the upper limit, the highest degree of bad luck, as it were, indicating the worst-case complexities.

Of course, if we assume that TM_A halts and hence that O does not remain undefined, then $f_A(n)$ is bounded, either polynomially or exponentially. To understand how, let us organise best algorithms and corresponding problems into a hierarchy of classes having increasing degrees of complexity. We can start from

(*P*) *the class of polynomial-time complexity problems*

These are problems which require algorithms whose time-complexity increases in constant linear or at most polynomial relation with the size of the input x. A polynomial is an algebraic expression consisting of a sum of terms, each of which is a product of a constant and one or more variables or indeterminates raised to a non-negative integral power. If there is only a single variable y, the general form is given by $a_0x^n + a_1x^{n-1} + a_2x^{n-2} + \ldots + a_{n-1}x + a^n$, for example $2x^4 + 3x^3 + 5x + 7$. When the highest power of the polynomial x (i.e. the degree *deg* of the polynomial) is 0 we have a constant time-complexity function, when deg = 1 we have a linear function, for deg > 1 (in the given example d = 4) we have a polynomial function. In each case, since the number of elementary operations required by TM to solve P with a data input x of size n – that is, the function $(O(TM_A, x)$ for $|x| = n)$ – increases with *n* no more rapidly than a polynomial in n, the algorithm implemented by TM is said to be executable in polynomial time and the problem itself to have a polynomial complexity. The number of operations is never larger than some constant multiple c of n raised to some fixed power k, that is, $O \leq c \times n^k$, so the complexity of problems in the class *P* grows slowly enough to make the corresponding algorithms usually computable by a *deterministic* Turing machine (or perhaps a group of them) efficiently in a reasonable time, that is, algorithms that solve polynomially bounded problems run in polynomial time. As an elementary example, you may think of an algorithm to find the treasure as $f(n) = 5R$, where 5 is the number of boxes to be searched in each room and R the number of rooms. Increases of R will not cause the complexity of the problem to escalate beyond control. Algorithms for problems in *P* are said to be polynomially bounded and efficient for run-time.

If TM is a non-deterministic Turing machine – that is, it consists of a guessing TM that writes a guessed solution on the basis of some arbitrary internal algorithm, and a deterministic TM that evaluates in polynomial time the guesses by a 1 or a 0, to check if the solution is correct – we can speak of

(*NP*) *the class of non-deterministic polynomial-time complexity problems*

This is the class of problems for which we can check solutions in polynomial time by a non-deterministic TM. The number of steps required by TM to *check* a solution of an *NP* problem is still a polynomial function of the size of the input. Without the *NP* class, many algorithms that are statistically tractable would not be considered computable within a reasonable (i.e. polynomial) time on the basis of strategy (1) (running faster) simply because of the limits affecting the linear process of a deterministic TM. Of course, every problem in *P* is also in *NP*.

Among *NP* problems, we find two important classes:

(*NP*-hard) *the class of non-deterministic polynomial-time hard complexity problems*

These are problems for which there is a polynomial-time reduction to *NP*-complete problems, and

(*NPC*) *the class of non-deterministic polynomial-time complete complexity problems* (*NP*-complete)

NP-complete problems are special problems in *NP*. If a problem is *NP*-complete then it is extremely unlikely (though this has not been proved) that there is an efficient algorithm to solve it *deterministically* in polynomial time. Two famous *NP*-complete problems are

- The travelling salesman problem: a salesman wishes to perform a tour of a given number of cities, calling at each city once and only once and travelling the minimum total distance possible, and
- William Hamilton's problem in graph theory: given a n-vertices graph – a collection of vertices and edges G (V, E) – we wish to discover whether

there is a Hamiltonian circuit in G (the calculation of the presence of a cycle of edges in G, i.e. a linear path, through which every n ∈ V is visited once and only once).

In terms of computational complexity, both problems are demonstrably equivalent.

A problem P_1 is said to be a member of the *NPC* class if and only if any other problem P_x in *NP* can be functionally reduced to it in polynomial time ($P_x < = p\ P_1$), that is, if P_1 is in *NPC* then it has the property that a polynomial-time solution for it would provide a polynomial-time solution for any P_x in *NP* as well. Of course, if a member of *NPC* could be proved to be functionally reducible to a problem in *P* this would prove the more general result *NP = P*. Whether this equation is correct is one of the most important open problems in computational theory. So far, it is known that $P \subseteq NP$ but all attempts to prove that *NP = P* have been unsuccessful. This is often, though not necessarily, interpreted as evidence that no *NP-complete* problem is actually *P*-solvable, so that $P \neq NP$ and $NP \supset P$. This remains only a reasonable conjecture.

Problems in *P* or *NP* are sufficiently economical in terms of resources required for their solutions. Computable problems for which no polynomially bounded algorithm is known but which can be solved by exponentially bounded algorithms, belong to a higher-order class of *intractable* problems, that is:

(EXP) the class of *exponential*-time algorithms, whose complexity increases according to a function that raises x to the power of its argument, i.e. $f\,n = x^n$.

Suppose one needs to make 5^R operations to discover the treasure, where R is still the number of rooms in the castle. The algorithm will be $O(5^R)$, and for any extra room Morgan Le Fay adds to the castle to hide her treasure one will have to carry out an exponentially higher number of operations.

Is there any way we can solve problems of class *EXP* via strategies (1) and (3) (running faster and scaling down the space)? We have seen that the answer is in the negative. Now that we know what a *NPC* or *EXP* problem is, we can describe intractable problems as problems which have no polynomial time solutions. There are *completely intractable* problems, i.e. problems that cannot be solved by any algorithm, such as the halting problem, Hilbert's tenth problem (solvability in integers of an arbitrary polynomial equation $P = 0$ with integral coefficients) or the several problems of "tiling the plane". In Chapter 2, we have defined them as *undecidable*. Then there are *decidable* but *intractable* problems, which are solvable in principle, but cannot be solved in polynomial time even if we use a non-deterministic system with the ability to pursue an unbounded number of independent computational sequences in parallel. We define these problems as *non-deterministically intractable*. Unlike polynomial-time problems, exponential-time problems are non-deterministically intractable and their solutions very quickly become impractical even for reasonably small values.

One of the most significant examples is the problem posed by the prime factorisation of integers. In Chapter 2, we encountered the multiplication of two primes 149×193 and the factorisation of their product 28,757. We can now say that multiplication belongs to P, while factorisation belongs to EXP. A five-digit number may require an hour's work to be factorised by trial and error, and although there are some good algorithms for relatively small integers, less than 120 decimal digits long, a 240-digit integer would already require billions of years to be factorised by the fastest algorithms available. This is owing to the fact that all universal algorithms devised so far for a "Newtonian" system have exponential complexity. The amount of time they need in order to find the prime factors of a number grows as an exponential function of the size of the number and very quickly the problem becomes computationally intractable, not in principle (recall the unbounded resources of a TM), but in practice. This is why systems for data encryption rely on factoring algorithms. No matter how far we improve the speed and the architecture of our present hardware, there is no way a *classical* computer can discover, in a reasonably short time, the factors that break the code if the number in question is a few hundreds digits long.

The potential growth in the computational performance of our present hardware is constrained by the laws of physics. A computer remains a physical device, time is a finite resource, and computable problems which demand too much of it are bound to remain forever unprocessable by monoprocessor machines, even if we know how to reach a solution, simply because there is not enough time to compute it. You may think of such problems as very distant planets that we know how to locate but shall never be able to visit, even if a whole colony of human beings was willing to travel for thousands of years.

The treasure in the castle can be beyond your reach. Or perhaps that is just how it seems. For, on the one had, we may hope that strategies (2) (improving the algorithms being used) and (4) (parallel computing) will allow us partly to overcome some of our hardware limits. After all, nobody has proved that there can be no polynomial-time algorithm for the factoring problem. On the other hand, there is one more radical strategy, concerning (1) and (3), which still needs to be taken into account. Conditions (1)–(4) try to improve the time-consuming nature of our search. In exploring the castle, we rely on the same basic sequential logic that determines the physical constraints of classic computers. The key word in classical computing is therefore *sequential time*, no matter whether it is shortened by spreading it over a number of parallel processors. Computational problems with an exponential-time degree of complexity prove that there is a physical limit to how far the *chronological features* of the hardware of a Turing machine working sequentially can be improved. But if *hardware* is constrained by *physics*, we may need to change the former (parallel computing) or the latter. Imagine you could step out of the castle and have a look at it as if you had a plan in front of you. You could see immediately where the treasure is, and get it at once, no matter how many rooms there are. Quantum computing attempts to step outside the physical limits of our standard computers and build a machine that enjoys such an external perspective, i.e. a discrete, non-deterministic Turing machine in which the physico-topological features of the hardware have been completely transformed. In theory, this means trying to overcome the constraints limiting our present Newtonian systems to take advantage of features offered by quantum systems. Stepping outside is a space move and the new key word becomes *quantum states*. In more detail, this requires a radically new way of codifying data and a new way of processing them.

Quantum computing

Conceptually, the architectures of a conventional and a quantum computer do not really differ: QCs are quantum TMs that implement algorithms that obey the laws of quantum physics, and it is possible to interpret quantum physics as a theory of physical information (on computational limits see Bennett and Landauer 1985; on quantum technology see Milburn 1996; Deutsch 1997 provides a conceptual approach). Data are uploaded as registers, which are then processed via logic-gate operations to achieve the desired computation under the control of an algorithm, and the results of the computation are encoded as further data registers until the output is finally made available to the user. The essential difference is precisely in the physics of the whole process. A conventional computer encodes, stores and processes discrete n-data registers according to a Newtonian physics which allows each bit of data to be only in one fully determined, definite state at a time. Hence a conventional bit is either 0/off or 1/on and can represent only a single value. A quantum computer QC, on the other hand, exploits the possibility of quantum states of atomic particles to store data registers in a *definable* but still *undetermined* quantum *superposition* of two states at the same time. The two logical states (known as "eigenstates") are represented by $|1>$ and $|0>$, and a quantum bit (*qubit*) is a two-level system that can be set in any superposition $|\psi>$ of these two *coexisting* states:

$$|\psi> = c_0|0> + c_1|1>$$

Now the coefficients c_i can vary, but we may simplify here by adopting the formula $a|0> + b|1>$, where the coefficients a and b (represented by complex numbers) are the amplitudes of each state normalised constant (so that $a + b = 1$), and can roughly be thought of as indicating the probability that the qubit will be found in that state (in other words, you can read $a|0>$ as loosely meaning "there is an 'a' number of chances that the qubit will be found in the 0 state"). This does not mean that a qubit has only a statistical existence, as some intermediate value between 0 and 1, or that it can be fuzzified. A qubit is actually in both the 0-state and the 1-state *simultaneously*, although possibly to different extents, which can be viewed as probabilities quantified by the amplitudes. It is a vacillating monad of information, and it is only once its state is observed or measured that it invariably collapses to either 0 or 1. This natural phenomenon of superposition, physically present in quantum-mechanical two-level systems such as spin-½ particles or two-level atoms, is strongly counter intuitive, for common sense finds it difficult to grasp how a qubit could be in two opposite states simultaneously. Unfortunately, conceptual explanations often prove even more incredible and metaphysically obscure than the factual explanandum they try to rationalise or make sense of. In this context, the philosophy student may perhaps take advantage of her acquaintance with Hegel's dialectics and look at quantum superposition $|\psi>$ in terms of *Aufhebung* (sublation), a process whereby contradictory positions are reconciled in a higher unity by being both annulled and preserved (*aufgehoben*) in their synthesis at the same time (an Hegelian example is finite and infinite in the synthesis of the absolute).

Once qubits are introduced as *aufgehoben* data units, the next step is to consider quantum logic gates that may perform Boolean operations upon quantum-mechanical superpositions of states, to generate other superpositions and eventually the desired output. Special logic-gates have to be devised to control the interaction between qubits and generate coherent change in their states. Having modified the very physics of information storage, the implementation of a probabilistic logic of computation of amplitudes must also be adopted. Quantum gates for logical operations such as NOT (this flips a spin-over) √NOT (this flips a spin only halfway, leaving it in a superposition of spin up and spin down) and XOR (the exclusive or) on qubits are perfectly possible mathematically. The desired output of quantum computations is obtained through the measurement of the quantum-mechanical probability amplitudes of the resulting qubits. Superposition, atomic interference to modify the state of qubits, quantum gates and operations on amplitudes finally make possible a QC whose computations involve two or more different qubits.

A QC can now be described as an exponential, non-deterministic Turing machine. To understand its extraordinary computational power, let us compare two data-register machines searching for a particular pattern among all possible combinations of 8 bits. A conventional 8-bit register computer can only operate sequentially on one of its 256 possible states at a time (2^8, all the 8-digits sequences that can be obtained from combinations of 0s and 1s). To prepare each state of a Newtonian register of n states a classical computer needs n operations. Take now an 8-qubit register QC. Let us assume, for the sake of simplicity, that the amplitudes of the superposition of each qubit are such that measurement of the qubit will result in the $|0>$ state with a "probability" of 0.5, and the $|1>$ state also with a "probability" of 0.5. We can load the quantum register in polynomial time to represent all 2^8 states simultaneously, because n elementary operations can generate a state containing 2^n possible states. Each of the 256 combinations has an equal probability of turning up with each measurement, and a single QC can now perform 2^8 operations at once, sifting through all the qubit patterns simultaneously. This is known as *quantum parallelism*, as opposed to standard parallel computing. In theory and simplifying a little, the elementary parallel system introduced in the section entitled "Parallel computing" as a network of Von Neumann machines would have to co-ordinate 2^8 PEs to achieve the same result in one operation. Having the whole matrix of 2^8 states in front of itself in one operation, a QC can explore all possible solutions of the problem simultaneously. Constructive and destructive interference with the qubits suppresses irrelevant patterns and enhances those that are interesting, and the QC finds the particular pattern it is searching for in only one computation. We have stepped outside the castle and found the treasure in a moment, by looking at the map, as it were.

The larger its register, the more exponentially powerful a QC becomes, and a QC with a register of 64 qubits could outsmart any network of supercomputers. Quantum computers, if physically implemented, would then represent utterly new types of machine, qualitatively alternative to our present VNMs. They could perform massively parallel computations, not by organising many processors working in tandem, but thanks to a quantum processor which would operate on coherent superpositions of qubits simultaneously. We can even speculate about the computational power of a network of QCs and quantum super-parallelism. QC could solve, in polynomial time, problems that we have seen require an exponential time for an ordinary computer. This also includes prime number factorisation, as Peter Shor proved by developing in 1994 the first quantum-mechanical algorithm for factoring efficiently (Shor 1994). Thanks to Shor's algorithm, a QC with the same clock speed as an ordinary PC could break the keys of any factoring-based cryptosystem, such as the widely used RSA, in a few seconds, while the problem remains simply intractable for a PC. Owing to the crucial importance of such a practical application, Shor's algorithm has had a remarkable impact and since its appearance, it has prompted a sudden increase of interest in quantum computing.

Quantum computing is a very young discipline. Richard P. Feynman was probably the first to address the possibility of a new quantum dynamics for computers that could mimic the behaviour of any finite physical object (Feynman 1982). In 1981, Paul Benioff applied quantum theory to computing problems, devising a quantum-mechanical simulation of a Turing machine. In 1985, David Deutsch devised a Turing-like conceptual model of a QC, proving that there is a "Universal QC" which can compute anything that a finite machine obeying the laws of quantum computation can compute (Deutsch 1985). Deutsch's important proof provides us with a quantum equivalent of the Turing Theorem for UTM: there exists a Quantum Universal Turing machine that can simulate any given Quantum Turing machine with only a polynomial slow-down. Since the 1980s then, the relationship between information theory and quantum mechanics has become increasingly clear, together with the potential advantages of a QC and the formidable engineering problems associated with its physical implementation. The potential advantages are intuitive. Such great computational power may force us to re-think the very concept of problems' complexity (Simon 1994). Not only would QCs make present applications in cryptography, based on factoring difficulties, obsolete, they would also provide new means to generate absolutely secure cryptosystems (based on wave-function collapse) and, more generally, transform into trivial operations statistical computations that are of extraordinary complexity. Physicists could then use QCs as powerful new modelling tools to investigate quantum mechanics' hypotheses and phenomena that are computationally too complex for our present technology.

Unfortunately, the difficulties in building an actual QC may turn out to be insurmountable. "Newtonian computing" is based on the fact that topological resources (space, location, stability of physical states, etc.) are not a major problem, but time is. Quantum computing deals with the chronological difficulties of Newtonian computing by means of an ontological shift in the theory of complexity. The relation between computational time and space is inverted and time becomes less problematic than space if it is possible to transform quantum phenomena of superposition, which are short-lasting and uncontrollable at a microscopic level, into quantum phenomena that are sufficiently long-lasting and controllable at a macroscopic level to enable computational processes to be implemented. Quantum computation is achievable only if this ontological shift becomes empirically feasible, and this in turn is possible only if we can design and build a technology that can

1   lower the technological level at which we can successfully control quantum phenomena. This includes the scalability of technical devices;
2   extend the time-length of the quantum phenomena supporting the computation. This means opposing the decay process, by which a quantum system dissipates energy in the environment, caused by the coupling of the system with the environment;
3   isolate the QC from the outside environment completely, while computations are taking place. This means adopting a completely reversible logic. The physics of "Newtonian" computation is such that whenever a bit of information is erased a small amount of energy is given up in the environment as heat (this is known as Landauer's principle, see Milburn 1996 for an introduction). Ordinary computers waste enormous amounts of energy because they implement an irreversible logic (you cannot reconstruct the input from the output), and thus they are coupled with the environment, through which they can get rid of their heat, but it is

possible (though far from easy) to devise reversible gates which in principle do not dissipate any energy into the environment, and therefore allow a QC to be fully isolated;

4 allow a QC to interact with quantum phenomena indirectly (any direct approach affects the nature of its reference) without causing their decoherence. To perform a successful quantum computation, a QC needs to maintain a coherent unitary evolution of the quantum phenomena involved until the computation is completed. The destruction of the coherent state is known as the phenomenon of decoherence and refers to the high propensity of quantum states to lose their superposition properties – what I have described as their *aufgehoben* equilibrium – through mutual interaction within the system;

5 satisfy (1)–(3) on a sufficiently large scale to generate a quantitatively usable amount of computational resources.

Without (1)–(4) there can be no efficient quantum computations, but it is doubtful whether each requirement can actually be satisfied to a satisfactory degree and, if so, whether the increasing implementations of these requirements are mutually compatible. The difficulty of the overall task of building a QC is shown by the fact that we seem to be coming close to wishing for a contradiction come true: quantum phenomena should retain their properties and yet modify them. We know that QCs are theoretically possible: the modellisation of virtual quantum machines has determined the development of research during the last decade. But so far the possibility of quantum computing on an interesting scale has been proven only mathematically, and in practice no elementary QC with the computational power of a pocket calculator has yet been built or shown to be realistically implementable. Constructing a QC may be as possible as balancing a hair on the head of a needle in a hurricane: there is nothing contradictory in it, but only God could do it. Down on earth, engineering a real QC means solving enormous difficulties concerning:

- the construction of reliable quantum gates;
- the generation of a sufficient amount of qubits;
- the "safety" of the qubits (complete isolation of quantum registers from the environment);
- the measurement of the output-qubits.

Wherever a quantum dichotomy/superposition can be generated there lies a potential QC, and several techniques have been devised to create actual qubits, on the basis either of light polarised in two perpendicular directions and hence the interaction of photons (in theory, photons passing through a stream of caesium atoms could form the basis of a XOR logic-gate), or on atoms' spins, or more often on cold, trapped ions (atoms with missing electrons, often of calcium) modified via a pulse of laser light, which can switch the ion from one energy level to the other. Computation could be performed by a series of laser pulses directed at two levels of one ion. In some cases, the technology in question is already well developed, e.g. in high-precision spectroscopy, yet the whole process remains so delicate (each pulse would have to operate without exciting any third level, or affecting any of the adjacent ions) and difficult that only a few laboratories in the world have the scientific and technological resources to set up such atomic-scale experiments and, so far, only the creation of a few qubits has proved to be possible (the limit, at the time of writing, is an ion trap housing at most 6 ions). Unfortunately, a working QC would need thousands of ions, vibrating in synchrony, and even if genetic difficulties could be solved, the construction of a QC may still turn out to be an impossible task because of a QC's extreme sensitivity to noise. A quantum system needs to be totally shielded from all interactions with any phenomenon outside itself. Two adjacent transistors can switch on and off independently and without any major problem caused by the environment or their mutual influence, but a qubit is an exceedingly fragile creature, whose safety is granted only if absolutely nothing happens to it. It cannot be touched by an air molecule, no light must shine on it, it cannot enter into unpremeditated relations with other qubits, indeed it cannot even be close to other qubits or prematurely measured, for in each of these cases the disturbed qubit stops being in superposition, vacillates no longer and settles into a definite digital state, making the whole computation useless. You can compare a QC to a machine which attempts to transport billions of very fragile crystal spheres (the zeros) and exceedingly unstable detonators (the ones) through extremely bumpy channels at the speed of light. Would the computer be able not to break any of them? Obviously not, which is why some device to assess the calculation reliability and some process for automatic error correction, similar to those used by ordinary computers, is being investigated for the construction of a QC. The redundancy approach is roughly that already adopted by Von Neumann himself: each qubit that needs to be "protected" from errors is bundled with other qubits whose only task is to act as bodyguards, as it were, and make sure that the boss-qubit reaches the end of the process safely. To some extent, when an error occurs (decoherence), its presence and impact can be computed and the original piece of information rescued. To stick to the analogy, a customer buys 12 crystal glasses but you send her 24, just to ensure that she is very likely to get at least the right number, if no more. In this case too, some steps have been made towards workable solutions.

Computer science will increasingly be the field where mathematics, nanotechnology, chemistry and physics interact, but whether QCs will ever become a new variety of desktops is hard to say. After all, biological computing using large-molecule systems or enzymes as memory registers has already proved to be not impossible, but absolutely impractical, and has been abandoned. For the foreseeable future, pessimism about real QC seems to be equally justified:

given the exponential time-scale of decoherence phenomena, it may not be possible to build a QC beyond the 10-qubit system, but then, who can predict what will happen in a hundred years? Major new breakthroughs in the technological treatment of superpositions, such as the present work done on quantum-magnetic phenomena, or in the construction of better materials may solve at least some of the present difficulties. Knowledge of quantum physical phenomena is still too limited for utter pessimism to be fully justified. Liquid QC is a good example. The most promising results (a QC that can add $1 + 1$, literally) have been obtained by abandoning the assumption that the quantum medium has to be tiny and isolated from its surroundings and using instead "seas of molecules" (the famous cup of coffee) to store the information. In a magnetic field, each nucleus within a molecule spins in a certain direction, which can be used to describe its state (e.g. spinning upwards = 1 and spinning downwards = 0) and nuclear magnetic resonance (NMR) can then be used to detect these spin states, while bursts of specific radio waves can flip the nuclei between spinning states.

Being equally in doubt, in 1997/8 DARPA funded a \$5 million Quantum Information and Computing Institute to investigate quantum computing and its applications. Dollars may not be sufficient to make something a reality, but have the extraordinary power of making one feel it is possible. All that can be said with some confidence is that at the end of the 1990s work on QCs was already fruitful for both disciplines involved, so the funds may not be wasted: computer scientists working on the physical constraints of conventional machines have provided new insights into innovative forms of calculation, error correction and data compression, while physicists have been able to investigate powerful ways of engineering and controlling quantum effects. The by-products and spin-offs of quantum computing may well prove more important and useful than the research project that is generating them, at least in the near future.

The usual question now, before moving to the next section: are we quantum computers? The mimetic temptation is constantly lurking and has attracted some philosophers and scientists working in the field. The technology and the physics change, but unfortunately the conceptual attitude does not, and nor do the problems affecting it. In a very vague sense, we are clearly "quantum beings". Since quantum mechanics appears to govern all physical systems at the microlevel, it must also be supposed that it regulates our lives as physical bodies in the world. In the same vague sense, then, we are also "Newtonian beings" at the macrolevel, mostly made up of water (H_2O makes up about 70 per cent of the human body). Yet none of us would try to explain the physical mechanics of Brutus' arm stabbing the body of Caesar by working on the level of interaction of masses of H_2O. It seems equally odd that we should try to explain the motivations of the former and the ambitions of the latter by looking at subatomic levels of energy superpositions. A perfectly satisfactory description of a computer can be given in terms of a Universal

Turing machine following algorithms to manage strings of binary symbols, but in the case of a person, a reliable and insightful description can only be given in terms of a conscious being, not of a biological machine. Of course, the organisational level matters, but it also matters whether the component or the composite result is more important. Quantum computing has been allied both to computational and non-computational views of the brain, yet analysis of consciousness according to one or the other model seems to follow a neo-Galenic approach[6] whose possible advantage, in the connectionist approach, is that of advancing a step further into the analysis of the atomic components making up a brain. No matter whether quantum neurophysiology is correct, a philosophy of mind based on it seems to be a further step in the wrong direction, towards the bottom-up explanation of human intelligence. Looking at a single platoon was insufficient to explain the behaviour of the whole army. Monitoring the actions of a single soldier will only make things worse.

Expert systems, knowledge engineering and formal ontologies

An expert system (ES) is a software application that can solve, or give advice on, a well-defined domain of problems in a particular field, thus performing problem-solving tasks that may otherwise be impossible or, more often, would require the intervention of a human expert. To achieve such seemingly intelligent behaviour as well as, if not better than, a human expert, an ES usually relies on:

1   a knowledge base (KB), i.e. a stored collection of topic-oriented knowledge appropriate for performing problem-solving tasks in a particular field, such as medical diagnosis, insurance planning or investment analysis. The knowledge base of an ES may consist of the rules and experience used by an expert to deal with problems in a particular field;
2   an inference engine, which generates an output of solutions/advice/ answers/ recommendations, integrating and interpreting inputs represented by (1) and by further data provided by the end user;
3   an interface for the I/O procedures required by (2).

For an ES "knowledge" is a set of facts, linguistically equivalent to declarative sentences assumed to be true, together with a set of inferential rules capable of generating new facts from existing ones. The KB incorporates both relevant data (knowledge-that) and experience (know-how) that have to be gained from experts and made fully explicit. Once collected, both types of information are converted into the format and sequence needed by the computer to answer the question or solve the problem. The inference engine contains a set of algorithms, known as universal production rules, which embody the general problem-solving methods and heuristic strategies determining the actions to be performed in each case. They have the logical form of an inference: *condition → action*, where the "condition" contains a series of patterns specifying the data that cause the rule to be applicable, and the "action" is a set of operations to be performed when the rule is applicable. These general inference rules should not be confused with the topic-oriented rules that are stored in the application domain, as instances of know-how. The inference engine automatically matches data against condition-patterns, and establishes which of them are satisfied and hence which specific rules are applicable. The proper actions are then performed sequentially, so that the ES may add or remove data during the process, thus further affecting the number of rules applicable. The process continues until there are no more conditions satisfied and rules to be applied and the output-solution can be issued. The interaction between end user and ES is normally via question–answer scenarios, and this explains why a friendly interface is important. By entering new data, or simply selecting pre-established alternatives from a list, the end user provides the problem-input. The program normally keeps on asking questions until it has reached a conclusion, which may then be a single suggestion or an array of alternatives, possibly arranged in order of likelihood.

Although no taxonomy is yet widely accepted, through the typology of end-users and knowledge bases, ESs can be distinguished into:

- AESs (aid ESs), which are meant to help experts to reach a solution. These are often "goal-driven": given a goal, e.g. a hypothesis to be falsified, the ES processes the available data to reach it;
- RESs (replacement ESs), which are supposed to interact directly with the layman, replacing the human expert. These are often "event-driven": the ES is activated and reacts to data provided by the user, by answering queries and solving problems;
- dynamic versus static ES, depending on whether the KB remains unchanged during the whole course of the problem solving session, or varies in both depth and breadth in connection with the process;
- KBS (knowledge-based system). This is the case when the ES contains mainly instances of knowledge-that, for example all reference materials available in a field, rather than know-how acquired by interviewing experts. A KBS is a program for relevant data mining and database queries (discovery of interesting regularities in large computer databases) that can also be used to extend the knowledge base of an ES.

There are many techniques, especially in the business sector, that may often be included in an ES:

- CBR (case-based reasoning) systems use a problem-solving technique that can compare and match similar patterns of information, representing previous and current situations or cases, and suggest courses of action based on previously solved occurrences. It is useful where heuristic knowledge is not available, and it is also the natural way for an expert to describe his or her knowledge – through examples, stories or cases.

- CP (constrained programming) systems are used to solve complex problems, with very large numbers of variables that can result in a combinatorial explosion when conventional programming techniques are used, through the most efficient allocation of resources. They use specialised "pruning" techniques that can constrain the problem space to a manageable extension. A CP does not always reach the optimum solution, but the advantage is that the proposed solution is usually effectively arrived at in a fraction of the time required by an exhaustive conventional search.

The "intelligent behaviour" of an ES depends as much on the quality of the data stored in its KB as on the logic, encoded in its inferential engine, that controls the application of the relevant rules. Expert systems are often described as being roughly equivalent to human experts, but in practice an AES may perform well above and a RES well below the level of an individual expert. This is why the former may include numeric simulation models, while the latter should be as user-friendly as possible and designed to interact with potential end-users who possess only ordinary mathematical and computing skills.

The advantages of ESs are many:

- They can help to analyse and hence give a better grasp of human expert knowledge.
- They can help to individuate, store, maintain, preserve, disseminate and reproduce expert knowledge.
- Their knowledge bases can be progressively increased, corrected and updated, although sometimes this implies having to resort to computer programming.
- Their logic is readily available: ESs can explain why further data are needed, and how and why certain conclusions were reached; they can describe the reasoning process through back-traces; and they can handle levels of confidence and uncertainty. This is extremely important for the assessment of the results of a session, for it helps to control the value and correctness of the system's conclusions.
- They have uniform behaviour: similar problems will always receive similar solutions. This means that an ES may make the same mistakes indefinitely, but will have no psychological or other human bias.
- Depending on the complexity of the software and the size of the KB, their implementation may still require powerful conventional hardware.
- They are easy to develop using specialised software tools, called ES shells. Shells contain an inference mechanism (backward chaining, forward chaining, or both), they require data to be entered according to a

specified format, and may include a number of other facilities, such as tools for writing hypertext, for devising friendly user interfaces, for interfacing with external programs and databases and so forth.

However, some of the shortcomings of ESs are equally significant, and should make clear why, again, commercial and scientific implementations of ES are the result of a LAI methodology:

- ESs are not universal but have only a narrow domain of "competence" and, as in the case of ANN, their flexibility is a type, not a token property.
- They can be brittle, i.e. unable to cope with problems that stretch their rules.
- They are non-creative and can hardly learn from past experiences and mistakes with sufficient flexibility.
- They cannot resort to common-sense knowledge (see the examples provided under the Cycorp entry in the webliography).
- They may easily incorporate erroneous rules or badly defined knowledge.

Failure to acknowledge such limitations has helped to spread a number of mistaken ideas about ES, three of which are of philosophical interest and should be corrected as follows.

(1) Only some forms of expertise and hence some kinds of problems are amenable to ES treatment.

ES literature often expresses contempt for the poor expert. She is often shown as being unable to define her inarticulate skills or experience by answering questions aimed at eliciting explicit knowledge in order to make her expertise subject to formal analysis by the knowledge engineer and translatable into a logical structure suitable to digital treatment. Yet the truth is that ESs can handle successfully only a limited range of well-defined problems or set of initial factors, which can be symbolically represented and whose solutions imply a selection from a definable group of choices and decisions based on logical steps. Broadly speaking, problems that concern not only information management but involve, for example, a reasonable degree of understanding of the issues at stake, subconscious, sublinguistic or subcognitive processes, or associative knowledge, are not amenable to ES solution. To think otherwise is to commit the fallacy of superarticulacy and presume, with Locke, that the mind is always utterly transparent to itself, having a complete and coherent articulation of all its subcognitive knowledge (note that this is a point that Descartes makes only with respect to the "cogito", and that Leibniz rightly rejects in favour of a more functionalist interpretation of the mind).

(2) ES techniques do not resemble human logic in their implementation.

ES strategies may, but do not have to, resemble what expert practitioners actually do. Problem-solving competence qualifies as know-how, hence as practical knowledge. However, practical knowledge is not readily exportable and importable, for it varies deeply, depending on the nature of the subject performing the action. Your knowledge-how to play tennis is utterly different from mine and above all from the knowledge-how that a robot would need to achieve the same result. Hence, to cope with a domain of problems ES techniques need not be like, and actually often differ from, what an expert would do in the same situation, although the aim is to reach the same result, if not a better one. It is interesting to note that knowledge engineers, being aware of the problem, have devised what is known in the literature as "the telephone test" to determine if a problem is amenable to an ES solution. If expert and end-user can solve a problem over the telephone, then an ES program is probably feasible. This mental experiment is clearly a version of Turing's Test. As a positive method, however, it is utterly unreliable. A politician and an economist may solve a number of problems over the telephone, or indeed by email, simply because they rely on a vast amount of commonly shared yet implicit knowledge, that may not be suitable for sufficiently explicit formalisation. The test is effective only as a negative method: if expert and end-user *cannot* solve a problem over the telephone then an ES program is very likely to be unfeasible as well.

(3) ES and fuzzy logic: confusion again

The reader may have noticed the strong similarity between an ES and a fuzzy system, and indeed many ESs today can be based on fuzzy logic. Fuzzy rule-based ESs can cope with degrees of uncertainty and satisfaction of the stated conditions through several methods, including certainty factors associated with rules and user data input, probabilistic inferences and the most significant results of tests; yet again, utterly ambiguous, vague or confused knowledge remains useless (recall the GIGO rule). This is why the logical analysis preceding the implementation of an ES is the most difficult stage. In this case too, the myth of a system capable to cope with a severe lack of information must be abandoned.

Knowledge engineering is the branch of computer science that designs ES, translating what needs to be done by a virtual expert system into what can be effectively achieved by a real program. If we are able to do some exercise in problem-solving procedures when discussing parallel computing, in knowledge engineering we can learn how to describe application domains by means of what are technically called, only a little misleadingly from a philosopher's perspective, *formal ontologies*.

According to a widely accepted approach, the development of an ES includes five highly interrelated and interdependent stages. If we concentrate only on the methodological and conceptual aspects, these can be roughly summarised thus:

(1) *Identification*, usually in collaboration with domain experts, of all the specific problems (the problem space) to be dealt with by the ES and hence of the kind of KB and inference engine required.

(2) *Conceptualisation* of the problem space (knowledge-base design). This implies determining the whole set of concepts and objects assumed to exist in the domain identified in (1), their relevant properties, the relations holding between them, the processes in which they may be involved and hence the corresponding control mechanisms for the actions and interactions under-lying the problem-solving tasks. Conceptualisation represents the initial stage in the construction of a formal ontology.

(3) *Formalisation* of (2) into a logic program (knowledge acquisition and knowledge-base construction), which transforms knowledge structures, problems, inference rules, control strategies and information flow into formal representations. The conceptualisation is specified into a formal ontology (see below) in this stage.

(4) *Implementation* of (3) into the language of the development shell and realisation of a working prototype. An ES can be implemented by using standard programming languages such as C or Visual Basic, or by using languages specifically designed for AI applications. The latter include LISP, which, as we have seen, provides special tools for manipulating lists of objects that have been found to be an underlying aspect of human reasoning, and PROLOG, which provides an inference engine. Furthermore, an ES can also be implemented by means of an expert system shell. A shell not only comes with an inference engine, so that the knowledge engineer only needs to supply the relevant knowledge, but it also provides reasoning tools such as

- rules for inferring new facts;
- demons which constantly check the current status of the ES, and activate if a set of conditions are met;
- when-needed methods. If the ES needs some data, a when-needed method for those data activates to obtain it from the user of the ES;
- when-changed methods. If key data in the ES change, this method activates and performs necessary actions relevant to that change.

(5) *Testing* of (4), including verification of accuracy. Epistemologically, the most interesting stages are the second and the third, and two points are worth remarking upon, before we address the ontology issue. First, working ESs are sometimes constructed by starting from what they can really do, that is, the problems they can successfully handle, rather than the needs of the end-users. This is the result of a clear understanding of the distinction between problems that are amenable to ES treatment and problems that prove untreatable, but it also clarifies why the end-users may often be dis-satisfied. It is the task of the knowledge engineer to keep the right balance between ES capacities and users' expectations. Second, as far as the intelligent behaviour of an ES is concerned, clearly the design and construction of the KB and the inference engine exploit the experts' know-how and the knowledge engineer's capacities. An ES should then be understood as a

sort of interactive archive of procedural and factual knowledge and not be confused with GOFAI projects. The construction of ESs belongs to that process of externalisation of the conceptual world of information and knowledge that I have already stressed in relation to the development of the Internet.

Looking now at the construction of an ES from the perspective of the design of the knowledge base rather than of the problem-solving tasks, stages (1)–(3) can be made more specific by comparing them to the three stages through which knowledge representation (KR) in a declarative language is achieved:

(1) selection of a domain of discourse or application domain, which can be referred to by using the concept of *possible world* (PW). By a PW I mean here a consistent scenario constituted by a set of entities with their properties and, possibly, their interrelations and processes. It may but usually does not have to be already instantiated;

(2) conceptualisation (that is, an abstract, informal and simplified view) of the PW we wish to represent formally. A conceptualisation encompasses a description of the concepts appropriate to, and the entities assumed to exist in PW, together with their properties, (possibly) the processes to which they are subject and, above all, the relations holding between them. The set of entities populating the PW is called the universe of discourse (note that this is often taken to be the true first stage of KR);

(3) a specification of the conceptualisation of the PW by means of a formal ontology Ω, which explicitly regiments the abstract conceptualisation into a logical model. The model may then become a concrete data structure amenable to processing. A formal ontology provides:

- a vocabulary, i.e. a mapping from the names of the entities in the universe of discourse to representational terms (the names of the defined entities, for example classes, instances, n-ary relations, functions, and individual constants). The terms thus represent the subject-oriented knowledge representation primitives of the ontology;
- a semantics, i.e. a set of definitions of the univocal meanings of the representational terms (the properties of the entities), based on other terms (simple equations), on conservative introductions (non-informative definitions of semantically empty labels) or "contentful" axiomatic postulates;
- a syntax, i.e. a set of axioms describing the actual or possible functions and mutual relations between the terms fully regulates their correct uses.

More intuitively, formal ontologies provide a vocabulary of formal concepts with a description of their mutual relations and of the ways in which they can correctly be used to represent, and (possibly) share, domain-oriented knowledge bases. An ontology Ω, together with a predicate logic establishing the vocabulary of logical symbols, their syntax and semantics, may then be understood as representing the language of KR and the basis for the construction of an expert system.

Ontologies were initially developed only as part of KB designs, but they clearly have enormous potential as mapping tools for repositories of organised knowledge in any context where it is important to have a full and explicit documentation of the domain of discourse, as Intel's WAVE project demonstrates (see the webliography). This pragmatic perspective must be kept in mind to understand three exigencies. Capturing and representing domain-oriented knowledge are two essential stages in the construction of any ES. Unfortunately, both processes are difficult, time-consuming and therefore expensive. Consequently, while many shells are available for developing production rules systems, realising the ontology from scratch remains one of the major costs in building an ES. The solution is to design ontologies that may be both *upgradable* and *reusable*, so that it becomes possible to maintain, increase, correct and improve them easily through time and import/export them across different projects. For example, the legal ontology of an ES dealing with human rights could be imported into the medical ontology of an ES dealing with patients' rights in a hospital, and new concepts, developed within the medical ontology, could be reused to upgrade the legal ontology. Knowledge sharing is of the utmost importance for any collaborative project but cannot be based only on reusability: inter-operability, based on interactive communication by way of message-passing, is equally vital. Special-purpose ESs can communicate with each other only if they can commit themselves to the same ontologies. A *sharable* ontology is therefore designed to allow such a degree of commitment, on the side of intelligent agents (groups of people and/or programs, including ES and other KB systems), as to make their efficient interoperability unproblematic. An ontology that allows future development (upgradable), inclusion into another ontology (reusable) and communication with other ontologies (sharable) is an *open ontology*, which minimises knowledge waste and redundancy, enhances collaboration and can be used both as an open catalogue of the subject domain and as an open vocabulary through which co-operating agents can interact. An ontology that satisfies all these conditions can be defined as *canonical*.

It was only in the 1990s that "green" methodologies that minimise waste and maximise reusability were adopted to promote standard KR languages and protocols for the construction of canonical ontologies. In this, a fundamental role has been played by the analysis of the concept of ontological commitment.

An ontological commitment is the procedural commitment *to* an ontology Ω and must be distinguished from a commitment *of* an ontology Ω to a particular methodology. Literature on the topic often overlooks this distinction, so I shall restrict the use of the term "ontological commitment" to the former case only, and use "Ω-commitments" to refer to the latter. We have seen that an ontological commitment consists in the explicit acceptance of an ontology among a community of intelligent agents. Now, recognition of degrees of commitment may be a purely "behaviourist" matter, for it refers only to the description level of the "epistemic" actions of an agent (knowledge-level) and not to the description level of its internal structure (the symbol-level representation used in the agent's internal knowledge base). According to such a behaviourist approach, two agents are said to be committed to the same ontology if and only if their observable actions are consistent with the definitions provided in the ontology. Although a plurality of heterogeneous agents may not refer to exactly the same ontology Ω, if they are committed to one they are capable of using a minimal vocabulary to pose logical queries and make logical assertions that are consistent with the description of the PW in question. If the actions of two agents are only Ω-consistent and the two agents cannot yet interoperate through Ω successfully because they commit themselves to completely different areas of Ω, then the two agents are said to be only minimally committed to Ω. If they can also interoperate by exchanging queries and assertions, then they are said to be also Ω-interoperative and maximally committed to Ω. The case of two or more agents sharing exactly the same ontology Ω is then only a specific case of maximal commitment, which grants that their interoperability is *complete*.

Ω-commitments have attracted less attention than ontological commitments but are of comparable importance. They can be organised into five types, and every intelligent agent shows a particular attitude towards each of them, either explicitly or implicitly.

(1) *Particularists versus universalists*: Libraries of specific ontologies are usually constructed bottom-up, by looking at particular domains of discourse. For example, the library of Ontolingua (see the webliography) contains ontologies such as 3D-Tensor-Quantities, Abstract-Algebra, Basic-Matrix-Algebra, Bibliographic-Data, Chemical-Crystals, Chemical-Elements. On the other hand, it is also possible to construct general ontologies top-down. This was the project carried out by the Cyc (see webliography), which attempted to construct an ontology of common-sense knowledge about the world that could then lead to more specific local ontologies. From the perspective of LAI, a "particularist" approach is to be preferred, for it grants almost immediate applicability and, when developed by a "green" methodology, ensures the modularity of the achievements. However, since specific levels of abstraction may vary depending on what the ontology is used for, and since, in terms of inclusion into another ontology, the more abstract an ontology is the more likely it will be reusable by other projects, it may be worth attempting to develop complete and coherent *core ontologies* (see Valente and Breuker's online article in the webliography) by means of a combination of top-down and bottom-up approaches, working at levels which are higher than the "particularist" yet lower than the "universalist", as in the case of canonical ontologies concerning whole fields such as medicine or computer engineering domains.

(2) *Platonist constructionism versus nominalist constructivism*: After (1), the next commitment is to the specific PW that needs to be conceptualised and "canonically ontologised". Note that here an a priori nominalist commitment regarding the existence of PW and its entities is probably harmful. Although physically instantiated PWs may presumably receive particular attention, a more tolerant, Platonist approach seems preferable, and knowledge engineering, being driven by real-world demands, has already included the ontologisation of non-physical domains as well, as the few examples from Ontolingua mentioned above suffice to prove. In a Platonist ontology with a *constructionist* approach, existence is equated to static representability, hence to logical consistency, both internal (stand-alone) and with respect to the system (networked), so the *construction* of a possible entity as a set of properties which is not contradictory in either respect is perfectly acceptable and constitutes the fundamental criterion for ontological admission. Philosophically, it is the objective consistency of a set of entities that makes possible the performance of subsequent actions. In a nominalist ontology with a *constructivist* approach, on the contrary, existence is equated either to actual existence, physically experienceable by a subject, or to algorithmic feasibility (perhaps via the analysis of a dedicated Turing machine) and dynamic provability again by a subject, so "merely" non-contradictory entities do not yet qualify for an ontological treatment. Philosophically, it is the range of subjective doings that settles the limits of what may count as being. However, since for an intelligent agent its own objective (agent-independent) ontology, with its description of the entities and their mutual relations, is all there is and represents the condition of possibility of any further actions, and since it is at least immaterial whether the objects in question are postulated as possible, identified as real, or accepted as finitely constructible, a Platonist–constructionist approach is not only viable but also preferable, for it allows a wider class of ontological libraries. In other words, ontologies are designed to support practical needs and a constructionist policy makes it possible to satisfy more of them. For scholarly problem-solving tasks, an ontology of Shakespearean characters may well be as acceptable and useful as an ontology of printed editions of Shakespeare's works, while a mathematical ontology will be easier to handle if the law of bivalence and proofs by means of *reductio ad absurdum* are available.

(3) *Substance versus function*: The third commitment is to the type of conceptualisation of the PW to be adopted. In principle, a conceptualisation could also be function-centred, but in practice it is usually object-centred. This is in line with the commitment in favour of a consistency-based ontology, made in (2), and influences both the range of possible ontologisations in (4) and the kind of logic adopted for their design in (5).

(4) *Static versus dynamic types of ontology*: Consistency-based PW and object-centred conceptualisations tend to generate static ontologies, based on structures of entities, class of entities, n-ary relations and functions. Dynamic

processes are left implicit, translated into relations or functions, or often disregarded. One may wonder whether things could not be improved.

(5) *The many logics of a formal ontology*: Which logic is most suitable for the design of an ontology and hence for KR? Ontologies appear to be usually committed to classic first-order predicate logic (a two-value logic including the law of bivalence), but second-order logic and non-standard or deviant logics (such as modal logic, *n*-values logics and fuzzy logic) may also be taken into consideration in the future, at least for representative needs, if not for inferential requirements. It must be remarked that reluctance to use deviant logics has often stemmed from nominalist attitudes, such as Quine's, which we have already remarked to be unjustified in this context (see (2)).

The previous Ω-commitments can be summarised by saying that the philosophy of canonical ontologies is constructionist and in line with a LAI approach, but that many methodological issues still require further study and clarification. Some of the most interesting problems, either conceptual or methodological, concern

- the logic of formal ontologies, including the study of the relations among sets of ontologies and of the diachronic development of ontologies;
- the possibility of a standard, ontological "interlingua" that may work as an ontological foundation of domain-oriented canonical ontologies;
- the distinction and investigation of meta-ontologies (ontologies of ontologies) versus ontological "super theories", i.e. general and abstract ontological tools such as set theory, mereology, topology, graph theory, systems theory, first- and second-order logic and modal logic;
- the exploration of ways in which problems posed by the typically multi-faceted character of ontologies (the presence of several viewpoints in one and the same domain of discourse; think for example of your role as an entity in the ontology of your institution and in the ontology of your cricket team) could be solved;
- the relation between formal ontologies, conceptualisations and taxonomic criteria (categorisation) of possible worlds;
- the expansion of ontologies so as to include causal, procedural and spatio-temporal languages, to mention only a few.

In working on similar problems, epistemology and knowledge engineering can be of mutual assistance. In epistemology, it is to be hoped that, on the one hand, we may be able to exploit the methodology of formal ontologies to study conceptual systems as well as to develop libraries of ontologies of ideas treated as artefacts/entities, and that, on the other hand, we may avail ourselves of the conceptual apparatus of formal ontology to articulate a general theory of critical constructionism, including the literary constructionism outlined in Chapter 4. In knowledge engineering, epistemological and methodological analyses may provide further conceptual clarifications and explanations to improve the present status of the field and help to design better applications. In 1996, in the presentation of the "Ontological engineering workshop: objectives and background", it was remarked that

> Ontological engineering currently is a craft rather than a science. . . . In workshops and in the published literature, ontologies are called important or indispensable in designing and building knowledge-based systems and in facilitating sharing and reuse of knowledge resources. It is evident that quite a number of research groups are building ontologies. It is less clear what design decisions are taken and how they contribute to the success (or failure) of the ontologies developed. Thus the danger of making the same mistakes over and over again is as real as the danger of inventing the wheel at several places simultaneously. Development of an ontology is a laborious and therefore costly process. The field would profit immensely if we could learn from each other's successes and failures. One way to lay down the dos and don'ts is in the form of systematic design practices. With so many groups working on the subject, it is possible to gather experiences and start articulating systematic design practices.
>
> (from http://wwwis.cs.utwente.nl:8080/kbs/EcaiWorkshop/
> objective.html)

Obviously there is plenty of useful work that philosophically minded engineers and mathematically minded philosophers can do together in this field.

Robotics, cybernetics and artificial agents

CHEAP LABOUR. ROSSUM'S ROBOTS. ROBOTS FOR THE TOPICS. 150 DOLLARS EACH. EVERYONE SHOULD BUY HIS OWN ROBOTS. DO YOU WANT TO CHEAPEN YOUR OUTPUT? ORDER ROSSUM'S ROBOTS.

One of the many ads on Internet? Not at all. These famous lines come from Karel Capek's play *Rossum's Universal Robots*, which opened in Prague in January 1921. They contain the first occurrence of "robot", a term coined by Capek and his brother from the Czech word "robota", which literally means "forced work or labour", coming from the Latin *robor* ("power", "force"). The play is staged in a factory that builds artificial agents. The plot centres on the conversion of such workers into military forces that eventually take over the factory and exterminate the whole of humanity. The end leaves open the question of whether the robots, which have lost the necessary know-how to reproduce themselves, may be on their way to becoming more human.

Philosophically rich and controversial, *RUR* was unanimously acknowledged as a masterpiece from its first appearance, and has become a classic of technologically dystopian literature. The neologism "robot" was, among other things, greatly successful. As early as 1924, we find that the Soviet Union propaganda film *Aelita* was also known as *The Revolt of the Robots*. Twenty years later, the young Isaac Asimov, who was born in Russia in 1920 and was well acquainted with Capek's terminology, introduced the word "robotics" in English, to indicate the scientific study and application of robots (*Runaround*, 1942).

Born as science-fiction terms, the concepts of "robots" and "robotics" have gradually become widely accepted in the scientific community in the past thirty years, and have merged with *cybernetics*, a term coined by Norbert Wiener (Wiener 1948; see also Wiener 1950 and 1964) from the Greek word *kybernetes* ("steersman" or "governor"), to indicate the interdisciplinary science of the communication, control and regulatory properties of complex, interacting systems, both biological and mechanical. Cybernetics developed during World War II as the investigation of the techniques and automatic-control mechanisms by which information is transformed into desired performance, and information concerning the actual results is made available to the system itself to allow it to determine its future course of action, through control mechanisms for feedback and self-correction. Theoretically, cybernetics had a much wider scope than robotics, for it could be viewed as the general science of systems of communication and control, both in living organisms and in machines that can acquire, process, communicate and employ information in order to perform practical tasks; but in its technical applications, as a branch of automation engineering, it has gradually become barely distinguishable from it.

Whether the fruit of a robotic or cybernetic approach, artificial agents are a very old fantasy. The ultimate ideal in the mechanisation of production is the perpetual motion machine: a machine that could produce more useful work or energy than it consumes, or a machine that, once set in motion, would be at least 100 per cent efficient at converting energy into work and hence could continue in motion indefinitely, without requiring any further input of energy. The first and second law of thermodynamics have proved both such projects to be impossible. Similarly, the ultimate ideal in the automatisation of action is the intelligent automaton, an artificial agent having its own power source, designed to be able to behave and respond to the environment independently of, and as intelligently as, any other ordinary human agent. For some time, computer science has tried to bring this dream true, yet since the 1980s there seems to be a tacit acceptance that this GOFAI project has failed too. In this case, however, there are no laws, comparable to those of thermodynamics, stating that forms of non-biological intelligence are impossible, so robots will always be possible entities in principle.

Mechanical automata are known to have been built as toys, or more often imagined as fictional creatures, for thousands of years and in utterly different cultures. Today, artificial agents can be distinguished into four families:

(1) *androids*, (2) *cyborgs*, (3) *robots*, (4) *webbots*. The order in the taxonomy is not merely alphabetic but also conceptual and technological.

The word *androi* in ancient Greek meant "men", and androids (or simply "droids") are biogenetically engineered agents, composed entirely of organic substances. They are mimetic, humanoid models, such as Frankenstein's, Rossum's and the famous NEXUS 6 Replicants that are to be "retired" by Deckard/Harrison Ford in *Blade Runner*. In the film, replicants differ from humans only in that they are emotionally immature, cannot help being completely self-controlled and lacking in any empathy. In one draft of the script we are told that a body is recognised to be that of a replicant only after a two-hour autopsy. As with Frankenstein's and Rossum's creatures, problems arise when the replicants begin to acquire a fully-human nature. For example, the new prototype Rachael is endowed with an experimental memory that provides her with a past as a background for her emotions. She takes for granted the fact that she is human. Conceptually, androids are the first and most natural kind of artificial agents ever imagined. Technologically, they belong to the realm of science fiction and philosophical mental experiments.

CYBernetic ORGanisms (*Cyborgs*) are partly human and partly mechanical agents. Although Wiener himself did not discuss the actual physical merger of living organisms and machines, their design originated from the field of cybernetics, and their actual possibility was suggested by Manfred Clynes and Nathan Kline, two NASA scientists who coined the word "cyborg" when arguing for the potential advantages of altering, replacing or augmenting the bodies of astronauts with exogenous components to make life in space more comfortable. In a generic way, many people could qualify as "cyborgs", having parts of their body replaced or augmented by prosthetic devices, false teeth, mechanical heart valves, contact lenses, or artificial bones, or dependent on mechanisms such as pacemakers and automatic biochemical pumps. In fiction, however, a true cyborg is an agent who has had his or her central nervous system mechanically or digitally modified. In theory, we could imagine having memory chips implanted in our brain and directly consultable "from within". Anyone could become a walking encyclopaedia and never forget dates or telephone numbers. More seriously, research into artificial ears and eyes – e.g. a miniature video camera wired to an electrode array implanted in the visual cortex of certain blind people – has been in progress for some time. Of course, the immense technological problems concern the way in which the biological neural network and the various mechanisms in question may be interfaced. So far cyborgs have remained either unfortunate human beings with a slightly improved body, or fictional characters.

With robots we enter into the realm of the technologically feasible. *RUR*'s robots are, in our terminology, androids, but the tension between biochemical reproduction and mechanical invention is already present even in the play. The older Rossum is a scientist who wishes to prove that a human being can be constructed in a laboratory. Although his techniques are different, his philosophy is as materialist and mechanist as Hobbes's and Dr Frankenstein's. Unlike the latter, in the play he is said to have failed in all his attempts to create a perfect human being. The younger Rossum, his son who takes over the project, is a pragmatic engineer, whose only aim is to provide a cheap labour force. His new robots are still biochemically-based, but lack any human features not directly useful for the performance of their industrial tasks, in short any emotional life. It is tempting to view the two Rossums as personifications of GOFAI and LAI respectively; and in so far as the former holds a mimetic and materialist perspective, while the latter limits himself to a task-oriented approach, the comparison may partially hold. Its obvious limitation, of course, lies in the overall idea of a carbon-based form of artificial and intelligent life. Real robots represent the merger of mechanical automata and computerised control systems. They do not take on a rather useless human appearance, such as *Star Trek's* Data, and at most they may vaguely resemble a limb, as in the case of industrial arms.

According to a fairly broad definition, a robot is any automatic machine that can be programmed to perform a variety of manual tasks, involving moving and handling objects, which would require some intelligence when performed by a human being. The problem with this definition is that it would even fit a washing machine: washing one's socks requires some intelligence, and the task is successfully achieved by the machine in its own way. Only an artificial agent would wash a pair of socks by quickly rotating them one way and another in a lot of hot water and soap for about an hour, but there is nothing intrinsically wrong with the procedure. However, we do not consider washing-machines and dishwashers authentic robots. Why? Because they create the environment with which they can interact. A washing-machine is in fact a whole microworld within which a particular task, and only that task, becomes achievable. It does not actually interact with the same environment in which we find ourselves as bodies, nor is it ready to cope with novelties coming from it. On the contrary, this is what computer-controlled industrial arms try to achieve, at least to some interesting extent.

To interact with its environment (*work envelope*) successfully, an industrial robot needs to be able to reach any possible point P in its space. The basic directions of movement in space are four: up and down, side to side, forward and backward and rotation, and we say that the arm has one degree of freedom for each direction in which a joint can go. Now, any P can be described by a set of three Cartesian co-ordinates {x, y, z} and an arm can reach any P only if it has at least six degrees of freedom. The human arm enjoys seven of them, for the shoulder has three (up and down, side to side, rotation) the elbow one (up and down) and the wrist another three (up and down, side to side, rotation), while jointed-arm robots can have from a minimum of six (in this case they are like a human arm, except for the rotation of the shoulder) and a maximum of twenty. The structure of a basic six-degrees jointed-arm robot consists in:

- a digital controller, i.e. a computer that co-ordinates the movements of the mechanical arm and may network the robot with other digital devices;
- an end effector, not necessarily resembling a human hand, suited for a specific task. It could even be a simple screwdriver and may be replaceable with other tools;
- sensors that can provide some feedback to the robot, keep it informed about the environment's and its own state and thus correct its movements if they deviate from the programmed patterns;
- an arm made of joints and links, whose task is to position the end-effector and sensors according to the instructions provided by the controller;
- a drive, that is, an engine that drives the links into their desired position.

Similar robots are the outcome of the merger of the Industrial Revolution and the information age. In 1956, George Devil and Joseph Engelberger, known as the fathers of robotics, formed "Unimation" the world's first robot company. Their vision was to construct industrial robots that could be integrated into a factory in the same way as business machines were part of an office. Five years later, General Motors adopted the first robot-worker, and in 1997, thanks to the advance in microelectronics, there were almost half a million robots in the world, a number that was likely to increase. Industrial robots are more efficient than human workers, in at least three respects – improved management control and productivity, no loss in continuous performance, consistent high quality production – and thus they are more competitive. They can do jobs that would be too dangerous, boring, repetitive or unhealthy for human beings, thus improving working conditions and the quality of life. In addition, they can help to lower the price of manufactured goods through the implementation of highly automated assembly lines.

Most robots are still only sophisticated variations of the model illustrated above; almost all of them are used in the motor industry, in electronics factories, aircraft manufacturing, warehouses and laboratories, but it is likely that in the future a wider variety of robotised agents will become more common in other contexts as well. In the course of this process, a more consistent adoption of a LAI approach will probably prove essential. Our present industrial robots are nothing more than microcomputer-controlled manipulators, entirely preprogrammed. Their mechanical arms are trained by physically moving them through the required motions, so that the controller can record all the movements and repeat them precisely. More generally, all kinds of robots, including mobile ones, can monitor their environment but lack independent processing of information on a wide scale, they are not creative or innovative, can take at most a very limited number of decisions, do not learn or significantly improve their behaviour through repeated trial and error, and have very little adaptability (as in the case of artificial neural networks, robots' adaptability is mainly a type, not a token feature). To make things worse, professional robots can cost anything between $50,000 and $200,000.

Yet none of the previous factors is sufficient to prove that they may not become as common as refrigerators or cars, artefacts which share with robots all the previous limits if not more (robots' price is probably only a consequence rather than a cause of their limited diffusion, and may dramatically decrease in time, like that of cars). The problem seems rather one of general strategy. Robots perform specific jobs flawlessly; there are a lot of jobs that we may like them to do for us, from cutting the grass in the garden to cleaning the carpet or driving our car home when we are too tired or have enjoyed an extra glass of wine. The question is that we still need to find a way to adapt the performance of such jobs to the capacity of our present or potential robots. We all wish to play the role of the Sorceror's Apprentice, but like Mickey Mouse we have not yet been capable of transforming tasks, which would require our kind of intelligence to be performed successfully, into stupid tasks that a robot may safely take care of, no matter whether they do them less economically than we would (e.g. the washing-machine) or even better than we do. On the one hand, there is a need to rethink the methods whereby the same result can be obtained via different processes: consider how differently from a human being the washing-machine operates. On the other hand, we need to transform the environment in which the task is performed and adapt it to the robots' capacities. Only when gardens are shaped and modified so as to make it possible for a robot to cut the grass, and streets are constructed to allow robotised buses to travel fast and safely will the relevant robots become a commodity. It is the environment of a robot that must become a bit more artificial, a contrived microworld in which objects, properties, relations and events are as narrowly and explicitly defined in advance as possible.

Two final considerations may now be in order. The first concerns a social issue. Robots are often viewed as a cause of unemployment, yet this is a superficial mistake, for more than one reason. Firstly, there are fewer than 500,000 robots currently active in the world and, in many cases, they are doing jobs that human beings should not or could not do anyway. Secondly, robotics has generated quite a number of new professions and jobs in other areas. Finally, the problem is, in any case, represented not by a robotised, jobless society, but by a society in which jobless people cannot live comfortably. Having a job, as opposed to having a practical activity or interest, is hardly a human need. It is an unfortunate necessity. Ask any student who has not yet become a workaholic. In so far as a robotised society produces more wealth and free time and distributes both resources fairly among its members, we may all wish to take our holidays and let our mechanical fellow-beings work for us. This is a typical philosophical statement, one might object. The reply is that, at best, this is a social and political issue to be solved, at worst, it can only be a "computopian" fantasy, not a dystopia.

The second consideration is ethical. In the philosophy of robotics we do not normally wonder whether we may be mechanical agents, but rather whether robots may ever achieve human status. Intelligence, consciousness, emotional life, bodily experience, communication skills and social relations are usually, if variously, recognised as the essential elements that would transform a robot into a person, and the possible acquisition of such properties, besides firing some idle speculations, unmasks a more interesting, master–slave dialectic that seems to affect our entire conception of co-operation and interaction with other entities, no matter whether artificial, animal or human, more generally. Robots are the equivalent of slaves. It is indicative that in *Star Wars* both R2D2 and C3PO are realistically viewed as friendly servants enjoying no rights. Now, masters wish to have autonomous agents (animals, slaves, robots, employees, assistants, etc.) capable of performing intelligent tasks on their behalf and possibly independently of their constant intervention. Intelligent "agenthood" is therefore intimately intertwined with the notion of delegation, which inevitably brings with it trust, accountability and responsibility. Necessarily then, the more the master delegates to the agent, the more the latter needs to become independent and autonomous, and the more likely it is that the master will lose control over it. Loss of control may then imply three different risks. On the one hand, the agent may not perform its task satisfactorily or as well as the master would have done in its place. This is not a major problem, as long as the master is able to regain control of the task in question or fix the problems. On the other hand, if the agent performs its tasks satisfactorily, the master may become wholly dependent on the agent (think of the boss without his secretary, the robotised factory without its robots, the professor without her teaching assistant) thus reversing the positions. Finally, even without dependency, the agent may, in any case, become completely autonomous and free itself from the master (so far this is possible only among human beings). The master is at least vaguely aware of such a dialectic and, in order not to allow the agent to become completely independent of himself, establishes rules that enable him to retain some essential control over the agent's behaviour and well-being. In robotics, Asimov translated such rules into his famous four laws:

0   A robot may not injure humanity, or, through inaction, allow humanity to come to harm.

1   A robot may not injure a human being or, through inaction, allow a human being to come to harm, unless this would violate a higher order law.

2   A robot must obey the orders given it by human beings except where such orders would conflict with a higher order law.

3   A robot must protect its own existence as long as such protection does not conflict with a higher order law.

The laws are clearly the master's rules and are far from being "robotically correct". Now, in human societies similar laws are not written, but this is precisely the advantage of dealing with intelligent agents: they grasp the rules on the fly when they get their first job, so you do not have to codify explicit instructions to make them understand the rules of the game. A careful study of our behaviour towards robots' actions is not only epistemologically relevant to our understanding of perception and agenthood, it may also significantly increase our grasp of the rules governing social structures and interactions.

Industrial robots have deeply affected their working environment in order to make possible their successful interactions. The industrial architecture of robotised factories is very different from that of "human" factories. This is reasonable. The more compatible an agent and its environment become, the more likely it is that the former will be able to perform its tasks efficiently. The wheel is a good solution to moving only in an environment that includes good roads. Let us define as "ontological enveloping" the process of adapting the environment to the agent in order to enhance the latter's capacities of interaction. We have seen that, presumably, home robots will have to prompt a higher degree of ontological enveloping to become everyday tools. Are there robots working in a totally enveloped environment? The answer is "yes". We call them "webbots".

Webbots are a new class of software agents, as one may easily guess from the origin of the word (WEB + roBOTS: the term is also used by html authoring tools, such as Microsoft FrontPage, to describe applications that allow simple interactive components to be added to Web pages without coding any instructions). Broadly speaking, webbots can be described as body-less, fully-digital robots, situated within a cyberspace (it could be the digital space of your hard disk, of a company's Intranet or the global space of the Internet) that may implement four features: pro-activity (they can take the initiative to perform tasks when required), autonomy (they can perform and control their operations without any external intervention), responsiveness (they can interact with the environment) and sociability (they can collaborate and negotiate with other agents and structure their tasks hierarchically).

Webbots operate interactively on another agent's behalf (usually a single end-user, but it could be a laboratory, another webbot, etc.) and can only act on other digital entities in the same space, though they themselves can be operated upon from without, by a human agent, and may "migrate" from one space to another, like any other software. They usually include a NLP (natural language system) interface for access. Webbots or a MAS (multi-agent system, a group of autonomous software agents equipped with their own instructions, collaborating on specific tasks) can for example search and query their environment, interact with it over time by performing information-based tasks that have been assigned to them by other agents, and thus pursue a large variety of different goals. A webbot may be an IRC or

MUD program (a Robo-Sysop) that provides some useful service, such as preventing random users from adopting nicknames already adopted by others, or simply chatting with you when nobody else is online, like the famous program called "Julia" (how would you feel if you were to discover that the fascinating Internet partner with "whom" you had a rather gallant if brief conversation was "only" a chatterbot?). Alternatively, it may be a cartoon that speaks to the human user and acts as a guide or teacher, or a Web program (sometimes also known as crawler or spider) that automatically explores cyberspace to retrieve documents, thus making search engines possible. A webbot may simply be a utility that constantly keeps the hard disk of your computer clean, compressed and virus-free. Webbots can be personalised to satisfy one's requirements, and this is a step forward with respect to the lack of flexibility shown by other intelligent agents. Predictably, the same webbot will in the future be able to perform a wide variety of completely different tasks, instantiating real token-flexibility. Their tasks are often humble, but are getting increasingly substantial, and webbots have started being employed in many business applications in the financial, manufacturing, retailing, electrinic commerce and travel industries. Their future includes not only work-flow co-ordination, but also didactic and ludic applications. Cyberspaces would be far more chaotic and polluted places without them. Webbots' power lies in the total ontological envelopment of their environment, for they are made of the very same digital stuff cyberspace consists of, and in the uniformity of their tasks, all information-based. Their potential has just begun to be exploited, but they already are one of the most successful applications of LAI.

The limits of LAI

At this point we should resist the temptation to put no limit on what LAI may be able to achieve in the future. The remarkably ingenious efforts made to transform a computer into something smarter than a mere electronic Abacus have always had the great advantage of being cumulative, but must remain subject to the conceptual limits of the technology in question. The "intelligence" of a computer lies entirely in its capacity to detect and process a *relation of difference* (usually, but not necessarily, binary), and proceed inferentially on its basis. It is an extraordinary capacity in itself, and a very powerful one too, when it is associated with the right logic – one can do a lot of extraordinarily complex mathematics or win a chess game with a Master just by carefully exploiting it – but whenever conditions of computability, epistemic-independence, experience-independence, body-independence and context-freedom are substantially unfulfilled, it nevertheless remains completely insufficient to *emulate* even the elementary intelligence of a guide-dog or a sheepdog, which grasps and deals primarily with the *relata* themselves. We must not forget that only under specially regimented conditions can a collection of detected relations of difference concerning some empirical aspect of reality replace direct experiential knowledge of it. Computers may never fail to read a barcode correctly, but cannot explain the difference between a painting by Monet and one by Pissarro. More generally, mimetic approaches to AI are not viable because knowledge, experience, bodily involvement and interaction with the context all have a cumulative and irreversible nature. For a human being (but the same observation may be extended to other animals), to know how to speak a language or demonstrate a theorem is not equivalent to mastering the whole sum of instructions required to perform the specific task in question well, nor does it consist in establishing a one-to-one relation between skilled capacities to do x and the correct list of instructions to do x. Any acquisition of a special skill or experience or capacity by a human being means the loss of a particular virginity. Once we have learnt how to read, we no longer see letters but words; through education not only do we no longer hear sounds but melodies, we also soon lose the capacity to hear a melody just as any melody, without perceiving it as classical music and then baroque music and then Handel's *Messiah* or our national anthem. Every step forward also means a loss. Human knowledge does not simply accumulate, it grows within a personal, social and cultural context, and it is always synthetic. It follows that, if an intelligent task can be successfully performed only on the basis of knowledge, experience, bodily involvement, interaction with the environment and social relations, no alternative non-mimetic approach is available, and any strong AI project is doomed to fail. To think otherwise, to forget about the non-mimetic and constructive requirements constraining the success of a computable approach, is to commit what we may call the Σ fallacy and to believe that, since knowledge of a physical object, for example, may in general be described as arising out of a finite series of perceptual experiences of that object, then the former is just a short notation for the latter and can be constructed extensionally and piecemeal, as a summation.

Given the nature of LAI, it is not surprising that it has come to acquire a much less ambitious approach than GOFAI's. Indeed, the pragmatic approach shown by contemporary trends in LAI allows one to foresee that, rather than generating new forms of intelligence, AI is and will remain a fruitful source of technological innovations only in so far as human intelligence is able to enlarge the number of processes that can be sufficiently "stupefied" to be carried on by a digital device. The failure of GOFAI is very far from entailing the impossibility of machines that can help us to think better, more efficiently and less expensively, or spare us tiresome tasks. The major advantage of computers in most commercial and real-life applications lies in their remarkable capacity to perform routine functions quickly, endlessly and fairly reliably. The millions of computers working all over the world perform tasks that require rigid repetition of fixed sequences of instructions without complaint or fatigue, without intelligence of any sort.

The view that I have tried to defend is that contemporary AI should be aiming at the creation not of a non-biological form of *Autonomous Intelligence*, but of an *Augmented Intelligence*, ours, and that future projects should be developed with an eye to this concept of a human, machine-aided intelligence. The failure of computational materialism has left us with the problem of explaining the genesis and nature of human intelligence and mental life, but it seems better and more honest to admit our ignorance and present lack of explanations than to endorse an incorrect theory.

Conclusion

The time available to each individual is a most precious resource because it is of finite, if unknown, length, is not transferable, and can be incremented only minimally, to an extent that is utterly insufficient when compared to the high demand. Despite this, the quality of one's time, and the degree of intensity and freedom with which one enjoys it, can be increased. Equally possible to increase are the number of potential packets of "(payable to) bearer time" represented by money, the "frozen time" with which it is possible to buy other people's real time and thus liberate or ameliorate one's own (money as time). The management of these variable aspects of time – quality, freedom and intensity of time, capitalisation of time-money – is at the root of many technological innovations, which can be organised into four groups, listed loosely in order of logical dependence:

1   materials technologies, which deal with the structure and properties of the physical world and provide the following three technologies with useful applications, essential to design, modify or create new realities;
2   "sanitary" technologies, which aim to "sanate" (enhance the quality of) our time, that is (a) to protract time, and (b) to reduce or (c) alleviate the time spent in spiritual and psycho-physical suffering;
3   time-saving technologies, whose aim is to liberate sane/sanated time;
4   entertainment technologies, which let us enjoy, or simply while away, our sane/sanated and liberated time.

Thanks to these technologies, humanity has been able to improve its condition. Individuals die despite their accumulation of time by means of (1)–(4), and since human beings are all necessarily more greedy (in the accumulation and conservation of time) than hedonistic (in the consumption of time), future generations always inherit part of the time liberated by their ancestors and solidified in material, financial and intellectual goods.

Let us now leave (1) and (2) to one side and concentrate on (3) and (4). The full utilisation of entertainment technologies leads to the transaction and consumption of free time and thus into a blind alley. Such technologies hedonistically consume whatever time has been liberated, producing amusement as *divertissement* and distraction in a philological sense, that is as a moving-away or diversion from the world. Television, cinema, video-games and so forth can all be seen as vectors that transfer packets of condensed time from users to providers, in exchange for tokens of time disengaged from the quotidian, which allow the user to step away from time for a while. If we analyse (3) and (4) in a purely logical sequence, the technologies that kill or while away free time occur at a secondary stage, when there are sufficient quantities of free time, both real and condensed. We can therefore disregard the entertainment technologies and concentrate on the condition of their possibility, namely the time-saving technologies. The technologies that liberate time have a life cycle that is both circular and virtuous. By saving humanity's time, they eventually allow it to devote an increasing quantity of time to further discoveries and technological inventions, which can then liberate still more time, and so forth. Societies with powerful time-saving technologies at their disposal end up liberating ever more of it, thus determining the expansion of the entertainment industry, which helps to consume the extraordinarily huge amount of free time now available to a increasingly large number of people.

Within the group of saving-time technologies, we may distinguish two sub-groups:

3(a) *The energy technologies*: These are technologies that deal with physical reality. They pursue the liberation of time through the increasingly efficient production, multiplication and transformation of energy, at an ever-decreasing cost; think for example of the lever, the wheel, the plough, the mill and the various kinds of engines. From the perspective of a philosophical anthropology, these are the technologies of the *homo faber*.

3(b) *The information technologies*: These are technologies that deal with the world of mental creations. They pursue the liberation of time through the implementation of increasingly efficient processes of information management, broadly understood, such as the creation, preservation, communication, elaboration and increment of information. In this case, there come to mind examples such as the abacus, the printer, the mechanical clock, the telegraph, the radio, the telephone, the transistor, the television (partly), and the computer, at least in its primary use. From the perspective of a philosophical anthropology, these are the technologies of the *homo sapiens*.

If we simplify a little, and leave aside all those cases in which the two types of technology are indissolubly merged, this time the order of the occurrence of (3a) and (3b) is not merely logical but historical as well. Many of the main steps in the production of energy at low cost have occurred before most of the corresponding transformations in the technology of information. This is owing to the fact that the extension of the information cycle – education, training, research, communication – to a high percentage of a population requires huge quantities of time, and time is initially made available only by the accumulation of power, which can be exercised on the world of things, and some exchangeable "bearer time". Thus, in its early stages of development, modern society is strongly characterised by a steady attention to the mechanisation of industrial processes and the corresponding generation of both new sources of energy and new means to exploit them. Humanity is willing to gain free time in exchange for the massification of production and on condition that DIY would stop being a necessary self-imposed commandment, and become a simple third-person invitation (organisation of labour).

Once a society equips itself with a sufficient store of energy technologies, their continuous employment begins to generate an increasing capitalisation of time, both as real free time enjoyed by the generation alive, and as durable and financial goods, inherited by future generations. The very success of industrial society soon results in a dramatic increase in the quantity of information generated and required by the proper functioning of the whole system of production as well as by the new service society that it brings about. The universe of organised information becomes such a rich and complex domain, and the various types of information such a precious resource – a good if not already a commodity – that managing procedures more and more urgently require a technology adequate to their scale and level of complexity. At some point, the quantity of wealth of time accumulated makes industrial society so complex, and the energy technologies that should liberate further time so refined, that the very possibility of continuing to free ever more time for an increasing number of people comes to depend on the technologies devoted to the management of information, the life-blood of the system. The time-saving process reaches a threshold of transformation, beyond which information technologies become at least as vital as energy technology and the system is ready to evolve from an industrial- to an information-based model. The only factor that is still missing is a technology that can make possible information management as efficiently as the energy technologies liberate time. The arrival of ICT in the 1950s has fulfilled this role in our society.

Thanks to ICT and computer science, the engineering of codified information, the infosphere has begun to produce the instruments necessary for its own management. This is the sense in which the computer has represented the right technology at the right moment. Although the military and strategic needs that arose during World War II, the Cold War, the war in Vietnam, etc., were crucial in providing the enormous resources necessary for computer science to take many of its first great steps, it should be clear that the "economic necessity" of ICT was already implicit in the Industrial Revolution. It was the accumulation of capital and the corresponding growth in complexity of the financial and industrial world during the nineteenth century that laid the ground for an explosive demand for a powerful information technology in the following century. Meanwhile the "cultural necessity" of ICT was a natural consequence of the growth of the infosphere, and therefore partly the offspring of the invention of printing and the mass production of books, in the form of mechanised reproduction of written language, as I have tried to show in the previous chapters.

Thinking is not only tiring, it is also time-consuming and becomes very tedious when demanded by repetitive and stylised tasks, those usually involved in the use and control of machines. It is not surprising, then, that the second industrial revolution has consisted in the development and application of self-regulating devices to control and improve services in general as well as manufacturing production and distribution. The mechanisation of industrial processes has been followed by their automatisation. Consequently, in a few decades physical goods and their mechanical production have become financially and culturally less significant than what makes both possible, namely an efficient management of information. This industrial revolution has been followed by the chip revolution, and the industrial culture, still so keen on concepts such as ownership, material objecthood, perceptible qualities and automatic processes, has been slowly supplanted by a manufacturing culture in which concepts such as control, information, algorithms, virtual visualisation and interactive processes play a more significant role. Engines and the energy industry have been displaced from their central position by computers and data management.

From the perspective of a philosophical anthropology, it is now useful to synthesise the previous analysis by saying that the passage from the energy technologies to the information technologies represents the passage from the *homo faber* to the *homo sapiens*, for this perspective helps us to uncover a paradoxical feature of contemporary info-dustrial societies. Human beings differ from other animals because they are sufficiently intelligent to wish that they could stop working and reasoning, and free enough to toil harder than other creatures to pursue both these aims in order to enjoy their free time. It follows that the *homo faber* and the *homo sapiens* are direct but only contingent consequences of the truly essential *homo ludens*. The fact that philosophers do not typically endorse this view only clarifies why they rarely qualify as champions of common sense. People appear to know better. Different cultures at different times have always mythicised the cosmological beginning of a working-and-reasoning age as the loss of a paradise, in which physical and mental activities are neither required nor pursued. It takes a *homo ludens* to eat the only fruit forbidden by God, unthinkingly and playfully. The afterlife is never seriously conceived of as a workshop, a library or a laboratory. Attempts to regain a heavenly state of leisure – to regain the *mythical* status of *homo ludens* by evolving through *homo faber* and *homo sapiens* into the *actual homo ludens* – have constantly led mankind to delegate both physical and mental toil to other agents of very disparate kinds.

The history of human emancipation has been, so far, not devoid of success. Nature, animals, technological devices and the labour of other human beings have all been employed to transform energy into force and to manage information. The paradox of the industrial and the information revolutions, however, is that in both cases the fundamental anthropological project seems to have failed, although nothing should have been more successful than the engine and the computer in sanating (healing) and liberating human time, developing *homo faber* into *homo sapiens* and then bringing both closer to extinction in favour of *homo ludens*. The industrial revolution and the automatisation of the industrial society have decreased the autonomy and independence of *homo faber* without eliminating the need for him altogether. The information revolution, with its mind-consuming work, has constantly increased the demand for intelligence, forever removing the possibility of a naive state of playful insipience from the prospect of *homo sapiens*. Since the end of the nineteenth century, it has become ever more evident that most employees can work less – the average working week in the EU is now some-what less than 40 hours – only on condition that at least some of them spend more time than their ancestors doing conceptual work. The management of industrialised society has turned out to require increasingly well-educated, properly trained, skilful individuals, capable of carrying out a growing number of intelligent tasks. If industrial society could still hope for the evolution of *homo faber* into a *homo sapiens* that could then approximate to *homo ludens*, the information society seems to have decreed the failure of this project: the sanation and liberation of time, reaching its culmination, has brought about boredom and sadness instead.

No matter whether one subscribes to Max Weber's suggestion that Protest-ant ethics had a significant influence on the development of capitalism (*The Protestant Ethic and the Spirit of Capitalism*), it seems that, in info-dustrial societies based on a "working culture", the increasing generation of free time and leisure simply exacerbates various forms of psychological depression and the suicide rate.[7] Mankind has always hoped to emancipate itself from work-ing for life's necessities, but once a huge, aggregate quantity of free time becomes available for the first time in history, what to do with it is a serious problem for millions of individuals. Is there any reason to hope that the fundamental anthropological project can be rescued? Modern technology is what has provided most of us with leisure time. It is only in this free time that *homo sapiens* can philosophise at liberty, Aristotle knew that already. Philo-sophy, however, precludes the human right to be naive, so after philosophy, the destiny of *homo sapiens* seems to be either to face ontological failure – to remain forever a *homo faber* or *sapiens* or, when this is no longer possible, to annihilate himself – or to move towards development into a *homo poieticus* (from *poiesis*, a creation, a making) of intellectual and spiritual realities. Such evolution cannot be achieved by attempting to regain a naive state of blessed insipience, a pre-intellectual condition of direct contact with reality. The very philosophical process that creates the possibility of a solution also obstructs this simple way out of the problem. The exit lies only ahead, at the end of the process of reflection, in a form of critical constructionism, according to which the mind designs the world that it inhabits and within which it operates. Critical constructionism does not while away the time sanated and liberated by technology, but employs it to emancipate the mind from reality, semanticising the latter (investing it with meaning by means of an ontologically oriented interpretation of design), hence to build and improve the infosphere on and through knowledge, and to develop the state of philosophical reflection into a state of playful mental enjoyment of construction. A simple (i.e. non-reflective) constructionist attitude and an ethic of achievement is what already unites all human endeavours. It is also the approach that we have seen constantly surfacing throughout this book, as the overlying theme in the evolution of the world of information and ICT. So there are reasons for hope. The project for a *homo ludens* may be rescued by transforming it into a project for a *homo poieticus*. What must be recognised is the need for a work of conceptual excavation and discovery: the constructionist trend in modern culture needs to become aware of its own nature and to acquire a more prominent role in shaping human actions, if it is going to be the basis for a new philosophical anthropology. Bringing to light (and this is the sense in which the work is foundationalist) the nature of critical constructionism in all its complexity was not and could not be the aim of this book. I hope it may the task of a future book on the philosophy of information.[8]

Notes

1 Properly speaking, a technology can be described as pervasive only if it is noticed for its absence. In this specific sense telephones and televisions are pervasive technologies. You would be surprised to find a house without a telephone, and I boast about the fact that I do not have a television set – while personal computers are becoming pervasive and for the Internet it is just a matter of time.

2 In medicine a CAT scan (computerised axial tomography scan) is a non-invasive method of X-ray imaging used for diagnosis, an alternative to exploratory surgery. The CAT scanner passes a narrow fan of X-rays through successive sections of the body. The output of the scanning is then converted by a computer into cross-sectional images and finally, using views taken from various angles, into a 3D model of the organ or tissue under analysis.

3 A poor VRE is simply a 3D environment which allows for a low degree of interaction from without via input devices such as a keyboard, a mouse or a joystick – standard 2D operating systems for personal computers such as Win95 do not yet satisfy even this criterion, unlike more sophisticated software developed for CAD applications. Rich VREs are characterised by 3D, morphing, physical constraints, e.g. effects of solidity, full and collective immersion of the subjects within the environment and direct interaction via data gloves. Morphing can be defined as computer-generated animation in 3D. In order to give the impression of metamorphosis of an object from one state into another, the computer needs first to generate a mathematical model of the beginning and the end of the process in 3D and then calculate all the transformations undergone by the virtual object's location, surface texture, colour, lighting, reflectiveness and transparency, to determine the values of each single dot, on the screen, that constitute the object.

4 In a system, homeostasis is the maintenance of a constant internal state of stability of all the conditions required by its efficient functioning.

5 Coupling is the technical word whereby we refer to the strength of interrelations between the components of a system (e.g. the modules of a program, or the processing elements of an artificial neural network). These interrelations concern the number of references from one component to another, the complexity of the interface between the components, the amount of data passed or shared between components and the amount of control exercised by one component over another. The tighter the coupling, the higher the interdependency, the looser the coupling the lower the interdependency. Completely decoupled components – systems with a null degree of interdependency – have no common data and no control flow interaction.

6 According to Galen, the great Greek physician, the human body was composed of four kinds of fluid: phlegm, blood, choler (yellow bile) and melancholy (black

bile). Physical and mental characteristics were explained by different proportions of humours in individuals. An excess of phlegm gave rise to a "phlegmatic", or calm, temperament and was associated with water; too much blood caused a "sanguine", or passionate, temperament and was associated with air; excess of yellow bile was behind a "choleric", or irascible, temperament and was associated with fire; and excess of black bile caused a "melancholy", or depressive, one, associated with earth. An imbalance of the humours could supposedly be treated by a corresponding diet.

7   In 1986, the highest suicide rates per million of the population were 430 for men in Finland and 199 for women in Denmark. In the United States the suicide rate in the age group between 15 and 24 tripled between 1950 and 1980 and suicide is now the third most common cause of death in this age group. In 1992, there were 3,952 suicides in England and Wales, about 78 per million of the population. Four times as many young men kill themselves as do women.

8   I seem to have a bad habit of ending books by referring to other future books. This note is only for the reader who may be interested in the connection between this conclusion and that occurring at the end of *Scepticism and the Foundation of Epistemology*. In both cases, I write that future work will be needed, but while here I am arguing that it will be crucial to develop a critical constructionism that may provide a unified philosophy of information and hence a theory of the nature of the infosphere, in *Scepticism* I suggested that the development of a negative anthropology is needed to understand the *emergence* of the infosphere. In what follows I have slightly revised the conclusion reached in that context.

The history of modern thought has been characterised by an increasing gap between mind and reality. It is a process of epistemic detachment which has been irresistible ever since it began, and quite inevitably so. Knowledge develops as mind's answer to the presence of the non-mental. It is the means whereby the subject establishes a minimal distance, and emancipates itself, from the object. The rise of dualism and the escalating interaction between traditional knowledge, as an object, and innovative knowledge, as a further reaction to it, has led to the emergence of a new world.

Today the infosphere is an artificial universe which becomes, to an ever-increasing degree, the very environment we inhabit, and whose challenges we must answer. It is a domain as completely autonomous from each of us, as individual minds, as the physical world is, and which, unlike the latter, is capable of infinite growth in extension and complexity. What is our relation to such an epistemic reality?

On the one hand, our situation is one of potentially full understanding of something that bears the stamp of total intelligibility. As I have tried to explain in *Scepticism*, it is only an apparent paradox that several centuries of constant growth of knowledge should have made us lose such closeness to the world of things, while providing another type of reality, an entire universe of codified information, which enfolds reality, and intentionally keeps it at distance from the mind. This new environment has been created by the human mind, and since we are totally responsible for its existence, we may also be confident of its potential full intelligibility.

On the other hand, in the process of studying the infosphere, the mind investigates its own product and hence is bound to be confronted with the inevitable dilemma represented by a self-referential assessment.

A radical reflection upon the reasons that prompt and sustain the incessant construction of the world of knowledge is badly needed, but no innovative theory capable of explaining and vindicating the phenomenon of the construction of the human encyclopaedia (the infosphere viewed from a purely epistemological perspective) can ever be based merely on the still dominant, but yet too naive, assumption of a human desire for knowledge for its own sake. A more negative anthropology is required, in order to make possible a new philosophy of knowledge as an ontology of knowledge.

The dualism of mind and reality; the self-reflective nature of knowledge; the emergence of the infosphere as the real habitat of mental life; the constructionist capacities of the mind; these are among the most innovative matters confronting our philosophical reflection today. They are not entirely new, for at least since the Renaissance the mind has constantly moved away from reality, intentionally constructing and refining its own cultural environment as an alternative to the world of nature. These issues are also far from having reached their ultimate development, and this is what makes their understanding a pressing question. They have certainly become more and more clearly discernible in the twentieth century. It is with respect to such new features of our knowledge and culture that Greek intellectualism becomes utterly inadequate and a new theory of the genesis of the epistemic relation between mind and reality is required.

Bibliography

Aleksander, I. and Morton, H. (1995) *An Introduction to Neural Computing* (International Thomson).

Anderson, A. R. (ed.) (1964) *Minds and Machines* (Englewood Cliffs, NJ: Prentice-Hall).

Auerbach, E. (1953) *Mimesis: The Representation of Reality in Western Culture* (Princeton, NJ: Princeton University Press).

Aukstakalnis, S. and Blatner, D. (1992) *Silicon Mirage: The Art and Science of Virtual Reality* (Berkeley, Calif.: Peachpit Press).

Baker, N. (1994) "Discards", in *The Size of Thoughts: Essays and Other Lumber* (London: Vintage, repr. 1997), pp. 125–81.

Baker, T. (1699) *Reflections upon Learning, wherein is shown the insufficiency thereof in its several Particulars. In order to evince the Usefulness and Necessity of Revelation* (London).

Barker, P. (1992) "Electronic Books and Libraries of the Future", *The Electronic Library* (10)3, pp. 139–49.

Barnes, J. (ed.) (1984) *Metaphysics* in *The Complete Works of Aristotle*, vol. 2 (of 2 vols) (Princeton, NJ: Princeton University Press).

Barrett, E. (ed.) (1988) *Text, ConText, and HyperText* (Cambridge, Mass.: MIT Press).

Barwise, J. and Etchemendy, J. (1993) *Turing's World* (Stanford. Calif.: CSLI and Cambridge: Cambridge University Press).

Barwise, J. and Etchemendy, J. (1998) "Computers, Visualization and the Nature of Reasoning", in T. W. Bynum and J. H. Moor (eds) *The Digital Phoenix: How Computers are Changing Philosophy* (Oxford: Blackwell), pp. 93–116.

Baudrillard, J. (1972, French orig.) *For a Critique of the Political Economy* (English trans. 1981, St Louis, Minn.: Telos Press).

Baudrillard, J. (1981, French orig.) *Simulacra and Simulations* (English trans. 1994, Ann Arbor, Mich.: University of Michigan Press).

Baudrillard, J. (1991, French orig.) *The Gulf War Did Not Take Place* (English trans. 1995, Bloomington, Ind.: Indiana University Press).

Bennett, C. H. and Landauer, R. (1985) "The Fundamental Limits of Computation", *Scientific American* (253)1, pp. 48–56.

Boden, M. A. (1987) *Artificial Intelligence and Natural Man*, 2nd edn (London: MIT Press).

Boden, M. A. (ed.) (1990) *The Philosophy of Artificial Intelligence* (Oxford: Oxford University Press).

Boden, M. A. (ed.) (1996) *The Philosophy of Artificial Life* (Oxford: Oxford University Press).

Bolter, J. D. (1984) *Turing's Man: Western Culture in the Computer Age* (Chapel Hill, NC: University of North Carolina Press).

Bolter, J. D. (1991) *Writing Space: The Computer, Hypertext, and the History of Writing* (Hillsdale, NJ and London: Erlbaum).

Boole, G. (1854) *An Investigation of the Laws of Thought, on Which are Founded the Mathematical Theories of Logic and Probabilities* (London: Walton & Maberly); repr. 1916 as *George Boole's Collected Logical Works* (Chicago, Ill., and New York: Open Court), vol. 2; repr. 1951 (New York: Dover).

Boolos, G. and Jeffrey R. (1989) *Computability and Logic*, 3rd edn (Cambridge: Cambridge University Press).

Bringsjord, A. (1998) "Philosophy and 'Super' Computation", in T. W. Bynum and J. H. Moor (eds) *The Digital Phoenix: How Computers are Changing Philosophy* (Oxford: Blackwell), pp. 231–52.

Brookshear, J. G. (1989) *Theory of Computation: Formal Languages, Automata, and Complexity* (Redwood City, Calif.: Benjamin/Cummings).

Brookshear, J. G. (1997) *Computer Science: An Overview*, 5th edn (Reading, Mass.: Addison-Wesley).

Burkhardt, H. and Smith, B. (eds) (1991) *Handbook of Metaphysics and Ontology*, 2 vols. (Munich: Philosophia Verlag).

Burkholder L. (ed.) (1992) *Philosophy and the Computer* (Boulder, Colo.: Westview Press).

Bush, V. (1945) "As We May Think", *Atlantic Monthly* (176)1, pp. 101–8.

Butler, C. (1985) *Statistics in Linguistics* (New York: Blackwell).

Bynum, T. W. and Moor, J. H. (eds) (1998) *The Digital Phoenix: How Computers are Changing Philosophy* (Oxford: Blackwell).

Carpenter, B. E. and Doran, R. W. (eds) (1986) *A. M. Turing's Ace Report and Other Papers* (Cambridge, Mass.: MIT Press).

Cassirer, E. (1996) *The Philosophy of Symbolic Forms*, 4 vols (New Haven, Conn., and London: Yale University Press).

Checkland, P. B. and Scholes, J. (1990) *Soft Systems Methodology in Action* (New York: John Wiley & Sons).

Christensen, D. E. (ed.) (1983) *Contemporary German Philosophy* (University Park, Pa: Pennsylvania State University Press).

Church, A. (1936) "An Unsolvable Problem of Elementary Number Theory", *American Journal of Mathematics* (58), pp. 345–63.

Churchland, P. M. (1990) *A Neurocomputational Perspective: The Nature of Mind and the Structure of Science* (Cambridge, Mass.: MIT Press).

Churchland, P. S. and Sejnowski, T. (1992) *The Computational Brain* (Cambridge, Mass.: MIT Press).

Clark, A. J. (1989) *Microcognition: Philosophy, Cognitive Science, and Parallel Distributed Processing* (Cambridge, Mass.: MIT Press).

Clark, A. J. (1993) *Associative Engines: Connectionism, Concepts, and Representational Change* (Cambridge, Mass.: MIT Press).

Clarke, A. C. (1967) "Technology and the Future", repr. 1972 in *Report on Planet Three and Other Speculations* (London: Pan Books), Ch. 14.

Cohen, D. I. A. (1997) *Introduction to Computer Theory*, 2nd edn (New York: John Wiley & Sons).

Cohen, J. (1965) "On the Project of a Universal Character", *Mind* (63), pp. 49–63.

Copeland, B. J. (1993) *Artificial Intelligence: A Philosophical Introduction* (Oxford: Blackwell).

Copeland, B. J. (1997) "The Broad Conception of Computation", *American Behavioral Scientist* (40)6, pp. 690–716.

Cutland, N. J. (1980) *Computability: An Introduction to Recursive Function Theory* (Cambridge: Cambridge University Press).

Dahlbom, B. and Mathiassen, L. (1993) *Computers in Context: The Philosophy and Practice of Systems Design* (Oxford: Blackwell).

Davis, M. (ed.) (1965) *The Undecidable: Basic Papers on Problems, Propositions, Unsolvable Problems, and Computable Functions* (New York: Raven Press).

Dawson, M. R. W. and Shamanski, K. S. (1994) "Connectionism, Confusion, and Cognitive Science", *Journal of Intelligent Systems* (4), pp. 215–62.

de Bury, R. (1970) *Philobiblon* (Oxford: Blackwell).

De Kerkhove, D. (1991) *Brainframes: Technology, Mind and Business* (Utrecht: Bosch & Keuning).

Dennett, D. C. (1978) *Brainstorms: Philosophic Essays on Mind and Psychology* (Cambridge, Mass.: MIT Press).

Dertouzos, M. L. (1997) *What Will Be: How the New World of Information Will Change Our Lives* (London: Piatkus).

Descartes, R. (1984) *The Philosophical Writings*, 2 vols, ed. J. Cottingham, R. Stoothoff and D. Murdoch (Cambridge: Cambridge University Press).

Detlefsen, M. (1998) "Gödel's Theorems", in *Routledge Encyclopedia of Philosophy*, vol. 4 (London: Routledge).

Deutsch, D. (1985) "Quantum Theory, the Church–Turing Principle and the Universal Quantum Computer", *Proceedings of the Royal Society*, series A (400), pp. 97–117.

Deutsch, D. (1997) *The Fabric of Reality* (Harmondsworth: Penguin Books).

Devlin, K. (1991) *Logic and Information* (Cambridge: Cambridge University Press).

Dewdney, A. K. (1989) *The Turing Omnibus: 61 Excursions in Computer Science* (Rockville, MD: Computer Science Press).

Dewdney, A. K. (1996) *Introductory Computer Science: Bits of Theory, Bytes of Practice* (New York: Computer Science Press).

Dijksterhuis, E. J. (1986) *The Mechanization of the World Picture: Pythagoras to Newton* (Princeton, NJ: Princeton University Press).

Dretske, F. (1981) *Knowledge and the Flow of Information* (Cambridge, Mass.: MIT Press).

Dreyfus, H. L. (1992) *What Computers Still Can't Do: A Critique of Artificial Intelligence*, 2nd edn (Cambridge, Mass.: MIT Press).

Dreyfus, H. L. (1998) "Philosophy of Artificial Intelligence: Responses to My Critics", in T. W. Bynum and J. H. Moor (eds) *The Digital Phoenix: How Computers are Changing Philosophy* (Oxford: Blackwell), pp. 193–212.

Dreyfus, H. L. and Dreyfus, S. E. (1988) "Making a Mind versus Modelling the Brain: Artificial Intelligence Back at a Branchpoint", in S. R. Graubard (ed.) *The*

Artificial Intelligence Debate: False Starts, Real Foundations (Cambridge, Mass.: MIT Press), pp. 15–44.

Dreyfus, H. L. and Dreyfus, S. E., with Athanasiou, T. (1986) *Mind over Machine: The Power of Human Intuition and Expertise in the Era of the Computer* (Oxford: Blackwell).

Eisenstein, E. L. (1993) *The Printing Revolution in Early Modern Europe* (Cambridge: Cambridge University Press).

Emmeche, C. (1991) *The Garden in the Machine: The Emerging Science of Artificial Life* (Princeton, NJ: Princeton University Press).

Erasmus, D. (1982) *Adages*, translated and annotated by R. A. B. Mynors (Toronto and London: University of Toronto Press), first published 1506.

Ess, C. (ed.) (1996) *Philosophical Perspectives on Computer-mediated Communication* (Albany, NY: State University of New York Press).

Feigenbaum, E. A. and Feldman, J. (eds) (1963) *Computers and Thought*, (New York: McGraw-Hill).

Fetzer, J. H. (1998) "Philosophy and Computer Science: Reflections on the Program Verification Debate", in T. W. Bynum and J. H. Moor (eds) *The Digital Phoenix: How Computers are Changing Philosophy* (Oxford: Blackwell), pp. 253–73.

Feynman, R. P. (1982) "Simulating Physics with Computers", *International Journal of Theoretical Physics* (21)6/7, pp. 467–88.

Feynman, R. P. (1985) *QED: The Strange Theory of Light and Matter* (Harmondsworth: Penguin Books).

Floridi, L. (1995) "The Internet: Which Future for Organised Knowledge – Frankenstein or Pygmalion?", UNESCO Philosophy Forum, Paris, 14–17 March 1995; various versions published in *International Journal of Human–Computer Studies* (43), 1995, pp. 261–74; *The Information Society* (9) 1996, pp. 5–16 and *The Electronic Library* (14) 1996, pp. 43–52.

Floridi, L. (1996) *L'estensione dell'intelligenza – Guida all'informatica per filosofi* (Rome: Armando).

Floridi, L. (1997a) "Computer-Mediated-Interaction: A Logical Analysis", National Conference, *Internet Meeting 1997, Internet and Intranet for Companies*, Centro Congressi Milanofiori, Assago, Milan, 15–17 May 1997 (Milan: Tecniche Nuove).

Floridi, L. (1997b) "Logic and Visual Thinking", in E. Lunani (ed.) *L'apporto dell'informatico nell'insegnamento delle discipline filosofiche*, Atti delle giornate di studio di Perugia, organizzate dall'IRRSAE dell'Umbria in collaborazione con l'Istituto Italiano per gli Studi Filosofici, 18–20 Marzo 1996 (Perugia: GESP Editrice), pp. 99–115.

Floridi, L. (1997c) *Internet* (Milan: Il Saggiatore).

Fodor, J. A. (1975) *The Language of Thought* (New York: Thomas Crowell).

Fodor, J. A. and Pylyshyn, Z. (1988) "Connectionism and Cognitive Architecture: A Critical Analysis", *Cognition* (28), pp. 3–71.

Forester, T. and Morrison, P. (1994) *Computer Ethics*, 2nd edn (Cambridge, Mass.: MIT Press).

Fox, J. (1981) "Towards a Reconciliation of Fuzzy Logic and Standard Logic", *International Journal of Man–Machine Studies* (15), pp. 213–20.

Galton, A. (1990) *Logic for Information Technology* (New York: John Wiley & Sons).

Galton, A. (1996) "The Church–Turing Thesis: Its Nature and Status", in P. Millican and A. Clark (eds) *Machines and Thought: The Legacy of Alan Turing*, vol. 1 (Oxford: Clarendon Press), pp. 137–64.

Garey, M. R. and Johnson, D. S. (1991) *Computers and Intractability – A Guide to the Theory of NP-Completeness* (New York: W. H. Freeman and Co.); first published 1979; the 1991 reprint contains a final note of update.

Genette, G. (1983) *Narrative Discourse: An Essay in Method* (Ithaca, NY: Cornell University Press).

Gillies, D. (1996) *Artificial Intelligence and Scientific Method* (Oxford: Oxford University Press).

Gödel, K. (1934) "On Undecidable Propositions of Formal Mathematical Systems", in M. Davis (ed.) *The Undecidable: Basic Papers as Problems, Propositions, Unsolvable Problems, and Computable Functions* (New York: Raven Press), pp. 41–74.

Goethe, J. W. von (1984) *Faust*, Parts I and II, ed. and trans. S. Atkins (Princeton, NJ: Princeton University Press); first published 1790–1832.

Goldstine, H. H. (1972) *The Computer from Pascal to von Neumann* (Princeton, NJ: Princeton University Press).

Golub, G. and Ortega, J. M. (1993) *Scientific Computing: An Introduction with Parallel Computing* (San Diego, Calif.: Academic Press).

Graubard, S. R. (ed.) (1988) *The Artificial Intelligence Debate: False Starts, Real Foundations* (Cambridge, Mass.: MIT Press).

Grim, P., Mar, G. and St Denis, P. (1998) *The Philosophical Computer: Exploratory Essays in Philosophical Computer Modeling* (Cambridge, Mass.: MIT Press).

Grossberg, S. (1988) *Neural Networks and Natural Intelligence* (Cambridge, Mass.: MIT Press).

Haack, S. (1979) "Do We Need Fuzzy Logic?", *International Journal of Man–Machine Studies* (11), pp. 437–45; repr. in Haack (1996) *Deviant Logic – Fuzzy Logic* (Chicago and London: University of Chicago Press).

Haack, S. (1996) *Deviant Logic – Fuzzy Logic* (Chicago and London: University of Chicago Press).

Hamilton, E. and Cairns, H. (eds) (1963) *The Collected Dialogues of Plato including the Letters*, 2nd edn with corrections (Princeton, NJ: Princeton University Press).

Harel, D. (1992) *Algorithmics, The Spirit of Computing*, 2nd edn (Reading, Mass.: Addison-Wesley).

Harry, M. J. S. (1990) *Information and Management Systems, Concepts and Applications* (London: Pitman).

Haugeland, J. (1985) *Artificial Intelligence: The Very Idea* (Cambridge, Mass.: MIT Press).

Heidegger, M. (1977) *The Question Concerning Technology and Other Essays* (New York: Harper & Row), first published 1949.

Heidegger, M. (1982) "Hebel – Friend of the House", in D. E. Christensen (ed.) *Contemporary German Philosophy*, vol. 3 (University Park, Pa: Pennsylvania State University Press).

Heim, M. (1993) *The Metaphysics of Virtual Reality* (New York: Oxford University Press).

Herken, R. (ed.) (1988) *The Universal Turing Machine* (Oxford: Oxford University Press).

Hockey, S. (1980) *A Guide to Computer Applications in the Humanities* (Baltimore, Md.: Johns Hopkins University Press).

Hodges, A. (1992) *Alan Turing: The Enigma* (London: Vintage), first published 1983.

Hodges, W. (1977) *Logic: An Introduction to Elementary Logic* (Harmondsworth: Penguin Books).

Hopcroft, J. E. and Ullman, J. D. (1979) *Introduction to Automata Theory, Languages and Computation* (Reading, Mass.: Addison-Wesley).

Hopfield, J. J. (1982) "Neural Networks and Physical Systems with Emergent Collective Properties", *Proceedings of the National Academy of Science* (USA) (79), pp. 2554–8.

Horgan, T. and Tienson, J. (1991) *Connectionism and the Philosophy of Mind* (Dordrecht: Kluwer).

Hyman, A. (1982) *Charles Babbage, Pioneer of the Computer* (Oxford: Oxford University Press).

Jeffrey, R. (1994) *Formal Logic: Its Scope and Limits*, 3rd edn (New York and London: McGraw-Hill).

Johnson, D. G. (1994) *Computer Ethics*, 2nd edn (Englewood Cliffs, NJ: Prentice-Hall).

Jones, N. D. (1997) *Computability and Complexity* (Cambridge, Mass.: MIT Press).

Jowett, B. (1953) *The Dialogues of Plato*, vol. I, *Meno* (Oxford: Clarendon Press).

Kazemier, B. and Vuysje, D. (eds) (1962) *Logic and Language* (Dordrecht: Reidel).

Kenny, A. (1978) *The Aristotelian Ethics: A Study of the Relationship between the Eudemian and Nicomachean Ethics of Aristotle* (Oxford: Clarendon Press).

Kenny, A. (1982) *The Computation of Style: An Introduction to Statistics for Students of Literature and Humanities* (Oxford: Pergamon).

Kenny, A. (1992) *Computers and the Humanities* (London: British Library Research and Development Department).

Klir, G. J. and Folger, T. A. (1988) *Fuzzy Sets, Uncertainty, and Information* (Englewood Cliffs, NJ: Prentice-Hall).

Kosko, B. (1992) *Neural Networks and Fuzzy Systems* (Englewood Cliffs, NJ: Prentice-Hall).

Kozen, D. C. (1997) *Automata and Computability* (New York: Springer-Verlag).

Lamb, W. R. L. (1957) *Meno* (Cambridge, Mass.: Harvard University Press).

Lancashire, I. (1988) *The Humanities Computing Yearbook 1988* (Oxford: Clarendon Press).

Lancashire, I. (1991) *The Humanities Computing Yearbook 1989–90* (Oxford: Clarendon Press).

Landow, G. P. (ed.) (1994) *Hyper Text Theory* (Baltimore, Md.: Johns Hopkins University Press).

Landow, G. P. (1997) *Hypertext 2.0: The Convergence of Contemporary Critical Theory and Technology*, 2nd edn (Baltimore, Md.: Johns Hopkins University Press).

Ledger, G. R. (1989) *Re-counting Plato: A Computer Analysis of Plato's Style* (Oxford: Clarendon Press).

Leibniz, G. W. (1968) *Zwei Briefe über das binäre Zahlensystem und die chinesische Philosophie*, (*Two Letters on the Binary System of Numbers and Chinese Philosophy*), ed. R. Loosen and F. Vonessen (Stuttgart: Belser-Presse).

Lévy, P. (1990) *Les Technologies de l'intelligence* (Paris: Editions La Découverte).

Lewis, H. R. and Papadimitriou, C. H. (1998) *Elements of the Theory of Computation*, 2nd edn (Englewood Cliffs, NJ: Prentice-Hall).

Longo, G. (ed.) (1991) *Philosophy of Computer Science, The Monist* (82)1.

Lucas, J. R. (1961) "Minds, Machines and Gödel", *Philosophy* (36), pp. 112–27.

Lucas, J. R. (1996) "Minds, Machines and Gödel: A Retrospect", in P. Millican and A. Clark (eds) *Machines and Thought: The Legacy of Alan Turing*, vol. 1 (Oxford: Clarendon Press), pp. 103–24.

Lunani, E. (ed.) (1997) *L'apporto dell'informatica nell'insegnamento delle discipline filosofiche*, Atti delle giornate di studio di Perugia, organizzate dall'IRRSAE dell'Umbria in collaborazione con l'Istituto Italiano per gli Studi Filosofici, 18–20 Marzo 1996 (Perugia: GESP Editrice).

Lyon, D. (1988) *The Information Society – Issues and Illusions* (Cambridge: Polity Press).

Lyotard, J. F. (1984) *The Postmodern Condition: A Report on Knowledge*, trans. G. Bennington and B. Massumi (Minneapolis, Minn.: University of Minnesota Press); first published 1979, as *La Condition postmoderne: rapport sur le savoir* (Paris: Éditions de Minuit).

Machlup, F. (1980–4) *Knowledge: Its Creation, Distribution and Economic Significance* (Princeton, NJ: Princeton University Press).

Machlup, F. and Leeson, K. (eds) (1978) *Information through the Printed World* (New York: Praeger).

Machlup, F. and Mansfield, U. (1983) *The Study of Information, Interdisciplinary Messages* (New York: John Wiley & Sons).

McKenzie, D. F. (1986) *Bibliography and the Sociology of Texts, The Panizzi Lectures 1985* (London: British Library).

McKnight, C. (1991) *Hypertext in Context* (Cambridge: Cambridge University Press).

McLuhan, M. (1964) *Understanding Media: The Extensions of Man* (Cambridge, Mass.: MIT Press), repr. 1994.

Meltzer, B. and Michie, D. (eds) (1969) *Machine Intelligence 5* (Edinburgh: Edinburgh University Press).

Metropolis, N., Howlett, J. and Rota, G.-C. (eds) (1980) *A History of Computing in the Twentieth Century: A Collection of Essays* (New York and London: Academic Press).

Miall, D. S. (ed.) (1990) *Humanities and the Computer, New Directions* (Oxford: Clarendon Press).

Milburn, G. (1996) *Quantum Technology* (St Leonards: Allen & Unwin).

Millican, P. and Clark, A. (1996) *Machines and Thought: The Legacy of Alan Turing*, 2 vols. (Oxford: Clarendon Press).

Mingers, J. (1997) "The Nature of Information and its Relationship to Meaning", in R. L. Winder, S. K. Probert and I. A. Beeson (eds), *Philosophical Aspects of Information Systems* (London: Taylor & Francis), pp. 73–84.

Minsky, M. L. (1967) *Computation: Finite and Infinite Machines* (Englewood Cliffs, NJ: Prentice-Hall).

Minsky, M. L. (1987) *The Society of Mind* (London: Heinemann); first published 1986.

Minsky, M. L. (1990) "Logical vs. Analogical or Symbolic vs. Connectionist or Neat vs. Scruffy", in P. H. Winston (ed.) *Artificial Intelligence at MIT, Expanding Frontiers*, vol. 1 (Cambridge, Mass.: MIT Press).

Minsky, M. L. and Papert, S. (1969) *Perceptrons: An Introduction to Computational Geometry* (Cambridge, Mass.: MIT Press); see also *Perceptrons, Expanded Edition*, (Cambridge, Mass.: MIT Press).

Mitcham, C. (1994) *Thinking through Technology: The Path between Engineering and Philosophy* (Chicago: University of Chicago Press).

Mitcham, C. and Huning, A. (eds) (1986) *Philosophy and Technology: Information Technology and Computers in Theory and Practice*, 2 vols (Dordrecht and Boston: Reidel).

Montague, R. (1962) "Toward a General Theory of Computability", in B. Kazemier and D. Vuysje (eds) *Logic and Language* (Dordrecht: Reidel).

Moor, J. H. (1985) "What is Computer Ethics?", *Metaphilosophy* 16(4), pp. 266–75.

Moret, B. M. E. (1998) *The Theory of Computation* (Reading, Mass.: Addison-Wesley).

Morrison, P. and Morrison, E. (ed.) (1961) *Charles Babbage and his Calculating Engines* (New York: Dover).

Negroponte, N. (1995) *Being Digital* (Cambridge, Mass.: MIT Press).

Nelson, T. (1974) *Computer Lib/Dream Machines* (Redmond, Wash.: Microsoft Press); 1987, a reissue, with some revisions.

Neuman, M. (1990) "An Introduction to the Analysis of Electronic Text in Philosophy", *The Computers & Philosophy Newsletter* (5), pp. 1–5.

Neuman, M. (1991) "The Very Pulse of the Machine: Three Trends Toward Improvement in Electronic Versions of Humanities Texts", *Computers and the Humanities* (25)6, pp. 363–75.

Neumann, J. von (1961–3) *Collected Works*, 6 vols, ed. A. H. Taube (Oxford: Pergamon Press).

Newell, A. (1990) *Unified Theories of Cognition* (Cambridge, Mass.: Harvard University Press).

Newell, A. and Simon, H. (1976) "Computer Science as Empirical Enquiry: Symbols and Search", *Communications of the Association for Computing Machinery* (19), pp. 113–26.

Nielsen, J. (1995) *Multimedia and Hypertext: The Internet and Beyond* (Boston and London: AP Professional); this is a revised and updated edition of *Hypertext and Hypermedia* (1990).

Nietzsche, F. (1903) *Vom Nutzen und Nachtheil der Historie für das Leben*, English trans. by R. Gray in *Unfashionable Observations*, 1995 (Stanford, Calif.: Stanford University Press).

Novalis, (1957) *Fragmente*, in *Werke Briefe Dokumente*, 4 vols, ed. E. Wasmuth (Heidelberg: Verlag Lambert Schneider); the citation in the text is from the second volume, fr. 1, p. 9.

Ong, W. J. (1982) *Orality and Literacy: The Technologizing of the Word* (London: Methuen), repr. 1990.

Orwell, G. (1949) *Nineteen Eighty-four* (London: Secker & Warburg).

Pagels, H. R. (ed.) (1984) *Computer Culture: The Scientific, Intellectual, and Social Impact of the Computer* (New York: New York Academy of Sciences).

Panofsky, E. (1953) "In Defence of the Ivory Tower" (The Association of Princeton Graduate Alumni, Report of the Third Conference held at the Graduate College of Princeton University), pp. 77–84.

Partridge, D. and Wilks, Y. (eds) (1990) *Foundations of Artificial Intelligence: A Sourcebook* (Cambridge: Cambridge University Press).

Penrose, R. (1989) *The Emperor's New Mind: Concerning Computers, Minds, and the Laws of Physics* (Oxford: Oxford University Press).

Penrose, R. (1990) "Précis of 'The Emperor's New Mind: Concerning Computers, Minds, and the Laws of Physics'", *Behavioral and Brain Sciences* (13), pp. 643–705.

Penrose, R. (1994) *Shadows of the Mind: A Search for the Missing Science of Consciousness* (New York: Oxford University Press).

Peirce, C. S. (1931–58) *Collected Papers*, ed. A. W. Burk (Cambridge, Mass.: Harvard University Press).

Pylyshyn, Z. W. (ed.) (1970) *Perspectives on the Computer Revolution* (Englewood Cliffs, NJ: Prentice-Hall).

Ramsey, W., Stich, S. and Rumelhart, D. E. (1991) *Philosophy and Connectionist Theory* (Hillsdale, NJ: Erlbaum).

Reza, F. M. (1994) *An Introduction to Information Theory* (New York: Dover); first published 1961.

Rheingold, H. (1987) *The Cognitive Connection: Thought and Language in Man and Machine* (Englewood Cliffs, NJ: Prentice-Hall).

Rheingold, H. (1991) *Virtual Reality* (London: Secker & Warburg); repr. 1992 (London: Mandarin).

Rich, E. and Knight, K. (1991) *Artificial Intelligence*, 2nd edn (New York: McGraw-Hill).

Roszak, T. (1994) *The Cult of Information* (Berkeley, Calif., and London: University of California Press); rev. edn of 1986 (New York: Pantheon Books).

Rucker, R. (1988) *Mind Tools: The Mathematics of Information* (Harmondsworth: Penguin Books).

Rumelhart, D. E. and McClelland, J. L. (eds) (1986) *Parallel Distributed Processing: Explorations in the Microstructure of Cognition*, 2 vols. (Cambridge, Mass.: MIT Press).

Russell, S. and Norvik, P. (1995) *Artificial Intelligence: A Modern Approach* (Englewood Cliffs, NJ: Prentice-Hall).

Saunders, L. (1993) *The Virtual Library: Visions and Realities* (London: Meckler).

Saussure, F. de (1983), *Course in General Linguistics* (New York: McGraw-Hill).

Savage, J. E. (1998) *Models of Computation: Exploring the Power of Computing* (Reading, Mass.: Addison-Wesley).

Schagrin, M. L., Rapaport, W. J. and Dipert, R. R. (1985) *Logic: A Computer Approach* (New York: McGraw-Hill).

Searle, J. R. (1980) "Minds, Brains, and Programs", *Behavioral and Brain Sciences* (3), pp. 417–57.

Searle, J. R. (1990) "Is the Brain's Mind a Computer Program?", *Scientific American* (262), pp. 20–5.

Self, J. (ed.) (1988), *Artificial Intelligence and Human Learning: Intelligent Computer Aided Instruction* (London and New York: Chapman and Hall).

Seyer, P. C. (1991) *Understanding Hypertext: Concepts and Applications* (Blue Ridge Summit, Pa.: Windcrest).

Shannon, C. E. (1948) "A Mathematical Theory of Communication", *Bell System Technical Journal* (27), pp. 379–423, 623–56.

Shannon, C. E. (1993) *Collected Papers* (Los Alamos, Calif.: IEEE Computer Society Press).

Shannon, C. E. and Weaver, W. (1975) *The Mathematical Theory of Communication* (Urbana, Ill.: University of Illinois Press).

Shapiro, S. C. (1992) *Encyclopedia of Artificial Intelligence*, 2nd edn (New York: John Wiley & Sons).

Shor, P. (1994) "Algorithms for Quantum Computation: Discrete Log and Factoring", 35th Annual IEEE Conference on Foundations of Computer Science, Santa Fe, New Mexico.

Shurkin, J. N. (1984) *Engines of the Mind: A History of the Computer* (New York and London: Norton).

Siegelmann, H. T. (1995) "Computation Beyond the Turing Limit", *Science* (268), 28 April, pp. 545–8.

Siegelmann, H. T. (1998) *Neural Networks and Analog Computation: Beyond the Turing Limit* (Boston, Mass.: Birkhäuser).

Siegelmann, H. T. and Sontag, E. D. (1994) "Analog Computation via Neural Nets", *Theoretical Computer Science* (131), pp. 331–60.

Simon, D. R. (1994) "On the Power of Quantum Computation", 35th Annual IEEE Conference on Foundations of Computer Science, Santa Fe, New Mexico.

Simon, H. A. (1996) *The Sciences of the Artificial*, 3rd edn (Cambridge, Mass.: MIT Press).

Simon, H. A. and Newell, A. (1964) "Information-processing in Computer and Man", in Z. W. Pylyshyn (ed.) *Perspectives on the Computer Revolution* (Englewood Cliffs, NJ: Prentice-Hall), pp. 256–73.

Sipser, M. (1997) *Introduction to the Theory of Computation* (Boston and London: PWS Publishing Company).

Skyrms, B. (1990) *The Dynamics of Rational Deliberation* (Cambridge, Mass.: Harvard University Press).

Sloman, A. (1978) *The Computer Revolution in Philosophy: Philosophy, Science and Models of Mind* (Hassocks: Harvester Press and New York: Humanities Press).

Smolensky, P. (1988) "On the Proper Treatment of Connectionism", *Behavioral and Brain Sciences* (11), pp. 1–74.

Smullyan, R. S. (1968) *First Order Logic* (Berlin and New York: Springer-Verlag).

Spinosa, G. (1990) "Philosophical Lexicography: The Lie and the Use of the Computer", *Computers and the Humanities* (24), pp. 375–9.

Stillings, A. *et al.* (1995) *Cognitive Science* (New York: MIT).

Sudkamp, T. A. (1997) *Languages and Machines*, 2nd edn (Reading, Mass.: Addison-Wesley).

Tannenbaum, R. (1988) *Computing in the Humanities and Social Sciences*, vol. 1, *Fundamentals* (Rockville, Md.: Computer Science Press).

Tapscott, D. (1996) *The Digital Economy, Promise and Peril in the Age of Networked Intelligence* (New York: McGraw-Hill).

Tapscott, D. and Caston, A. (1993) *Paradigm Shift, The New Promise of Information Technology* (New York: McGraw-Hill).

Taylor, R. G. (1997) *Models of Computation and Formal Languages* (Oxford: Oxford University Press).

Teschner, G. and McClusky, F. B. (1990) "Computer Alternatives to the History of Philosophy Classroom", *Teaching Philosophy* (13), pp. 273–80.

Thagard, P. (1988) *Computational Philosophy of Science* (Cambridge, Mass.: MIT Press, Bradford Books).

Tiles, M. and Oberdiek, H. (1995) *Living in a Technological Culture: Human Tools and Human Values* (London: Routledge).

Toffler, A. (1980) *The Third Wave* (New York: Bantam Books).

Tunnicliffe, W. R. (1991) *Mathematics for Computing* (Englewood Cliffs, NJ: Prentice-Hall).

Turing, A. M. (1936) "On Computable Numbers, with an Application to the Entscheidungsproblem", *Proceedings of the London Mathematics Society*, 2nd series (42), pp. 230–65; correction published in vol. 43 (1936), pp. 544–6; repr. in M. Davis (ed.) (1965) *The Undecidable: Basic Papers on Problems, Propositions, Unsolvable Problems, and Computable Functions* (New York: Raven Press).

Turing, A. M. (1948) "Intelligent Machinery", National Physical Laboratory Report, B. Meltzer and D. Michie (eds) (1969) *Machine Intelligence 5* (Edinburgh: Edinburgh University Press).

Turing, A. M. (1950) "Computing Machinery and Intelligence", *Mind 59* (236), pp. 433–60.

Vamos, T. (1991) *Computer Epistemology: A Treatise in the Feasibility of Unfeasibility or Old Ideas Brewed New* (Singapore: World Scientific Publishing Co.)

Van der Lubbe, J. C. A. (1997) *Information Theory* (Cambridge: Cambridge University Press); first published 1988.

Van Gelder, T. (1995) "What is Cognition, if not Computation?", *Journal of Philosophy* (92), pp. 345–81.

Van Gulick, R. (1998) "Chinese Room Argument", in *Routledge Encyclopedia of Philosophy*, vol. 2 (London: Routledge).

Varela, F. J., Thompson, E. and Rosch, E. (1991) *The Embodied Mind: Cognitive Science and Human Experience* (Cambridge, Mass.: MIT Press).

Weizenbaum, J. (1976) *Computer Power and Human Reason* (Harmondsworth: Penguin Books); repr. 1984.

Wiener, N. (1948) *Cybernetics or Control and Communication in the Animal and the Machine* (Cambridge, Mass.: MIT Press); rev. edn 1962.

Wiener, N. (1950) *The Human Use of Human Beings: Cybernetics and Society* (Boston, Mass.: Houghton Mifflin).

Wiener, N. (1964) *God and Golem, Inc.: A Comment on Certain Points Where Cybernetics Impinges on Religion* (Cambridge, Mass.: MIT Press).

Williams, M. R. (1997) *A History of Computing Technology*, 2nd edn (Los Alamos, Calif.: IEEE Computer Society Press).

Winder, R. L., Probert, S. K. and Beeson, I. A. (1997) *Philosophical Aspects of Information Systems* (London: Taylor & Francis).

Winograd, T. and Flores, C. F. (1987) *Understanding Computers and Cognition: A New Foundation for Design* (Reading, Mass.: Addison-Wesley).

Winston, P. H. (ed.) (1990) *Artificial Intelligence at MIT, Expanding Frontiers*, vol. 1 (Cambridge, Mass.: MIT Press).

Woolley, B. (1992) *Virtual Worlds: A Journey in Hype and Hyperreality* (Oxford: Blackwell).

Zadeh, L. A. (1965) "Fuzzy Sets", *Information and Control* (8), pp. 338–53.

Zimmermann, H. J. (1991) *Fuzzy Set Theory and Its Applications*, 2nd edn (Dordrecht; Kluwer).

Index